RE-IMAGINING CULTURAL STUDIES

The Promise of Cultural Materialism

RE-IMAGINING CULTURAL STUDIES

The Promise of Cultural Materialism

Andrew Milner

First published 2002

SAGE Publications Ltd
6 Bonhill Street
London EC2A 4PU

SAGE Publications Inc
2455 Teller Road
Thousand Oaks, California 91320

SAGE Publications India Pvt Ltd
32, M-Block Market
Greater Kailash - I
New Delhi 110 048

British Library Cataloguing in Publication data

A catalogue record for this book is available from the British Library

ISBN 0 7619- 6113 5
ISBN 0 7619 6114 3 (pbk)

Library of Congress Control Number available

Printed and bound in Great Britain by Athenaeum Press, Gateshead

Contents

Acknowledgements

As ever, acknowledgement is due to Verity Burgmann, my friend, comrade and lover, and to our three sons, David, James and Robert. I am indebted, too, to friends, colleagues and students in the Centre for Comparative Literature and Cultural Studies at Monash University, especially Jeff Browitt, Claire Colebrook, Anthony Elliott, Kevin Hart, Douglas McQueen-Thomson, Gary Pearce, Kate Rigby, Gail Ward and Chris Worth; and, in the Centre for Research in Philosophy and Literature at Warwick University, Christine Battersby, Andrew Benjamin, Hanping Chiu, Stephen Houlgate, Heather Jones and Jacqueline Labbe; to staff at the Monash University Library and at the Warwick University Library; and to Tina Briggs and other staff in the Accommodation Office at Warwick University. I owe various debts of gratitude to Jennifer Bowen, Craig Brandist, Roger Bromley, Maria Elisa Cevasco, Sue Cockerell, Ann Dudgeon, Sean Homer, John Iremonger, Sheila Jones, Andrew Keogh, Stephen Knight, John Milner, Richard Milner, Joyce and Phil Morton, Colin Sparks, Kaye Stearman, Ian Syson, Terry Threadgold, John Tulloch and Frank Webster. Fred Inglis and Terry Eagleton spoke to me about Williams, the latter on more than one occasion. Chris Rojek at Sage was interested and encouraging. Acknowledgement is due to the Australian Research Council, which funded this project with grants totalling $A 18,295, and to the Faculty of Arts at Monash University, which provided a grant of $A 5,000. Last but not least, thanks are due to John Forster, my Sixth Form English teacher, who first introduced me to Leavis, Williams and Hoggart, Liverpool poets, the Royal Shakespeare Company and Pelican Books. I alone bear responsibility for the argument that follows.

For Verity

1

Cultural Materialism
and Cultural Theory

A spectre is haunting Europe - the spectre of Communism. All the Powers of old Europe have entered into a holy alliance to exorcize this spectre. (Marx and Engels, *The Communist Manifesto*)

But effective exorcism pretends to declare the death only in order to put to death. As a coroner might do, it certifies the death but here it is in order to inflict it. This is a familiar tactic. The constative form tends to reassure. The certification is effective. It wants to be and it must be in *effect*. It is *effectively* a performative. But here effectivity phantomalizes itself. It is in fact [*en effet*] a matter of a performative that seeks to reassure but first of all to reassure itself by assuring itself, for nothing is less sure, that what one would like to see dead is indeed dead ... In short, it is often a matter of pretending to certify death there where the death certificate is still the performative of an act of war or the impotent gesticulation, the restless dream, of an execution. (Derrida, *Specters of Marx*)

The spectre that haunted Europe in 1848 seems to have been exorcised, at least for the moment, at least from the eastern half of the continent. But its theoretical counterpart - Marxism as distinct from Communism - continues to haunt what the western academy has come to know as 'Cultural Studies'. Thirty years ago it would have been merely truistic to call attention to the Marxian origins of the new proto-discipline. But these have been progressively occluded in subsequent histories, especially those centred on categories like 'culturalism', 'structuralism' and 'post-structuralism', which still powerfully inform the (proto-)

discipline's collective wisdom and pedagogical strategies (Johnson, 1979; Turner, 1996). Here, thinkers and writers who had imagined themselves to be Marxists tend to be transformed retrospectively into 'culturalists' or 'structuralists'. The most influential such account is almost certainly Stuart Hall's famous essay, 'Cultural Studies: Two Paradigms', first published in 1980 in the journal *Media, Culture and Society*, and subsequently much republished elsewhere. Hall's representative culturalists were Richard Hoggart, Raymond Williams and E.P. Thompson; his structuralists Louis Althusser and Claude Lévi-Strauss; his post-structuralists (though this is not the term used) Jacques Lacan and Michel Foucault.[1] Hall's decision to compound Williams and Thompson, both self-declared 'Marxists', with Hoggart, who was nothing of the kind, is one example among many of what Paul Jones has termed 'the myth of "Raymond Hoggart"' (Jones, 1994).[2] We might note that Hall also worked hard to bracket together Althusser and Lévi-Strauss. This didn't quite amount to a 'myth of Claude Althusser', since Althusser was clearly more of a structuralist than Williams had ever been a 'culturalist'. But the conflation was intended, nonetheless, to remind Hall's readers of Althusserian Marxism's 'immense theoretical debt' to non-Marxist structuralism (Hall, 1980, p. 64).

This strange status of Marxism in Cultural Studies, as a part of the intellectual furniture so routinely present as to be barely worth commenting upon, hardly mattered in the 1970s when Hall began work on this essay. Its longer-term significance would become apparent, however, during the postmodern 1980s, when Marxism went from being *de rigueur* to *passé* in what seemed like the blink of an eye. As Elizabeth Grosz recalled in the admittedly extreme case of Althusser himself: 'His name is ... rarely mentioned today, and always in hushed tones' (Grosz, 1989, p. 235). But if Althusser had compounded the sin of Marxism with the crime of uxoricide, a similar forgetting overtook even those with more exemplary private lives: in short, the entire argument was effectively 'forgotten'. So the earlier Marxist interest in social class was suddenly 'decentred' by an increasing preoccupation with the cultural effects of other kinds of cultural difference - gender, race, ethnicity, sexuality - and by the growing influence of post-structuralism and postmodernism. It then became possible for Cultural Studies to rewrite its own history as if there were only ever culturalists, structuralists and postmodernists, never any Marxists at all. This book will be about Cultural Studies and about how it developed from earlier disciplinary forms in the humanities and social sciences. But it will also and of necessity be about Marxism and about the contribution made by various Marxist thinkers to the creation of the 'conditions of possibility' for Cultural Studies. More specifically, it will explore the particular kind of 'Marxism' associated with the work of Raymond Williams, for which he himself coined the term 'cultural materialism'.[3] As signifiers, neither Cultural Studies nor cultural materialism nor Marxism are readily attachable in any uncomplicated fashion to transparently available signifieds. We must say a little more, then, about what exactly we will choose to mean by each of these terms

Cultural Studies and Cultural Theory

Let us begin with Cultural Studies, by any standards an unusually polysemic sign. Its various senses have tended to cluster around four main sets of meaning: as an interdiscipline; as a political intervention into the existing disciplines; as an entirely new discipline, defined in terms of an entirely new subject matter; and finally, as a new discipline, defined in terms of a new theoretical paradigm. No doubt, other available definitions remain in play, but these four seem especially prominent. The first was clearly that intended by Hoggart in the initial proposal to establish a Centre for Contemporary Cultural Studies at the University of Birmingham. Here Cultural Studies was understood as an interdisciplinary postgraduate research field, which would recruit from among people already trained in 'the social sciences, history, psychology, anthropology, literary study'. For Hoggart, Cultural Studies was - and still should be - a 'field of study', rather than a discipline: 'the student should have an initial discipline outside Cultural Studies,' he has written, 'an academic and intellectual training, and a severe one' (Hoggart, 1995, p. 173). There is a clear echo here of F.R. Leavis's earlier conception of an English School requiring its students 'to come to fairly close terms ... with ... other disciplines' (Leavis, 1948, p. 57). For Hoggart, the enterprise was to be much more fully interdisciplinary than for Leavis, but literature would still be its single 'most important' element (Hoggart, 1970, p. 255). The second conception, that of Cultural Studies as a kind of political intervention, is more readily associated with Hall, Hoggart's immediate successor as Director of the Birmingham Centre. For Hall, the 'seriousness' of Cultural Studies is inscribed in its 'political' aspect: 'there is something *at stake* in cultural studies,' he has insisted, 'in a way that ... is not exactly true of many other ... intellectual ... practices' (Hall, 1992, p. 278). Similarly 'political' conceptions recur throughout the Cultural Studies literature, even in the 'Introduction' to Simon During's widely used textbook reader, where its 'engaged form of analysis' is described as one of the discipline's two distinguishing features (During, 1999, p. 2).

A third conception sees Cultural Studies as a new discipline defined in terms of a new subject matter, that is, as the study of popular culture. Shorn of pretension to both interdisciplinarity and political relevance, this is perhaps the most 'modest' of the four meanings and the most readily compatible with pre-existing disciplinary structures. There can be no doubt that Cultural Studies had indeed emerged in part by way of a quasi-populist reaction against the cultural elitism of older forms of literary study: all three of the discipline's widely acknowledged 'founding fathers', Hoggart, Thompson and Williams, were committed to the study of popular or working-class culture. However, none of these had imagined Cultural Studies as coextensive with the study of the 'popular arts'. But in the subsequent history of the Birmingham Centre and of Cultural Studies more generally, it has often appeared as such. Hence the growing sense of Cultural Studies as a sociology or ethnography of mass media consumption, nicely symbolised in Hall's appointment to the chair in sociology at the Open University and eventual election as President of the British Sociological Association. The development of such sub-specialisms as Communication and Media Studies is clearly an important legacy of this kind of Cultural Studies. We should add, however, that there is also an 'immodest Cultural Studies', a fourth option defined in terms of a new paradigm, connecting the study of the popular to the study of the 'literary'. In this definition, Cultural Studies represents a shift not so much in empirical subject matter as in theoretical paradigm. This conception was important for Hoggart, but even more especially so for Williams, whose 'empirical' work quite systematically transgressed the boundaries between elite and popular cultures: he was as interested in television and the press as in canonical literature and drama. Hence his insistence that, as concepts, both 'literature' and 'criticism' were 'forms of a class specialization and control of a general social practice, and of a class limitation of the questions ... it might raise' (Williams, 1977a, p. 49).

This sense of the 'literary' as one element among others within the more general processes of 'writing' and 'communication' became characteristic of Williams's later work. But it is present elsewhere too. It informs Anthony Easthope's understanding of the 'double movement' by which 'literary study becomes increasingly indistinguishable from cultural studies' and 'cultural studies makes incursions into the traditionally literary terrain of textuality' (1991, p. 65). It is present in Tony Bennett's sense of Cultural Studies as fundamentally concerned with 'the relations of culture and power' (1998, p. 53). If this latter description is overly Foucauldian (and designed with intention to divert Cultural Studies towards policy studies moreover), it clearly gestures in the same direction as Williams and Easthope, towards what might be termed a 'social-scientific' study of all culture, whether elite or popular, in both its textual and extra-textual aspects. No doubt, there is something to be said for all four senses of the term 'Cultural Studies': they each register important aspects of different phases in its theoretical and practical development. But there is a cumulative logic to this development, nonetheless, which suggests that the greater promise lies with the fourth conception: not in the discovery of a new empirical subject matter, nor even in the deconstruction of the disciplinary boundaries that demarcated literature from fiction, art from culture, the elite from the popular; but rather, in the development of new methods for the analysis of both.

Definition is a dangerous business, I know, so let me settle for pastiche. Borrowing from the textbook procedures of the dismal science of economics, we might productively 'define' Cultural Studies as the social science of the study of the production, distribution, exchange and reception of textualised meaning. I use the term 'social science' here, not in any strongly positivist sense, such as one finds in high structuralist semiology or functionalist sociology, but in the much looser sense of a discipline, the primary purposes of which are description and explanation rather than judgement and canonisation. The term 'textualised meaning' denotes a concern with signifying practices in general rather than literature or art or the mass media in particular. Finally, 'production, distribution, exchange and reception' are intended to denote an interest in how texts are produced and received, how they are productive, and with the practices that articulate them and that they articulate, as well as with texts 'in their own right'. Such concerns are necessarily political, of course, since all texts are always produced and received in contexts significantly affected by the structures of social power.

If this is indeed what we mean by Cultural Studies, then its intellectual novelty, in relation both to humanist literary criticism and to positivist social science, has been primarily theoretical in character. This book will be about theory, then, or 'Theory' as it is sometimes written in the United States. By this I mean something very different from either philosophy or the older discipline-specific theories deployed by the 'modern' humanities and social sciences: a new and, some would argue, distinctly 'postmodern', type of transdisciplinary theorising. Fredric Jameson cites Foucault as the exemplary instance of this kind of 'undecidable' genre, which takes as its object not so much a particular class of phenomena as the textualisation of the phenomenal in general (Jameson, 1998a, p. 3). For Jameson, Theory is very specifically post-structuralist: he uses the terms more or less interchangeably to denote 'very precisely a postmodernist phenomenon' in which 'depth is replaced by surface'. Thus understood, Theory is characterised by an in principle opposition to depth models, be they hermeneutic (inside/outside), dialectical (appearance/essence), psychoanalytic (latent/manifest), existential (authenticity/inauthenticity) or semiotic (signifier/signified) (Jameson, 1991, p. 12). But if Theory is both transdisciplinary and textual, as it clearly has been, then it need not necessarily be post-structuralist. Indeed, Jameson himself writes Theory of a distinctly transdisciplinary and textual character, while nonetheless maintaining a clear distance between himself and what remains of post-structuralism (however we define that term). If the doctrinal challenge represented by Foucault's genealogy and Derridean deconstruction provided the initial occasion for the emergence of Theory, as it clearly did, then the challenge has been taken up by Jameson's depth models, so that hermeneutics, Marxism, psychoanalysis and semiotics (but perhaps not existentialism) have themselves been progressively reconstructed as transdisciplinary approaches to textual and cultural analysis.

At one level, this might be read as a triumph for anti-postmodernism. Hence, Perry Anderson's gloating conclusion that the 'capture of the postmodern ... has set the terms of subsequent debate ... the most significant interventions ... have ... been Marxist in origin' (1998, p. 78). But if Jameson's Marxism has captured the postmodern, there is also an important sense in which the postmodern has captured it[4] - as also hermeneutics, psychoanalysis and semiotics. For all Jameson's own professed fidelity to the legacy of Adornian Critical Theory (Jameson, 1990), it is clear that his work has acquired a distinctly postmodern character: at the most obvious of levels, its central object is postmodern late capitalism; at another, it has become increasingly transdisciplinary, moving away from his own disciplinary background in Comparative Literature toward such distant objects as film and architecture; at a third, it is as textualist as any post-structuralism (Jameson's lifework is above all an extended labour in textual commentary). As Anderson notes, no previous Marxist would ever have conceded, let alone insisted, that Marxism is a 'great collective story', that it is, in short, a grand narrative (Anderson, 1998, p. 53; Jameson, 1981, p. 19). Analogous 'postmodernisations' are readily observable in iek's psychoanalysis, Eco's semiotics or in the mutation of post-Gadamerian hermeneutics into reception theory. The point here is neither to bemoan nor to celebrate the transformation of theories into Theory, but merely to note its more general significance. Almost everyone who worked in the humanities and social sciences, whether in the United States or Canada, Britain or Australia, at any time during the last three decades of the twentieth century, would have encountered Theory of this kind. Whether appalled by its poverty, like Thompson, or attracted to its glamour, like Terry Eagleton, there was no doubting its cultural salience (Thompson, 1978; Eagleton, 1996a, pp. 191-2). Even Hoggart, as unlikely a theoretician as any, would eventually admit, albeit a little disingenuously, that 'one does not wish to undervalue the importance of theory and the need for theoretic languages' (1995, p. 177).

For myself, I will readily concede to Hoggart that we must earn the right to use theory, that 'it must not be made into a charm, or a prop; or a waffle-iron to be banged on top of the material' (ibid., p. 178); in short, that good theory must be about something. That said, I would also want to insist that many of the older disciplinary boundaries and their attendant theories have in fact become increasingly irrelevant to a society in which everyday life has become progressively media-encultured, and in which hitherto relatively autonomous, non-market institutions for the regulation of value have become progressively assimilated into each other by way of the market. Like it or not - and in many ways I don't - the postmodern cultures of the late twentieth and early twenty-first centuries have become so thoroughly media-tised, commodified and relativised as to demand very different modes of analysis from those Hoggart had learnt from English Literature. Ironically, the initial recognition that this might be so was registered at its clearest in Cultural Studies, Hoggart's own intellectual bequest to the Anglophone academy. This is not meant to suggest that the future belongs of necessity to some kind of 'post-disciplinarity'.[5] On the contrary, transdisciplinary Theory seems likely to be a transitional form, through which the older disciplines are recomposed into new ones more appropriate to postmodern culture. Just as hermeneuts and Marxists have learnt to become Theorists, so deconstruction has itself become increasingly 'grounded' (in the law, for example). As Jameson notes, Theory is already confronted by a renewed impetus toward disciplinary re-differentiation: 'philosophy and its branches are back in force' (1998, p. 94). We might add that Cultural Studies is itself increasingly subject to calls for 'disciplinisation' (Bennett, 1998, pp. 53-9).

Western Marxism and Cultural Studies

If Cultural Studies is best defined in terms of its theoretical novelty, then what exactly were the sources for this paradigm shift? The name, of course, came from Hoggart, but the more general intellectual framework can plausibly be read as deriving from, or at least significantly anticipated by, three relatively distinct primary sources - respectively, Frankfurt School Critical Theory, Cambridge English, and the French 'structuralist' reworking of Saussurean linguistics into a general semiology - and one important secondary source, through which each of these was refracted, the 'sixties' (which in practice meant the 1970s) 'New Left', as constructed at Birmingham and elsewhere. Against much of the received wisdom in contemporary Cultural Studies, I want to call attention here to the distinctly Marxist character of each of these three primary sources. Which leads us to the second of our three key terms, that is to Marxism itself, or, to be more specific, to what Merleau-Ponty had termed 'Western Marxism'. By this he meant the tradition of critical Marxism developed in Western Europe, especially in Germany, in more or less deliberate opposition to official Communist Marxism (Merleau-Ponty, 1974, pp. 7, 30-58). This sub-variant of the Marxist tradition had been centrally preoccupied with what Cultural Studies would later recognise as 'culture': its characteristic thematics were human agency, subjective consciousness, and hence 'ideology'. As Anderson observed: 'Western Marxism ... came to concentrate overwhelmingly on study of *superstructures* ... It was culture that held the central focus of its attention' (1976, pp. 75-6). At the point of its initial inception during the early 1920s, this stress on agency and consciousness had served to underwrite a 'leftist' rejection of political fatalism, in favour of the immediate possibilities of revolution. As the moment of revolutionary optimism failed, however, the emphasis shifted towards an analysis of the system-supportive nature of cultural legitimations. Whether in celebration of the emancipatory potential of human self activity, or in recognition of the debilitating and disabling power of ideological legitimations, culture provided Western Marxism with its key explanatory category.

That the Institut für Sozialforschung at the University of Frankfurt, the so-called 'Frankfurt School' of Theodor Adorno, Max Horkheimer and Herbert Marcuse, later Jürgen Habermas and later still Axel Honneth, has been broadly 'Marxist' in theoretical inspiration seems almost self-evident. For all its undoubted elitism and for all its political antipathy to the more 'extreme' elements in the sixties' student movement, the School's general theoretical outlook was very obviously Marxist. Adorno might have called in the police to evict the student radicals from his Institut and Habermas might have described them as 'red fascists' (Leslie, 1999, p. 120; Adorno and Marcuse, 1999, p. 128). But it is impossible to read Adorno and Horkheimer's *Dialectic of Enlightenment* except in relation to the Marxist tradition. And even Habermas, a much less obviously Marxian thinker than Adorno, could still declare as late as 1979 that he valued 'being considered a Marxist' (1979, p. 33). In any case, it was Marcuse, rather than Adorno, who bore the primary responsibility for transmitting the Frankfurt School legacy to the English-speaking world, where what we know as Cultural Studies first became established. *Dialectic of Enlightenment* remained unavailable in English translation until 1972, while *One-Dimensional Man* became part of the intellectual furniture of the radical sixties (Adorno and Horkheimer, 1972; Marcuse, 1964). The Marcusean argument was thus simultaneously both more clearly Marxist than that in Adorno and Horkheimer and also much more influential in New Left debates (Adorno and Marcuse, 1999).

Cambridge English in its specifically Leavisite formation is as near to a German or French intellectual 'school' as anything in twentieth-century British intellectual history. In retrospect, it might even warrant acknowledgement as a distinctive 'Cambridge School'. Clearly, neither F.R. nor Q.D. Leavis was in any sense a Marxist, though their anti-utilitarianism ran strangely parallel to the work of the Frankfurt School. But if we extend the sense of a 'Cambridge School' to include both Williams and the young Eagleton, then the lineage acquires a more Marxian character. This extension seems warranted, moreover, if only because there is no doubting Williams's debt to Leavis: 'The immense attraction of Leavis lay in his cultural radicalism', Williams would explain: 'It was the range of Leavis's attacks on academicism, on Bloomsbury, on metropolitan literary culture, on the commercial press, on advertising, that first took me' (Williams, 1979a, pp. 65-6). Even Eagleton shared in something of this. As he explained in a 1985 interview, Cambridge in his undergraduate days:

> was ... buzzing with the Leavis argument ... There was a sense in which, by a kind of negative identification, if one was a working-class student reading English one might easily become a Leavisite. The Leavisites were seen both as a victimised minority and as attempting ... to speak in broader critical terms ... during the 1960s, Cambridge remained in many ways the centre. (Eagleton, 1985, p. 131)

A Cambridge 'tradition' can thus be plausibly read as leading from the Leavises to Williams and Eagleton, rather than to Hoggart, that is, as progressively acquiring a distinctly Marxist inflection.

A similar inflection informs general semiology. The key figure here was neither Lévi-Strauss nor Althusser, but rather Roland Barthes. It was Barthes who initiated the post-Second World War revival of Saussurean semiology in *Mythologies*, first published in French in 1957, though not in English translation until 1973. Barthes was *the* 'French structuralist' of the 1960s, *Mythologies* itself an enormously influential text on Anglophone Cultural Studies. It was also a much more 'Marxist' text than we now tend to allow. Its central theoretical argument, that in bourgeois society myth is 'depoliticized speech' (Barthes, 1973, p. 142), clearly rehearses Marxian thematics already available in the work of Sartre and Brecht. Jameson has described it as part of a 'universal crystallization of Marxism among French intellectuals', occasioned in part by the influence of Brecht's 1954 and 1955 *Théâtre des nations* visits to Paris, which included productions of *Mother Courage* and *The Caucasian Chalk Circle*. Jameson's conclusion warrants repetition:

> Barthes's dealings with 'nature' ... represent a creative and explosive wiring together of the Sartrean philosophical polemics and the Brechtian practical and aesthetic estrangements of the same illusion of stasis and the eternal. The Brechtian origin of some of these themes and positions might help us to recover some of their original political content as well. (Jameson, 1998b, p. 172)

So Adorno and Habermas, Williams and Eagleton, even the young Barthes, can be read as 'Marxists'. But why should this matter? Let me be clear that I am not really concerned to demonstrate that these Marxists were 'correct'; nor to complain that they have been given insufficient credit (though I am inclined to think both statements more or less true). What interest me, rather, are the ways in which Western Marxism came to constitute something like a 'condition of possibility' for the emergence of Cultural Studies. To put the case as succinctly as possible: in order to be able to imagine a social science of the study of both elite and popular cultures, it was necessary to become relatively 'distanced' from both. And Western Marxists were, in fact, so distanced, simultaneously opposed both to the elitist complacencies of establishment 'high culture' and to the commercialism of capitalist 'popular culture'. By comparison, most conservative, liberal and social-democratic intellectuals were far too closely implicated in the former, many (mostly American) liberals and some (mostly European) social-democrats too closely in the latter, to be able to establish the required critical distance. No doubt, the Leavises shared in this dual antipathy, but, as Eagleton hinted, they were unusual in this respect: theirs was a peculiarly eccentric biographical trajectory, defined in terms of its radical intellectual isolation, and thus unlikely to be replicated elsewhere in the culture.

Critical Theory, left Leavisism and general semiology each by turn rehearsed all four of our versions of Cultural Studies and they did so, moreover, in much the same cumulative fashion. So Critical Theory defined itself in 'totalistic' opposition to the discrete disciplines of 'traditional theory' (Horkheimer, 1972), but also as a kind of political intervention into the discipline of sociology, in short as a 'critical sociology' (Adorno, 1976). Likewise, it defined the 'culture industries' as a crucial part of its subject matter, but also insisted that they be understood in relation to high culture. Much the same can be said of Barthes and Williams, with linguistics and English Literature respectively substituted for sociology. From the specific standpoint of Cultural Studies, however, Williams's achievement is the greater, since he was able to define more explicitly than either Adorno or Barthes the strongest sense of the project, as a non-canonising, social-scientific, study of all aspects of the production and reception of all texts, whether elite or popular. By comparison with Hoggart, Williams used the term 'Cultural Studies' only sparingly, though it is certainly present in his last unfinished book (Williams, 1989a, pp. 151-62). During the late 1970s and early 1980s he had seemed to prefer the idea of a 'cultural sociology': at one point he even chose to describe Cultural Studies as 'a branch of general sociology' (Williams, 1981, p. 14). But, whatever the term, the project Wiliams pursued was recognisably still that of the Cultural Studies he had first mapped out in *The Long Revolution*(Williams, 1965).

Culture and Cultures

The title of Jameson's *The Cultural Turn* serves to remind us that all postmodern 'Theory', not only that explicitly identified with Cultural Studies, is in fact a kind of cultural theory - as distinct, say, from economic or political theory. At one level, of course, this distinction is spurious, since in mass-mediated societies the economic and the political are themselves increasingly encultured. But Theory has tended to ignore the strictly economic or political aspects of political economy: even Jameson's famous invocation of Ernest Mandel's *Late Capitalism* is oddly gestural (Jameson, 1991, pp. 35-6; Mandel, 1975). If Theory is relatively easily defined, culture is much less so. We have said that Cultural Studies is the study of the production, distribution, exchange and reception of textualised meaning. In this most general of senses, then, 'culture' refers to the complex of institutions, artefacts and practices that make up our symbolic universe: to art and religion, science and sport, education and leisure, but not to the polity or the economy. As that which is neither work/class/exploitation nor war/power/oppression, culture becomes 'the heart of a heartless world', to borrow Marx's description of religion (Marx, 1975a, p. 244). But just as religion in the abstract translates in practice into religions in the bitterly contested plural, so too culture readily translates into cultures. Hence its almost talismanic status during the so-called 'culture wars' of late twentieth-century America, where it could denote simultaneously both the canonical high 'culture' of established academic tradition and the ethnic, sexual, generational and gendered 'counter-cultures' of the 'new social movements'. Outside the United States, these particular culture wars found only faint echo, except as objects of vicarious participation. This is not to suggest that the cultural relativism (or pluralism) characteristic of the 'postmodern condition' had failed to register elsewhere, only that in America its political effects were uniquely concentrated in the institutions of higher education. In other times and in other places, culture wars were more typically fought out, in more violent fashion, for example between actual or putative nation-states. As Geoffrey Hartman observes, culture is 'an inflammatory word that kindles actual wars' (1997, p. 14).[6] The peoples of the Balkans have learnt to their cost that cultural identity can come at a higher price than in New York or Sydney.

Culture is a good thing, then, but dangerously so. Little surprise that Williams should have described it as 'one of the two or three most complicated words in the English language' (Williams, 1976a, p. 76). Hartman notes this complexity, but also the way in which its use proliferates - 'camera culture, gun culture, service culture, museum culture, deaf culture, football culture' - so that it becomes a kind of 'linguistic weed' (1997, p. 30). Williams and Hartman have each attempted to trace the intellectual history of the concept. In its earliest meanings, both in English and in French, it referred to the tending of natural growth, either in animals or in plants, as it still does in compound words like agriculture and horticulture. Williams dated the word's metaphorical extension, to include human development, from the early sixteenth century in English usage; and its earliest use as an independent noun, to refer to an abstract process, from the mid-seventeenth century (Williams, 1976a, pp. 77-8). Both Hartman and Williams attach a crucial significance to the legacy of German

Romanticism, where German *Kultur* was troped against French *civilisation*, as human nature in opposition to mechanical artifice. Hartman begins with Fichte and Schiller, Williams with Herder, and both see Wordsworth, Coleridge and Matthew Arnold as central to the English refashioning of the trope, although Williams also called attention to Carlyle (Hartman, 1997, pp. 205-7, 210; Williams, 1963, pp. 54, 85, 136; Williams, 1976a, pp. 78-80). In its initial formulations, Williams's history remained determinedly 'English', leading to Eliot, F.R. Leavis, Orwell and by implication himself. Hartman's (which includes Williams) is much more cosmopolitan and leads to Spengler, Benda, Nazism and Heiner Müller. Different histories tell different stories: for Williams, the idea of culture held out the promise of emancipation; for Hartman, 'the fateful question' as to whether a truly 'generous' idea of culture is possible remains only 'precariously' open (Williams, 1963, pp. 322-33; Hartman, 1997, pp. 192-3). The difference is partly that between the 1950s and the 1990s, partly that between Britain and continental Europe, partly between Europe and the United States, but partly also a difference of substance over what exactly to make of all this complexity.

In his first major book, *Culture and Society 1780-1950*, Williams had identified four important kinds of meaning that attached to the word: as an individual habit of mind; the state of intellectual development of a whole society; the arts; and as the whole way of life of a group or people (Williams, 1963, p. 16). In the later *Keywords*, originally intended as an appendix to *Culture and Society*, but significantly amended and augmented thereafter, only the latter three usages remained in play (Williams, 1976a, p. 80). Later still, his sociology textbook, *Culture*, would reintroduce the first usage, grouping it together with the second and third as 'general', and contrasting these with the fourth, more specifically 'anthropological' meaning (Williams, 1981, p. 11). Here he also distinguished between the word's physical and human applications; between its positive and negative connotations; its use as a noun of process and as a noun of configuration; its politically radical and politically reactionary applications; and so on. Much of this clearly foreshadowed Hartman's account. Williams was clear, however, that these confusions and complications belonged to our 'culture', if we may so use the term, rather than to any fault either in his analysis or in the word itself: 'These variations ... necessarily involve alternative views of the activities, relationships and processes which this complex word indicates. The complexity, that is to say, is not finally in the word but in the problems which its variations of use significantly indicate' (Williams, 1976a, p. 81). The range and the overlap of meanings, the distinctions simultaneously elided and insisted upon, are all in themselves 'significant' (ibid., p. 80).

For Hartman, the crucial such distinction is that between 'culture' as a general ideal, 'a "republic of letters" in which ideas can be freely exchanged' and '*a* culture' as 'a specific form of embodiment or solidarity'; the crucial need to protect the former against the latter (Hartman, 1997, pp. 36, 41). Hence, the special significance to cultural discourse of literature in general, poetry in particular: 'to provide counterexamples to disembodied thought and unearned abstraction' (ibid., p. 61). For Williams, the crucial distinction was that between the term's literary-critical and aesthetic applications, on the one hand, its sociological and anthropological ones, on the other. Thus:

> the concept of 'culture' ... became a noun of 'inner' process, special-ized to its presumed agencies in 'intellectual life' and 'the arts'. It became also a noun of general process, specialized to its presumed configurations in 'whole ways of life'. It played a crucial role in defi-nitions of 'the arts' and 'the humanities', from the first sense. It played an equally crucial role in definitions of the 'human sciences' and the 'social sciences', in the second sense. (Williams, 1977a, p. 17)

Culture, then, may be counterposed to society, as 'art'; but the two may also be defined very nearly coextensively, as the non-political, non-economic, residually 'social'. The conjunction in the title of *Culture and Society* is thus no less ambiguous a term than either of the nouns: it can imply an essentially external relation of aggregation or opposition; or, conversely, an essentially internal relation of near inclusion.

There is a clear parallel between Hartman and Williams here, since 'culture' is to 'a culture' as 'arts' is to 'a whole way of life'. Note the difference, however. Where for Hartman the distinction runs between a generality and a particular, a general public sphere and a singular sub-culture, for Williams it ran between two generalities, the arts and the whole way of life. While for Williams society remained a generali-ty, or a commonality, for Hartman it has become a multicultural plu-rality of particulars: he acknowledges as much when rehearsing Lloyd and Thomas's earlier objections to the supposed 'over-identification' between Williams and the conservatism of the 'culture and society' tradition (Hartman, 1997, p. 139; Lloyd and Thomas, 1995). We shall return to the competing claims of the 'common culture' and politico-social multiculturalism in the chapters that follow. For the moment, however, suffice it to note that this is an issue of quite fundamental significance, both theoretically and practically. Williams's own views are very clear. The fundamental ambiguity between culture as art and culture as society, he held, arose very directly from out of the deep structures of the modern world. For it is only in societies roughly sim-ilar to our own, that is, those constructed by the 'long revolution' as democratic or quasi-democratic nation-states and capitalist economies, that 'culture' and 'society' become excluded from politics and economics. The ambiguities in the terms culture and society, and in their mutual relations, as also the currency of both in contemporary discourse, thus bear witness to the deeply problematic status of each in a society the driving imperatives of which are characteristically political and economic. This process, by which 'culture' (and with it 'society') becomes the more theoretically and discursively salient the more effectively it is extruded from the 'practical' business of life, is nicely caught in Williams's account of the concept's evolution in nineteenth-century English thought. Culture, he observes, had emerged:

> as an abstract and an absolute: an emergence which ... merges two general responses - first, the recognition of the practical separation of certain moral and intellectual activities from the driven impetus of a new kind of society; second, the emphasis of these activities, as a court of human appeal, to be set over the processes of practical social judgement and yet to offer itself as a mitigating and rallying alternative. (Williams, 1963, p. 17)

Idealism and Materialism

Hartman and Williams are agreed that culture thus understood, that is, as separate from and yet superior to economics and politics, was initially the creation of European Romanticism. As such, it denoted the arts, and perhaps especially literature: 'Poets are the unacknowledged legislators of the world', wrote Shelley (1931, p. 109). But the importance of art, and the ultimate legislative power of poetry, reside in their status as an expression of the distinctive 'spirit' of a people. Thus, art as 'culture' is counterposed to the mechanism of modern industrial 'civilisation'. This more properly 'social' sense of the term, already present in Romanticism, was later foregrounded in the twin 'social sciences' of anthropology and sociology. For Emile Durkheim, the 'founding father' of French anthropology, it was precisely the 'collective consciousness' of tribal culture which allowed us to distinguish between pre-industrial 'mechanical solidarity' and the 'anomie' of a modernity still chronically incapable of 'organic solidarity' (Durkheim, 1964, pp. 129-32, 353-73). For the early German sociologists, such as Max Weber and Ferdinand Tönnies, the opposition ran between status and class, *Wertrationalität* (value rationality) and *Zweckrationalität* (purposive rationality), *Gemeinschaft* (community) and *Gesellschaft* (association), feudalism and capitalism (Tönnies, 1955, pp. 37-9; Weber, 1948, pp. 180-95; Weber, 1964, p. 115). In each case, modern society was understood as distinctively and unusually asocial, its economic and political life characteristically 'normless' and 'value-free', in short, uncultured.

This sense of culture as a superior ideal, informing the whole way of life of whole peoples, as a matter of fact in pre-modern societies, perhaps only ideally so within modernity itself, is often characterised as 'idealist'. The latter term derives from philosophy and, in its more restricted uses, is applied to the 'classical idealism' of late eighteenth-century and early nineteenth-century German thought, most importantly to Kant and Hegel. It is clear, however, that roughly analogous notions subsequently became central to the development of English literary criticism and German sociology. The former was influenced by German idealism by way of English and German Romanticism, especially through Coleridge (Coleridge, 1972); the latter by way of a late nineteenth-century revival in neo-Kantian philosophy; and the debt is very real in each case. This is much less obviously so for French anthropology: Durkheim's 'idealism' points forward to structuralism and semiotics, rather than back to Romanticism or German idealism. But in its implicit valorisation of tribal unity over industrial anomie, and in its location of the source of that unity in the collective consciousness, it significantly reproduces two of the characteristic tropes of Anglo-German idealism. Moreover, in its subsequent appropriation by British 'social anthropology', the Durkheimian corpus was significantly 'naturalised', and thereby subsumed into a wider idealist tradition.

The obvious contrary instance in modern western thought, that of a 'materialism' stubbornly resistant to the lures of idealism, was provided by the British tradition of philosophical utilitarianism, and by its various intellectual progeny, notably the disciplines of economics and political science, perhaps also behaviourist psychology. For Thomas Hobbes, the central seventeenth-century precursor of modern English political philosophy, the initial datum for any adequate understanding of human social behaviour was to be neither religion nor art, nor manners nor morals, nor anything else subsequently acknowledged as 'culture', but rather the physical movement of the material human body: 'life itself is but motion, and can never be without desire, nor without fear' (Hobbes, 1960, p. 39). The body and its desires and fears, to pursue pleasure and to avoid pain, provided utilitarianism with a fundamental measure from which to deduce the nature of political and economic systems, both real and ideal. This has proven an immensely fertile intellectual enterprise, as the cumulative achievements of modern economic theory, to take the obvious example, clearly attest. But utilitarianism has been almost entirely unsuccessful, by contrast, as a point of entry into the understanding and explanation of culture. This is so for the most obvious of reasons, that in a strictly utilitarian system there can be *no* culture, *no* society, but only a plurality of discrete individual actors connected to each other either through the immediately economic contracts of the market place or through the compulsions of the state, itself conceived as the effect of a supposedly pre-political 'social contract'. As Margaret Thatcher famously insisted: 'there is no such thing as society. There are individual men and women' (quoted in Bradley, 1998, p. 2). On this view, culture, whether understood as art or as society, is reduced to an aggregate of individual commodities, each for sale in the market place of individual taste, its value determined solely by the revealed preferences of the aggregate of individual cultural consumers. As the nineteenth-century utilitarian philosopher, Jeremy Bentham, insisted: 'push-pin is of equal value with ... poetry' (1962, p. 253).

A rigorous materialism, such as that proposed by Hobbes and subsequently pursued by modern economic theory, is thus fundamentally unable to conceive of the cultural as meaningfully distinguishable from the economic and the political. For it is in the nature of culture, as defined by both poetry and anthropology, that it possess both an internal order of its own and certain clearly coercive, or at least compulsive, properties *vis-à-vis* the individual. Culture *cannot* be reduced to a simple matter of individual preference, mere taste. 'Poetry is the most philosophic of all writing,' wrote Wordsworth, 'its object is truth, not individual and local, but general and operative' (Wordsworth, 1952, p. 394); and later, 'the Poet binds together by passion and knowledge the vast empire of human society' (ibid., p. 396). For Durkheim, 'the collective consciousness is the highest form of the psychic life, since it is the consciousness of the consciousnesses ... outside of and above local contingencies, it sees things only in their permanent and essential aspects, which it crystallizes into communicable ideas' (1976, p. 444). Doubtless, both Durkheim and Wordsworth (and, indeed, Shelley) overstated their case. But, even if the truth of poetry is perhaps not quite so general, the unacknowledged legislature perhaps not quite so powerful, the consciousness of the consciousnesses perhaps not quite so permanent and essential, then each sentiment captures a part, nonetheless, of what many of us experience as the most basic of truths about our 'culture': that our art, our religion, our morals, our knowledge, our science, are not simply matters of private preference, but rather possess an 'objectivity' the validity of which is barely touched upon by notions such as that of taste; in short, that we belong to our culture at least as much as it belongs to us. It is this experience, this 'truth' if we like, which is radically unamenable to analysis in terms of the utilitarian schema. Whatever else utilitarian political economy may have achieved, it remains constitutionally incapable of an adequate theory of culture.

There are weaker versions of materialism, however, which insist not so much on the exclusion of the cultural as on its merely secondary character. The most important of these historically has been Marxism itself. As the American sociologist, Talcott Parsons, once observed, there is a sense in which Marxism might be considered simply a sub-variant of the more general utilitarian tradition (Parsons, 1949, p. 110). But this is a part only, and the lesser part at that, of the truth. In fact, Parsons's own clear lack of interest, even perhaps antipathy, led him to a serious underestimation of the continuing debt owed by Marx both to German idealism and to Romanticism. The main trajectory of Marx's mature intellectual career is still probably best understood in relation to the distinctively British tradition of utilitarian and quasi-utilitarian political economy. But his early intellectual formation had been shaped, nonetheless, by German Romanticism and by Hegelianism. The resultant synthesis, while increasingly conducted in the language of political economy, continued to rehearse a number of important idealist thematics, most obviously those present in the theories of alienation and 'commodity fetishism', and in the implicitly invidious comparison between use-value and exchange-value (Marx, 1970, pp. 71-83; Marx, 1975b, pp. 327-30). Marx's *magnum opus* is thus not so much an extension as a *critique* of political economy, to borrow the words of its subtitle.

Marxian materialism was thus able to reserve a place for culture, albeit, in the more historically persuasive formulations, an essentially secondary one. The best known of these, and almost certainly also the most influential, was the so-called base/superstructure formula, in which 'the economic structure of society' was deemed 'the real foundation', which gives rise to a legal and political 'superstructure', and thence to correspondent 'definite forms of social consciousness'. These latter, which are described as 'religious, artistic or philosophic' (Marx, 1975c, pp. 425-6), are not specifically defined as superstructures by Marx himself, but the elision routinely occurs in most subsequent 'scientific' Marxisms. Obvious instances here include the Russian Marxists, Georgei Plekhanov (Plekhanov, 1978) and Andrey Zhdanov (Zhdanov, 1977). Less well known internationally, but of greater local significance to the English-speaking world, were the British Marxist literary critics, Christopher Caudwell and Ralph Fox (Caudwell, 1946; Fox, 1979). Here, as elsewhere in 'scientific socialism', the separate existence of culture as a 'relatively autonomous' realm, neither directly reducible to nor coextensive with the economy, is readily conceded. But its role remains epiphenomenal, an adjunct to, effect of, or even, in Caudwell's unfortunate phrase, a 'secretion' from (Caudwell, 1946, p. 29), the 'economic base'.

For much of the twentieth century, cultural theory was polarised between idealist accounts, most obviously those proposed by traditional literary humanism, but also those deployed in both post-Weberian sociology and post-Durkheimian anthropology, and materialist accounts, normally of a specifically 'vulgar' Marxist kind. Comparing such idealisms and materialisms, Williams observed that 'the importance of each position ... is that it leads ... to intensive study of the relations between "cultural" activities and other forms of social life ... The sociology of culture, as it entered the second half of the twentieth century, was broadly compounded of work done from these two positions' (1981, p. 12). In the 1960s and 1970s, however, new theoretical paradigms were brought into play, which sought to establish the materiality of culture itself. As Williams continues: 'a new kind of convergence is becoming evident ... it differs in its insistence that "cultural practice" and "cultural production" ... are not simply derived from an otherwise constituted social order but are themselves major elements in its constitution ... it sees culture as the *signifying system* through which necessarily ... a social order is communicated, reproduced, experienced and explored' (ibid., pp. 12-13). Williams himself could write with peculiar authority here quite simply because his own 'cultural materialism' had come to provide the paradigmatic instance, in the English-speaking world at least, of precisely this new kind of convergence.

Cultural Materialisms

Which takes us finally to our third key term. This book is about Cultural Studies, cultural theory and Marxism, but it is also about the particular kind of cultural theory to which Williams gave the name, and which Hartman finds by no means entirely unsympathetic: cultural materialism. Williams coined the term to denote his own break from an older tradition of British Communist Marxism, on the one hand, and that distinctly British version of literary humanism associated above all with the Leavises, on the other. There are a great many books on cultural theory (it is a veritable growth industry), a growing number on cultural materialism and even a few on Williams. Most of the material on cultural theory remains depressingly uniform, however, in its celebration of postmodern 'difference': a touch of Foucault and Deleuze, a dash of Derrida, combined to produce a wry knowingness, ideally neither shaken nor stirred. Much of the commentary on cultural materialism tends to conflate it with Stephen Greenblatt's 'new historicism', as an emergent orthodoxy in post-Foucauldian literary studies. So, for example, Howard Felperin describes cultural materialism as the 'counterpart in Britain' of the new historicism (Felperin, 1990, p.1), while Scott Wilson treats new historicism as 'the bastard offspring of ... cultural materialism' (Wilson, 1995, p. 55). Kiernan Ryan has even claimed that cultural materialism and new historicism have together 'become the effective horizon of advanced literary study' (Ryan, 1996, p. ix). In a similar vein, Wilson insists that cultural materialism and new historicism 'now constitute the new academic order ... in Renaissance studies' (Wilson, 1995, p. viii). If this is so - and I am by no means entirely persuaded - then this must be a rather different cultural materialism from that of Williams himself, for whom it had been an explicitly 'Marxist theory' (Williams, 1977a, p. 5). Marxism is distinctly unfashionable these days and there is, of course, no necessary virtue in fidelity to an argument's foundational statement, nor any necessary vice in theoretical revision. But insofar as Williams was both a socialist and a (very peculiar) Marxist, his position remains as unassimilable to new historicism as it once was to Hoggart's.

Much of this contemporary 'cultural materialism' derives from Jonathan Dollimore and Alan Sinfield, rather than from Williams.

Dollimore himself readily admits to borrowing the term from Williams, but nonetheless describes his own cultural materialism as growing 'from an eclectic body of work ... which can be broadly characterised as cultural analysis'. He adds that this work includes: 'the considerable output of Williams himself, and, more generally, the convergence of history, sociology and English in cultural studies, some of the major developments in feminism, as well as continental Marxist-structuralist and post-structuralist theory, especially that of Althusser, Macherey, Gramsci and Foucault' (Dollimore, 1994a, pp. 2–3). But this surely is not cultural materialism: rather, it is Cultural Studies itself, in the sense that we have been using the term here. And if cultural materialism is reduced to Cultural Studies in this fashion, then the effect is very different from that intended by either Dollimore or Sinfield: in short, to elide the specifically Marxist contribution to the development of the field. John Higgins has taken understandable exception to Dollimore and Sinfield's apparent failure to register the specificity of Williams's argument. 'At least as far as Williams was concerned,' he writes: the "term" cultural materialism was intended to have a clearly defined conceptual content ... which would put it at odds with ... "Marxist-structural and post-structuralist theory"' (Higgins, 1999, p 172). Higgins is surely right to insist on this difference, no matter how much one might sympathise with Dollimore and Sinfield, or with Greenblatt, in their attempts to recast literary studies as a sub-branch of Cultural Studies. For, in truth, Williams's cultural materialism was never intended simply as coextensive with Cultural Studies, but rather as a particular argument within and even against it.

Let us say a little more, then, about Williams himself and about his own cultural materialism. At the time of his early death, at the age of 66 in January 1988, he was still widely regarded as the most important 'left-wing' figure in post-war British intellectual life. He had taught in adult education and later at Cambridge University, where he was Professor of Drama until his retirement in 1983. His various contributions, as a literary critic, as a central source of inspiration for Cultural Studies, as a key figure in the New Left intelligentsia, even as a 'realist' novelist, were all widely acknowledged. Little wonder, then, that his death should have come as a 'fearful shock' to the British Left (Inglis, 1995, p. 1). As Higgins recalls: 'progressive intellectuals throughout the world mourned the passing of one of the foremost socialist thinkers, intellectuals and cultural activists of the postwar period' (1999, p. 1). I cannot speak for the world, but something very like this certainly occurred in Melbourne, where I live and work (cf. Levy and Otto, 1989). In retrospect, however, it seems surprising how little of this extensive eulogy and commentary was devoted to Williams's work as a theorist (with or without the capital 'T'). For the main part, it tended to deal either with his status as a grand old man of the Left (Blackburn, 1988) or with his contribution to the development of contemporary Cultural Studies (Garnham, 1988). Cornel

West's 1988 memorial address to the National Film Institute described Williams memorably as 'the last of the great European male revolutionary socialist intellectuals born before the end of the age of Europe' (West, 1995, p. ix). The tribute was real, but as Prendergast would later observe, its 'emphasis on endings and closures ... implies a perspective of completion' (1995, p. 1). Even the most impressive of the memorials, Eagleton's collection of *Critical Perspectives* (Eagleton, 1989a), had announced on its rear cover that it included essays on Williams's work 'as a literary critic, as a student of popular culture, as a novelist and as an analyst of contemporary politics and society', but not, significantly, as a theorist. Distance from the immediate shock has failed to rectify the situation. Indeed, Williams has increasingly been subject to something of the same kind of forgetting that overcame Marxism more generally. The extended treatment of his work promised by *Media, Culture and Society* (Sparks, 1988, p. 133) failed to materialise. The co-editor of a (largely) American collection would soon conclude that 'though he has ... been dead for less than five years, he is already part of a different political age' (Dworkin, 1993, p. 54). Inglis's peculiarly eccentric pseudo-biography remained determinedly hostile to the theoretical writings: reading Williams, by turn, as the Left's lost leader who might have been 'a great politician' and as a kind of Richard Hoggart fallen among theoreticists, it judged the excursions into theory both 'redundant' and 'unreadable' (Inglis, 1995, pp. 205, 249).

I suspect this under-appreciation of the sheer theoretical novelty of Williams's writing derives in part from the fact that Anglophone audiences still tend to think of 'Theory' as an essentially French affair (though, to be fair, that is certainly not the import of West's memorial). I will argue here for a much more positive assessment of Williams's significance as a cultural theorist. What exactly are we to understand, then, by Williams's sense of the term 'cultural materialism'? He had first used it in a short essay published in the hundredth issue of the journal, *New Left Review*, to which he had been a long-standing contributor. Cultural materialism, he explained:

> is a theory of culture as a (social and material) productive process and of specific practices, of 'arts', as social uses of material means of production (from language as material 'practical consciousness' to the specific technologies of writing and forms of writing, through to mechanical and electronic communications systems). (Williams, 1980a, p. 243)

The position would be 'spelled out more fully', he added, in *Marxism and Literature* and in the book that would eventually be published in England as *Culture*, in the United States as *The Sociology of Culture*. There is an important sense in which these two books do indeed 'spell out' the theory, and they will, then, command much of our attention in the pages that follow, most especially in chapter four, where Williams's cultural materialism is elaborated upon in some detail. But we should note also Williams's insistence, in the 'Introduction' to *Marxism and Literature*, that cultural materialism had been 'a position which, as a matter of theory, I have arrived at over the years' (Williams, 1977a, p. 5). Its pre-history, as part of a much longer intellectual evolution, therefore also demands our attention. That history, as articulated both in Williams's own work and in that of his more directly relevant predecessors and contemporaries, will be surveyed in the two chapters which immediately follow. Chapters 2 and 3 will be devoted to the complex question of Williams's earlier 'left culturalism' and its doubly ambivalent relationship to Leavisism on the one hand, Marxism on the other. That such a legacy exists seems incontrovertible: as late as 1979, and while commenting on *Marxism and Literature*, Williams would still insist that, 'I was trying to say something very much against the grain of two traditions, one which has totally spiritualized cultural production, the other which has relegated it to secondary status' (Williams, 1979a, pp. 352-3). His initial negotiation of this relationship finds expression most importantly in *Culture and Society* and *The Long Revolution*, first published in 1958 and 1961, respectively. These two works will provide a central focus for our third chapter. But Williams was by no means working in an intellectual or political vacuum. His reaction against Leavisism had been shared, in part at least, by Hoggart; that against Communist Marxism by Thompson. Their work, as also the wider context of the radical intellectual culture of the 1950s and early 1960s, will require further examination at this point.

In *Marxism and Literature*, Williams described cultural materialism as 'a theory of the specificities of material cultural and literary production within historical materialism' (1977a, p. 5). This latter term is Marx's, and it therefore comes as little surprise that Williams should here view cultural materialism as 'in its specific fields ... part of what I at least see as the central thinking of Marxism' (ibid., pp. 5-6). We are under no obligation, however, to concur in this judgement. Bennett, for example, has insisted that there is nothing especially Marxist about cultural materialism; and that other intellectual traditions, most notably feminism and Foucauldian post-structuralism, are actually more properly 'historical materialist' than Marxism itself (Bennett, 1990, pp. 13-14, 35-6). From a position much more sympathetic to Marx, and to the base/superstructure metaphor, Eagleton has argued that Williams's cultural materialism is not so much non-Marxist as pre-Marxist: 'it returns us back *before* Marx's full development of historical materialism, to the earlier philosophical contentions between materialism and idealism' (Eagleton, 1989b, p. 169). In an obituary written shortly after Williams's death, Nicholas Garnham, one of his very few occasional co-authors (Garnham and Williams, 1986), and indeed a self-confessed cultural materialist in his own right (Garnham,

1983), chose to stress that 'Williams's importance lies precisely in his at times highly critical but nonetheless lifelong allegiance ... to historical materialism as an intellectual project' (Garnham, 1988, p. 130). Clearly, the connection between Williams's cultural materialism and other materialisms, historical and otherwise, remains a matter for some considerable controversy, not least in the ranks of his admirers, among whom one could count Bennett, Eagleton and Garnham. The point at issue here is most certainly not Marxism as it had been understood in Communism, but rather a whole series of more recent, and in truth more intellectually interesting, materialisms, most obviously Western Marxism, but also the various post-structuralisms which have in different ways emphasised the 'materiality of the sign'.

This question, that of the relation between Williams's cultural materialism and other, contemporaneous, would-be 'materialist' theories of culture, will be broached in Chapter 4, further explored in Chapters 5 and 6, and 'resolved', if only provisionally, in the concluding, seventh chapter. Chapters 5 and 6 take as their theme the various disciplinary, or at least proto-disciplinary, forms of intellectual inquiry that have been significantly influenced either by Williams himself, or by more generally cultural-materialist notions, or, more commonly, by a combination of each. Chapter 5 deals with what has come to be known as Cultural Studies, with what the Leavises had understood as 'mass civilization', Chapter 6 with literary studies, with what they had meant by 'minority culture'. These matters are discussed primarily in relation to Anglophone intellectual culture. In Chapter 7, however, we proceed to a necessarily tentative, although by no means entirely provisional, comparison between British cultural materialism and those developments in late twentieth-century German and French thought most commonly canvassed as its rough equivalent, in particular Habermas's theory of communicative action, Foucault's post-structuralist 'genealogy' and the cultural sociology of Pierre Bourdieu. This last chapter, as also the book itself, finally concludes with a discussion of the respective relevance of these various theoretical humanisms and anti-humanisms, not only to the would-be academic discipline of Cultural Studies, but also to the wider prospects for a more general, emancipatory politics.

Notes

1 Hall identified three main lines of development that lay outside the two main paradigms: Lacanian psychoanalysis, the political economy of culture and Foucauldian 'difference theory' - in short, 'classical' base/superstructure Marxism and post-structuralism (1980, pp. 70-1).

2 Jones's sense of the myth is inspired, in the first place, by Williams's own recollection that: 'One newspaper went so far as to refer, seriously, to a book called *The Uses of Culture* by Raymond Hoggart' (Williams, 1970).

3 Strictly speaking, this was not an original coinage, since the same term

had previously been used by the anthropologist, Marvin Harris (Harris, 1968). However, Williams does not seem to have been familiar with Harris's work.

4   Anderson's apparent triumphalism is also belied by his own subsequent assessment that 'the Right has provided one fluent version of where the world is going ... after another' (2000, p. 19).

5 This is a putative fifth conception of Cultural Studies canvassed in the early issues of the *International Journal of Cultural Studies*. The modish use of the prefix aside, it is difficult to see how it differs substantially from the earlier sense of the interdisciplinary (cf. Hartley, 1998, pp. 5-8).

6   Hartman cites Benda's early use of the term 'la guerre des cultures' in exactly this context (Benda, 1927, p. 33; Hartman, 1997, pp. 1-2).

2

Politics and Letters

What I have most wanted to do ... is to make political writing
into an art ... looking back through my work, I see that it is
invariably where I lacked a *political* purpose that I wrote lifeless
books ... (Orwell, 'Why I write')

Shallow:	Give me pardon, sir: if, sir, you come with news from the court, I take it there's but two ways, either to utter them, or to conceal them. I am, sir, under the king, in some authority.
Pistol:	Under which king, Bezonian? speak, or die.
Shallow:	Under King Harry.
Pistol:	Harry the Fourth? or Fifth?
Shallow:	Harry the Fourth.
Pistol:	A foutre for thine office! Sir John, thy tender lambkin now is king; Harry the Fifth's the man. (Shakespeare, *Henry IV Part II*, iv)

Trained in the discipline of English Literature at Cambridge, Williams
derived much of his initial critical vocabulary from F.R. Leavis, whose
work had provided English Literature with its dominant paradigm
during the middle decades of the twentieth century. Leavis in turn
stood in close relation to a much older tradition of 'literary' specula-
tion about the relationship between culture and society, in which the
claims of culture, understood both as art and as 'way of life', had been
counterposed, normally antithetically, to those of an industrialised or
industrialising, 'mechanical' or materialist, 'civilisation'. In the late

nineteenth and early twentieth centuries, this tradition had become institutionally organised, both in Britain and in the wider British Empire, into the academic discipline we now know as 'English'. Perhaps its most extreme formulation is in Leavis's own work, in the journal *Scrutiny* which he inspired, and more generally in the 'Leavisism' of his close collaborators, most obviously Q.D. Leavis, but also, for example, Denys Thompson and L.C. Knights.[1] Williams was never actually a student of Leavis, but the friends and collaborators with whom he co-founded the journal *Politics and Letters* in 1947, Wolf Mankowicz and Clifford Collins, were 'regularly taught by him' (Williams, 1979a, p. 67). Formed by the biographical experience of Welsh working-class life - he grew up in the small village of Pandy near the Anglo-Welsh border, his father a railwayman and a trade unionist - Williams was also a lifelong socialist. As a student at Cambridge, he had very briefly been a member of the British Communist Party; he was a Labour Party supporter during the 1950s and 1960s; an enthusiast for various New Left causes, especially the Campaign for Nuclear Disarmament; co-author in 1967 and 1968 of the *May Day Manifesto* (Hall et al., 1967; Williams, 1968a); and in his last years a fairly close associate of the left-inclined Welsh nationalist party, Plaid Cymru. Such political involvements led to an enduring interest in Marxist and quasi-Marxist versions of social and cultural theory. In one sense, then, the key to an understanding of Williams's intellectual evolution consists of an appreciation of how he variously negotiated his own doubly ambivalent relationship to Marxism and to Leavisism. Williams himself and his younger interlocuters from the *New Left Review* chose to represent this relationship as that between 'politics and letters', the title of the journal he had co-edited at Cambridge during 1947 and 1948, and also of the collection of 1979 'interviews with New Left Review'. Recalling the earlier journal in the later interviews, Williams explained that: 'Our intention was to produce a review that would ... unite radical left politics with Leavisite literary criticism' (1979a, p. 65).

This peculiar amalgam of Leavisite criticism and Marxian socialism has led many commentators, notably his own former student, Terry Eagleton, to describe Williams's early work as 'Left-Leavisism' (Eagleton, 1976, p. 22). The young Eagleton found his erstwhile mentor guilty, by turn, of an 'idealist epistemology, organicist aesthetics and corporatist sociology', all three of which had their roots in 'Romantic populism' (ibid., p. 27). Initially at any rate, Williams had been inclined to concede something to the force of this argument. He would soon insist to the contrary, however, that:

> What is suggested by the term Left-Leavisism is a coherent position which has moved somewhat along the political spectrum. This is a false diagnosis because it leads to the projection of the whole

complex onto the entire work. In fact, it was the elements of inco-
herence which were to prove decisive. (Williams, 1979a, p. 195)

No doubt, Williams was as entitled as anyone to insist on the incoher-
ence in his own early work (the immediate occasion for these remarks
is *Drama from Ibsen to Eliot*, 1952). But there is a certain obtuseness,
nonetheless, in this refusal to acknowledge the extent to which a loose
combination of Leavisite criticism and leftist politics had indeed
become a relatively 'coherent' argument, from the mid-1950s on, both
in his own work and in British intellectual life more generally, especially amongst the profession of English teachers. In retrospect, I find
little difficulty in detecting exactly this combination at work amongst
those who taught me English Literature at a North of England 'gram-
mar school', that is, a selective state high school, during the mid to late
1960s.

John Higgins has recently argued very persuasively that it was not
so much Leavis, as T.S. Eliot, who provided 'the single most powerful
influence' on Williams's thinking about drama; and rather less persuasively that this significantly undermines the view of Williams's
early work as Left-Leavisite (Higgins, 1999, p. 22). In itself, this stress
on Eliot clearly provides a useful corrective to an overly Leavisian
reading of Williams. For, as Williams himself explained, he had been
able to 'find no help at all in the Cambridge tradition' (Williams,
1979a, p. 192), when confronted by the central theoretical problem in
his early work on drama, that of the attempt to understand naturalism
as a form. And Eliot's verse drama had indeed seemed to suggest a
way forward beyond naturalism, to have 'brought us to a point at
which ... a solution can be envisaged' (Williams, 1952, p. 270). But
these amendments need not necessitate the wholesale revision Higgins
seems to envisage. To the contrary, whatever their differences over the
drama, the more general argument in Leavis and Eliot remains much
more compatible than Higgins will allow. Leavis had himself vigorously championed Eliot's poetry and there were clear and acknowledged intellectual affinities between the academic and the poet, affinities which became the more marked, moreover, as Leavisism acquired
an increasingly conservative character in the years after the Second
World War. Asked to explain the impetus to write *Culture and Society*,
Williams would pointedly identify Eliot and Leavis as the writers
whose work he had sought to counter (Williams, 1979a, p. 97). There
seems little reason to doubt his word. We will need to take account,
then, of Eliot as well as of Leavis, acknowledging their differences by
all means, but also seeking to register their many underlying affinities.
What kind of literary criticism was it, then, that Williams first encountered in the Leavises and Eliot? And what kind of Marxism in the
British Communist Party?

(Politics and) Letters

It is characteristic of Leavis that he should have attempted no formal statement of the principles by which his literary and cultural criticism is guided. The nearest to such a formulation is in the essay, 'Literary Criticism and Philosophy', written in reply to a challenge to defend his position 'more abstractedly' from the philosopher, René Wellek. 'Your insistence on a firm grasp of the actual,' Wellek had charged, 'presupposes you in the direction of a realist philosophy' (1937, p. 376). Leavis's response was to counterpose the poet's concern with the 'concrete' to the philosopher's with the 'abstract'. 'The critic's aim', explained Leavis, 'is, first, to realize as sensitively and completely as possible this or that which claims his attention'; and then to situate the work under consideration into a hierarchy of judgement, by reference to other similar such works, that is, to 'an organization of similarly "placed" things, things that have found their bearings with regard to one another, and not a theoretical system determined by abstract considerations' (Leavis, 1962a, p. 213). Leavis's resistance to explicit theorisation finds ultimate expression, therefore, in the famous dictum that: 'My whole effort was to work in terms of concrete judgements and particular analyses: "This - doesn't it? - bears such a relation to that; this kind of thing - don't you find it so? wears better than that?"' (ibid., p. 215). This insistence on the concrete analysis of specific literary texts has all the appearance of traditional English empiricism. But appearances can be deceptive. Leavis's formulation can avoid an explicit statement of evaluative criteria only because it assumes the existence of values already common to the literary critic and to his or her readers: the values are unstated but present nonetheless. And these specifically literary values in turn form part of a wider system of cultural, social and historical evaluation. By contrast, Eliot was a much more explicitly 'systematic' thinker: hence, the very serious attempt to fashion a specifically Christian social theory, drawing on such explicitly 'theoretical' resources as Hegelian philosophy, Durkheimian anthropology and Mannheimian sociology. But much that is made explicit in Eliot runs parallel to the implicit logic of Leavis's own unsystematised 'system'. Let me call attention here to what seem to be five especially salient features, all but one of which is present, with varying inflections, in both Eliot and Leavis: an organicist aesthetic; an anti-utilitarian social critique troped around the antithesis between culture and civilisation; a pessimistic, even apocalyptic, historicism; a militant understanding of the social role of the intellectual; and a more general cultural nationalism.

That Leavis's and Eliot's respective aesthetics represent variants of organicism, structurally analogous to the great systems of classical German idealism, has become something of an intellectual commonplace. Eliot's organicism is apparent, for example, in his insistence that literary culture is the creation, not of an aggregate of individual writers, but of 'the mind of Europe ... which abandons nothing *en route*' (Eliot, 1963a, p. 16). A similar organicism is apparent in Leavis's sense of literature as 'essentially something more than an accumulation of separate works: it has an organic form, or constitutes an organic order in relation to which the individual writer has ... significance and ... being' (Leavis, 1962a, p. 184). The centre of Leavis's intellectual effort consisted, then, in an attempt to map out the tradition of the English novel on the one hand, the tradition of English poetry on the other, each imagined in exactly such organicist terms. Conceived thus, the literary tradition is not simply an artefact of the critical enterprise, but rather an objective 'fact' of cultural history itself. It follows that, for Leavis, writing which sits uncomfortably with 'the tradition' is not properly 'literature' at all: the obvious instances here include both popular fiction and the contemporary avant-garde. Leavis's organicism is operative both at the level of the cultural tradition as a whole and at that of the individual literary work. At this second level, it finds expression in the aesthetic ideal of an organic unity of form and content. This notion informs the invidious comparison between Lawrence and Joyce, for example, by which the latter is judged inferior on the grounds that 'there is no organic principle determining, informing, and controlling [the work] into a vital whole' (Leavis, 1962b, p. 36). Perhaps the point is made most explicitly, however, when Leavis identifies the central weakness of Flaubert's *Madame Bovary* as 'the discrepancy between the technical ("aesthetic") intensity, with the implied attribute of interest to the subject, and the actual moral and human paucity of this subject' (ibid., p. 22).

The organic properties of 'great' literature derive, moreover, from the organicism of human social life, at least in its 'normal', 'healthy' forms. Thus the central category of Leavis's aesthetic, hinted at in Wellek's charge of a tendency towards realism, is that of a commitment to 'life' itself as a value. For Leavis, great literature is that which can render a form adequate to the expression of life: 'the major novelists ... count in the same ways as the major poets, in the sense that they are significant in terms of that human awareness they promote; awareness of the possibilities of life' (Leavis, 1962b, p. 10). Leavis was vehemently opposed to aestheticism, in the sense of *l'art pour l'art*. Hence, his insistence that the defining characteristic of the great English novelists is that 'they are all distinguished by a vital capacity for experience, a kind of reverent openness before life, and a marked moral intensity' (ibid., p. 17). Conrad, for example, is in Leavis's view, 'one of those creative geniuses whose distinction is manifested in their being peculiarly alive in their time - peculiarly alive *to* it' (ibid., p. 32). Leavis's assessment of English poetry runs along similar lines, so that the central weakness of the nineteenth century is its other-worldliness, its flight from reality, and, correspondingly, Eliot's significance is in his ability to 'invent techniques ... adequate to the ways of feeling, or modes of experience, of adult, sensitive moderns' (Leavis, 1938, p. 25). 'Life', in Leavis's sense of the word, is by no means identical with reality, but rather a value to be set against many aspects of the real. Perhaps the most precise statement of what he meant by the term is in his commentary on Blake: 'To be spontaneous, and in its spontaneity creative, is of the essence of life, which manifests itself in newness that can't be exhaustively reduced to the determined' (Leavis, 1972a, p. 15). Such non-determined, spontaneous creativity remains profoundly antithetical to a contemporary civilisation Leavis judged irredeemably utilitarian in character. So understood, that is, as a 'canon' of 'great works', the literary tradition came to provide the comparatively new academic discipline of English Literature with its central subject matter. By excluding the merely 'fictional', and much else besides, Leavis's aesthetic enabled a relatively precise definition and demarcation of the subject's intellectual and institutional boundaries.

For both Eliot and Leavis, the general culture bore a similarly organic form to that of the specifically literary. In *Notes Towards the Definition of Culture*, Eliot deployed precisely such an expanded, anthropological, sense of the term, as referring to 'all the characteristic activities and interests of a people', everything from Derby Day and Henley Regatta, through Wensleydale cheese and boiled cabbage, to Gothic churches and Elgar (Eliot, 1962, p, 31). In a later appendix, he proposed something very close to a formal definition: 'By "culture"', he writes, 'I mean first of all ... the way of life of a particular people living together in one place. That culture is made visible in their arts, in their social system, in their habits and customs, in their religion' (ibid., p. 120). Here as elsewhere, the reference to religion is especially significant: for Eliot, the culture of a people is necessarily an 'incarnation' of their religion (Eliot, 1962, p. 33). Hence, the gloomy prognosis, outlined at some length in *The Idea of a Christian Society*, that unlimited industrialisation might generate a generalised detachment from tradition and an alienation from religion, and thereby, in effect, the demise of culture (Eliot, 1982, p. 53). A culture, in Eliot's sense of the term, is the common property of a whole people. It will be consciously understood only by the cultural elites of the society, but nonetheless embodied in the unconscious texture of the everyday lives of other classes. So he writes that:

> What is important is a structure of society in which there will be from 'top' to 'bottom', a continuous gradation of cultural levels ... we should not consider the upper levels as possessing *more* culture than the lower, but as representing a more conscious culture ... I incline to believe that no true democracy can maintain itself unless it contains these different levels of culture. (Eliot, 1962, p. 48)

As a description of the class structures of mid-twentieth-century capitalist society, this seems almost risible. But the model is less that of Attlee's Britain (the book was first published in 1948) than an idealised version of medieval Christendom, where class is understood in overwhelmingly 'functional' terms. In principle, then, culture is not for Eliot a minority resource to be disseminated through education, but is already more or less consciously present in the lives of all classes. We should add that this will be especially so in 'healthy' societies, such as Eliot imagined medieval Europe to have been, but much less so in the increasingly non-Christian world conjured into being as part of what Williams would term 'the long revolution'.

For Leavis, as for Eliot, literary and non-literary culture were inextricably connected: in a healthy culture, there is 'behind the literature, a social culture and an art of living' (Leavis, 1962a, p. 190). For Leavis, as for Eliot, such cultural health must entail some kind of unity of sophisticated and popular cultures. Pre-industrial England provided Leavis with the exemplary instance of an 'organic community', in which such unity between the sophisticated and the popular had still remained possible. In *Culture and Environment* and again in the later *Nor Shall My Sword*, Leavis relied heavily on George Sturt's *The Wheelwright's Shop* to establish this sense of what the organic community had entailed: 'Sturt's villagers expressed their human nature, they satisfied their human needs, in terms of the natural environment; and the things they made ... together with their relations with one another constituted a human environment, and a subtlety of adjustment and adaptation, as right and inevitable' (Leavis and Thompson, 1960, p. 91). Such community remained the implicit ideal, by comparison with which contemporary society would be judged and found wanting. But Leavis also placed more explicit emphasis than had Eliot on elite culture, or 'minority culture' to use his own phrase. For Leavis, the essential value of a common culture devolved upon its capacity to sustain such a culturally superior minority. 'In their keeping', he writes, 'is the language, the changing idiom, upon which fine living depends, and without which distinction of spirit is thwarted and incoherent. By "culture" I mean the use of such a language' (Leavis, 1948, p. 145). This stress on language is distinctively Leavisite: it explains the peculiar significance for Leavis of *literary* culture (the equivalent role in Eliot is played by religion); and also the power of his insistence on the need for a close reading of literary texts. For it is in the language itself, at its most literary, that the truths of life are most clearly formed.

Both Leavis and Eliot were deeply critical of modern, mechanical civilisation and both subscribed to what was in effect a theory of cultural decline. In his essay on 'The Metaphysical Poets', Eliot had compared the early seventeenth-century English poets, Chapman, Donne, Lord Herbert of Cherbury, with those of the nineteenth century, such as Tennyson and Browning. He concluded that in the Metaphysicals, and by implication in all previous poetry, there had existed what he termed a 'unified sensibility', in which thought and feeling retained an essential unity. During the seventeenth century, however, and especially in the work of Milton and Dryden, a 'dissociation of sensibility' had set in from which English culture has never recovered. 'The difference is not a simple difference of degree between poets', he writes: 'It is something which had happened to the mind of England' (Eliot, 1963b, p. 287). Elsewhere, Eliot stressed that this dissociation had been 'a consequence of the same causes which brought about the Civil War' (Eliot, 1968, p. 34). Their eventual outcome would be capitalist industrialisation, which will in turn press the logics of dissociation towards their own terrible terminus: 'more insidious than any censorship', Eliot argued, 'is the steady influence which operates silently in any mass society organized for profit, for the depression of standards of art and culture' (Eliot, 1982, p. 66). In similar fashion, Leavis identified the dominant values of modern British society as essentially utilitarian, or in his own memorable phrase, 'technologico-Benthamite', and thus essentially hostile to 'life'. In contemporary society, Leavis comments, 'there is a dawning unselfrecognised conviction that we can get on, and get on better, without much life' (Leavis, 1972a, p. 33). The cultural logic of such a civilisation will militate against life, insofar as it is essentially materialistic, and will thereby reduce all problems of value to the level of crude material acquisition. In a highly public response to C.P. Snow's 1959 Rede Lecture, Leavis described Snow as wholly representative of a world 'in which the vital inspiration, the creative drive, is "Jam tomorrow" (if you haven't any today) or (if you have it today) "More jam tomorrow"' (Leavis, 1962c, p. 25).

Such materialism was, in Leavis's view, by no means a merely 'ideological' phenomenon. Quite the contrary, it arose as a direct consequence of the process of technological change precipitated by the industrial revolution. 'Technological change has marked cultural consequences,' writes Leavis: 'There is an implicit logic that will impose, if not met by creative intelligence and corrective purpose, simplifying and reductive criteria of human need and human good, and generate, to form the mind and the spirit of civilization, disastrously false and inadequate conceptions of ... ends' (Leavis, 1972a, pp. 94-5). Thus, the material process of mass production has two main cultural consequences, 'levelling-down' and 'standardization', each of which is essentially inimical to life. Technological change was, for Leavis, destructive of both individuality and creativity, and tended toward the reduction of all human beings to the status of passive respondents to external material forces. Technologico-Benthamite civilisation is thus increasingly inhabited by 'the worker whose routine work, requiring or permitting no creative effort on his (sic) part, and no large active interest - little more, in fact than automatisms - leaves him (sic) incapable of any but the passive and the crude' (ibid., p. 87). For Leavis, as for Eliot, a society such as this is of necessity hostile to art. Hence, the particularly gloomy prognosis for poetry in the modern world:

the finer values are ceasing to be a matter of even conventional concern for any except the minority capable of the highest level.
Everywhere below, a process of standardization, mass-production,
and levelling-down goes forward, and civilization is coming to mean
a solidarity achieved by the exploitation of the most readily released
response. So that poetry, in the future, if there is poetry, seems likely to matter even less to the world. (Leavis, 1938, pp. 213-14)

But poetry is only the extreme case of a more general problem. In fact,
the whole of literature, art and humane culture is threatened by the
material dynamics of contemporary society. As Leavis himself would
recall of the group involved in producing *Scrutiny*: 'The dialectic
against which we had to vindicate literature and humane culture was
that of the external or material civilization we lived in' (1963, p. 5).
That dialectic found its clearest impress in popular fiction on the one
hand, commercial advertising on the other. Q.D. Leavis elaborated
upon the culturally deleterious consequences of the former in her
influential *Fiction and the Reading Public*:

This for the sensitive minority is no laughing matter: these novelists
are read by the governing classes as well as by the masses, and they
impinge directly on the minority, menacing the standards by which
they live ... These writers ... work upon and solidify herd prejudice
and ... debase the emotional currency by touching grossly on fine
issues. (Q.D. Leavis, 1979, p. 65)

F.R. Leavis and Denys Thompson devoted much of their attention to
the latter in *Culture and Environmen*(Leavis and Thompson, 1960), a
manual for English teachers designed in part to educate their pupils in
effective resistance to advertising. As we noted in Chapter 1, Leavis's
anti-utilitarianism at times runs strangely parallel to Frankfurt School
Marxism. But the Leavises themselves clearly understood Marxism in
much the same fashion as did Parsons, as in essence merely a sub-variant of utilitarianism. Since utilitarian capitalist civilisation was
already materialist, it followed that Marxist materialism would prove,
not so much a solution to, as an exacerbation of, its most fundamental
problems: 'to aim at solving the problems of civilization in terms of the
"class war" is to aim ... at completing the work of capitalism and its
products' (Leavis, 1932, p. 213).

For the Leavises, as for Eliot, the previous 300 years could best be
characterised as a process of disintegration and decline. In Leavis's
version, however, the problem arose quite specifically as a result of
industrialisation, and not, therefore, as a result of whatever it was that
had caused the Civil War (a set of causes which must include the
Protestant Reformation). The destruction of the old organic community and its replacement by a more recent, and inorganic, industrial civil-

isation became one of Leavis's central preoccupations: 'Its destruction ... is the most important fact of recent history'. And Leavis had little doubt as to the adverse consequences of this 'vast and terrifying disintegration' (Leavis and Thompson, 1960, p. 87). To Snow's essentially benign account of the industrial revolution, Leavis would retort that: 'This ... is mere brute assertion, callous in its irresponsibility ... the actual history has been ... incomparably and poignantly more complex than that' (Leavis, 1962c, p. 24). Crucially, the breakdown of the organic community had produced a rupture between sophisticated and popular cultures. In Shakespeare or Marvell or Bunyan, Leavis explained, we find clear evidence of a cultural unity between the sophisticated and the popular: 'Bunyan shows how the popular culture to which he bears witness could merge with literary culture at the level of great literature' (Leavis, 1962a, p. 191). But with the Augustans this unity disappears and 'sophisticated culture cuts itself off from the traditional culture of the people'. The immediate consequence of industrialisation had been the almost total elimination of the older popular culture: 'By Wordsworth's death, the Industrial Revolution had done its work and the traditional culture of the people was no longer there' (ibid., p. 192). In the longer term, sophisticated culture would itself become increasingly obsessed with 'dream worlds' and so correspondingly divorced from 'life'.

As Leavis himself came to recognise, this 'actual history' was not history as conventionally understood by most historians. Indeed, his gloomy historicism ran directly contrary to much of the dominant historiographical wisdom. So when Leavis sought to distance his work from the immediately cognate discipline of history, he did so on the grounds of the latter's positivist empiricism. This was not simply, as it is sometimes represented, a matter of his stress on the 'internal' analysis of the literary text, as opposed to the 'external' analysis of the text's historical context. Much more importantly, what was at stake here was the centrality of evaluation, both as applied to the text and as applied elsewhere. As becomes clear, for example, from Leavis's criticisms of the historian, G.M. Trevelyan, the relevant questions of value pertain as much to historical context as to literary text. The unanswered, because unasked, questions in Trevelyan, Leavis insists, are:

> What, as a civilization to live in and be of, did England offer at such and such a time? As we pass from now to then, what light is thrown on human possibilities - on the potentialities of civilized life? In what respects might it have been better to live then than now? What tentative conception of an ideal civilization are we prompted towards by the hints we gather from history? (Leavis, 1962a, p. 200)

It is this sense of history (and sociology) as inadequately concerned with problems of value which led Leavisism to its own peculiarly militant sense of the social role of the intellectual, and of the special nature of English studies in relation to that role.

For all the obvious theoretical affinities between Eliot and Leavis - an organicist conception of culture, the central antithesis between culture and civilisation, the theory of cultural decline - Leavis's pessimism is finally less unremitting. The reason should be obvious: Eliot's insistence on the priority of religion over culture had left him more positively sympathetic than Leavis to the Catholic Middle Ages, correspondingly more fearful of an unlimitedly industrialising and secularising future. Eliot's Anglo-Catholicism thus precluded the possibility of a meliorist strategy such as Leavis would attempt to pursue through literary education. Stripped of Eliot's Christian medievalism, and rendered compatible, if not with secularism, then at least with Nonconformist Protestantism, Leavis's own version of idealist social theory aimed to transform the literary minority into an intellectual church militant. For Eliot, the cultural elite will tend to attach itself to the dominant class: 'An élite must ... be attached to *some* class' he wrote, 'it is likely to be the dominant class' (Eliot, 1962, p. 42). For Leavis, by contrast, the literary intelligentsia was to be trained precisely in opposition to the dominant classes. So English Literature would become, not merely one discipline amongst many, but rather a rallying point for the defence of humane values against the depradations of utilitarian civilisation.

Central to Leavis's programme of action was the role of the ideal English School, outlined in his *Education and the University*. The implicit logic of technological change can be reversed, we have seen, if met by 'creative intelligence' and 'corrective purpose'. And the primary source of such an effort was to be located here in the English School. The 'literary mind', Leavis argued, is the central kind of mind: 'an intelligence with the sensitiveness, the flexibility and the disciplined mature preoccupation with value that should be the product of literary training' (Leavis, 1948, p. 55). As such, there is nothing merely 'literary' about the literary mind: Leavis's model English School would aspire to assess the cultural value of whole communities, whole civilisations. Though recognising this entailed that 'everyone would have been required to come to fairly close terms ... with other fields of special study' (ibid., p. 57), the central informing virtues would nonetheless be those of the literary mind. 'In any period', wrote Leavis, 'it is upon a very small minority that the discerning appreciation of art and literature depends.' This minority:

> constitute the consciousness of the race (or a branch of it) at a given time. For such capacity does not belong merely to an aesthetic realm: it implies responsiveness to theory as well as to art, to science and philosophy in so far as these may affect the sense of the human situation and the nature of life. (Leavis, 1948, pp. 143-4)

'English' thus ceases to be a specialist discipline and becomes, in effect, the consciousness of the race. Such grand claims led Leavis by an almost inescapable logic to the view, aired in the polemic against Snow, that the English School would 'generate in the university a centre of consciousness (and conscience) for our civilization' (Leavis, 1962c, p. 30). The fundamental radicalism of the Leavisite project inhered, then, in this rejectionist stance toward the already established intellectual culture, here represented by the hapless C.P. Snow. As Francis Mulhern observed, Leavisism aspired to create 'an intellectual formation of a type virtually unknown in and deeply alien to English bourgeois culture: an "intelligentsia" in the classic sense of the term, a body of intellectuals dissociated from every established social interest' (1981, p. 326).

For all its distinctly unEnglish intellectual sectarianism, Leavisism also came to embody a form of often quite virulent English cultural nationalism. For much of its history, English studies has been justified on nationalist grounds: the 1921 Newbolt Report on the teaching of English, for example, had recommended that the subject be established in the schools precisely as the centre of a national education in national consciousness (Baldick, 1983, p. 95). No doubt, there is a nationalist aspect to Eliot: born and brought up in the United States, he had become English by a deliberate act of conversion, which embraced not only British naturalisation but also High Tory politics, High Anglican religion and High Royalist monarchism. But for Eliot the mind of England was always also part of the mind of Europe. By comparison, Leavis's insistence that the proper subject matter for the discipline was to be, not cultural texts in general, not even 'literary' texts in general, but rather English literary texts in particular, betrays a more aggressively nationalist sensibility. When in the 1960s it was finally proposed to include foreign writers in a new Cambridge paper on the novel, Leavis argued that the study of Proust and Kafka 'would be a misdirection. There is nothing relevant there' (Williams, 1984a, p. 117). Such cultural nationalism is evident in Leavis's improbable affirmation of the non-arbitrary nature of the English sign. As we have seen, he believed that it was in language itself, in its most literary moments of articulation, that the truths of a particular culture are most clearly formed. For Leavis, the English language in its 'Shakespearean use' was possessed of the peculiar property that its 'words seem to do what they say' (Leavis, 1972b, p. 58). This view clearly informs his famous dismissal of Milton: 'He exhibits a feeling *for* words rather than a capacity for feeling *through* words' (ibid., p. 53). Milton's use of English was so consistently remote from the spoken language, Leavis argued, that even 'habituation could not sensitize a medium so cut off from speech - speech that belongs to the emotional and sensory texture of actual living and is in resonance with the nervous system' (Leavis, 1972a, p. 54). The particular judgement on Milton is actually less significant here than the more general conception of the English language. For if the language is indeed thus, then the subject matter of literary studies must needs be constituted out of the Englishness of the language itself. Furthermore, the Englishness of the language is in turn an expression of the Englishness of the people and of their erstwhile common culture. The result is a nationalistic preoccupation with the superior virtues, if not exactly of the contemporary English, then of their peasant ancestors and the legacy of the pre-industrial organic community they bequeathed to the language.

Politics (and Letters)

During the 1930s, almost exactly contemporaneously with the development of the *Scrutiny* group, Marxism, or at least a certain account of it, had come to exercise a considerable albeit temporary influence over significant sections of the British intelligentsia. This new Communist Marxism was especially influential amongst the natural scientists on the one hand, writers and literary critics on the other. The latter group included C. Day Lewis, W.H. Auden, Stephen Spender, Christopher Caudwell, Edward Upward, Ralph Fox and Alick West. Indeed, Leavis himself was clear that *Scrutiny* had developed in part by way of response to the Marxist challenge: 'We were anti-Marxist - necessarily so ... intelligent, that is, a real interest in literature implied a conception of it very different from any that a Marxist could expound and explain ... Marxist fashion gave us the doctrinal challenge' (Leavis, 1963, p. 4). Williams himself was a member of the Communist Party from 1939 to 1941, despite subscribing to what he later remembered as 'a cultural stance in opposition to ... "party attitudes" to literature - which we criticized as narrow and stuffy' (Williams, 1979a, p. 46). For Williams, the appeal of Communist Marxism remained political rather than literary, and was in any case essentially short-lived. By the late 1940s, the three editors of *Politics and Letters* 'were convinced that we were the most radical element in the culture ... we regarded the Communist Party as irrelevant because of the intellectual errors it had made' (ibid., p. 66). Williams would never resume his membership, but his interest in, and relation to, Marxism as an intellectual system were to prove more enduring.

As noted in Chapter 1, Marx's own Marxism had reserved the term 'superstructure' for the politico-legal order, as distinct from the cultural. Moreover, Marx's own formulations were distinctly cautious: 'the forms of social consciousness', he wrote, 'correspond' to 'the economic structure of society'; the 'mode of production', he continued, 'conditions' the 'general process of ... intellectual life'; and, while 'economic conditions' can be 'determined with ... precision', this is not the case for the 'ideological forms' (Marx, 1975c, pp. 425-6). No doubt, the central analogy with construction (foundation/superstructure) and the powerfully evocative reference to the precision of natural science do indeed combine so as to suggest a process of mechanical causation, where the economy is the cause and culture the effect. Much of that suggestion is nonetheless belied by the carefully qualifying verbs, 'correspond' and 'conditions', rather than 'causes'. Whatever Marx's intentions, however, Communist Marxism very clearly adhered to a strongly deterministic version of the base/superstructure model. Neither Marx nor Engels had ever actually elaborated any kind of pre-scriptive theory of aesthetics, and both appear to have enjoyed fairly catholic literary tastes. There are, nonetheless, very many references to literary matters scattered throughout their published and unpublished writings. And Engels, in particular, engaged in a series of private 'lit-erary' correspondences where he employed the category of 'realism' as an informal criterion of aesthetic value. In a letter to Margaret Harkness in April 1888, for example, he wrote that: 'Realism, to my mind, employs, besides truth of detail, the truthful reproduction of typical characters under typical circumstances' (Marx and Engels, 1947, p. 41). Here and in other letters to Minna Kautsky and Lassalle (ibid., pp. 40-63), Engels in effect appeals to a set of fairly convention-al, contemporary notions about realism so as to make immediate, and in truth fairly casual, judgements on contemporary writing. Nonetheless, these and similar remarks were taken up by Communist Marxism as the basis for a more generally prescriptive theory of liter-ary value. To this combination of economically determinist sociology and realist aesthetic, Communist Marxism also added an immediate diagnosis of contemporary capitalist society as crisis-ridden; a critique of contemporary bourgeois culture as decadent; and a sense of the Communist Party as performing a leadership function in culture as well as in politics. In the specific case of British Communism, more-over, all this was further compounded by a quasi-Romantic sense of the social mission of the creative writer. We have seen that Marx and Engels were only ever very distant sources for this peculiar doctrinal amalgam. How, then, had it evolved? The answer lies, first, from the 'orthodox Marxism' of the Socialist Second International, especially as represented by Georgei Plekhanov; second, from the exigencies of Soviet Communist policy, as laid down by Lenin, Stalin and other party functionaries, such as Andrey Zhdanov and Karl Radek; third, from the native intellectual traditions British Marxists drew upon, most obviously Romantic anti-utilitarianism.

Though not himself a Communist, Plekhanov was a key influence on the formation of Communist theories of culture. In *The Development of the Monist View of History*, he had described culture as the complex product of an interaction between psychology and economy, in which the latter plays the determining role, the former the adaptive: 'Psychology adapts itself to economy. But this adaptation is a complex process ... on the one hand the "iron laws" of movement of the "string" ... on the other ... on the "string" ... there grows up the *"garment of Life" of ideology'* (Plekhanov, 1956, p. 265). In the later *Art and Social Life*, he represents art as the twin product of biology on the one hand, material history on the other. Thus: 'The ideal of beauty that obtains at a given time ... has its roots partly in the biological conditions of development of the human species, ... partly in the historical conditions in which this society ... arose and existed' (Plekhanov, 1978, p. 23). Plekhanov conceived this material history as operating in a very peculiar fashion, however, that is, as imposing itself directly upon the art work via the medium of the work's own artistic content. Content was thus equated with the realistic representation of material history, not in the sense of a particular set of cultural conventions designed to create the illusion of an accurate depiction of some extra-textual reality, but rather that of a genuinely accurate depiction of a genuinely extra-textual reality. Artistic form thereby becomes a superstructure, the material base of which is artistic content, understood as somehow coextensive with historical reality itself: 'the value of a work of art is determined, in the last analysis by its content' (ibid., pp. 19-20). And so, artistic realism becomes the measure of literary value: 'when a work distorts reality, it is a failure' (ibid., p. 63). What in Engels had amounted to little more than conventionally informed personal preference is here transformed into a prescriptive aesthetic. For Plekhanov, the 'allegedly artistic exercises' of bourgeois modernisms such as Cubism are the product of 'individualism in the period of bourgeois decay', an individualism which condemns the artist 'to barren preoccupation with his own private and empty experiences and sickly, fantastic inventions' (ibid., pp. 53-5). All three themes, the determining base and determined superstructure, artistic realism as a valorised mode of cognition, and the decadence of non-realistic bourgeois art forms, were to be taken up and elaborated by the 1934 Soviet Writers' Congress, at which the new Communist cultural policies of 'socialist realism' and 'revolutionary romanticism' were first announced.

In his opening speech to the Writers' Congress, Zhdanov counterposed Soviet socialist realism to bourgeois literary decadence in terms clearly reminiscent of Plekhanov. The success of Soviet literature, Zhdanov observed, 'is an expression of the successes ... of our socialist system' (1977, p. 17). For Zhdanov as for Plekhanov, under 'socialism' as much as under capitalism, great art serves so as to 'express' social reality. And for Zhdanov as for Plekhanov, the greatness of great art consists precisely in this indebtedness to reality: 'Our Soviet writer', he explains, 'derives the material of his works of art ... from the life and experience of the men and women of Dnieprostroy, of Magnitostroy' (Zhdanov, 1977, p. 20). To achieve this 'means knowing life so as to be able to depict it truthfully', he continues, 'not simply as "objective reality", but to depict reality in its revolutionary development' (ibid., p. 21). By contrast:

> The present state of bourgeois literature is such that it is no longer able to create great works of art ... Everything now is growing stunted - themes, talents, authors, heroes ... Characteristic of the decadence and decay of bourgeois culture are the orgies of mysticism and superstition, the passion for pornography. (ibid., p. 19)

Later in the Congress, Radek would proceed along similar lines: from the general proposition that 'literature is a reflection of social life' (Radek, 1977, p. 74); to an intemperate denunciation of Joyce's *Ulysses* as a 'heap of dung, crawling with worms, photographed by a cinema apparatus through a microscope' (ibid., p. 153); to a celebration of realism as 'reflecting reality as it is, in all its complexity, in all its contrariety, and not only capitalist reality, but also that other, new reality - the reality of socialism' (ibid., pp. 156-7). The precise extent to which Soviet Communist leaders believed their own rhetoric remains a decidedly moot point. Certainly, a truly realistic account of 'the reality of socialism', such as Solzhenitsyn would eventually produce in *One Day in the Life of Ivan Denisovich, Cancer Ward* and *The First Circle*, would have earned its 1934 author a prominent part in the Show Trials of the late 1930s. Indeed, even as it was, that fate befell many of the Congress participants, not least Nikolai Bukharin, whose contribution on poetry and poetics figured prominently in the 1935 English language edition of the main Congress speeches. Assuming their subjective sincerity, however, one is still struck by the apparent contradiction between a pseudo-deterministic sociology, which insists that the base determines the superstructure, and a voluntarist prescriptive aesthetic, which insists that it should do so. Were the sociology valid, then the aesthetic would thereby be rendered very nearly redundant.

Very nearly, but not entirely so. In Soviet Communism itself, sociology and aesthetic were reconciled by virtue of the Communist Party's self-proclaimed role as intellectual 'vanguard' or 'midwife of history'. Communist Marxism claimed to derive this notion from Lenin's 1902 pamplet *What Is To Be Done?*, written while the Bolsheviks were in opposition rather than government, and addressed to expressly political rather than cultural questions. Whether by legitimate inference or not, its arguments were generalised to include virtually all matters of post-revolutionary intellectual life. Lenin himself had argued that revolutionary-socialist consciousness could only be imported into the working class from external, party-political sources. 'Class political consciousness', he had written, 'can be brought to the worker *only from without* ... from outside the economic struggle, outside the sphere of the relations between the workers' (Lenin, 1970, p. 123). Left to themselves, he observed, the workers are 'able to work out merely trade-union consciousness' (ibid., p. 80). Nor was this simply a matter of relatively 'higher' and 'lower' levels of the self-same proletarian consciousness. On the contrary, for Lenin trade-union consciousness was ultimately a vehicle for *bourgeois* ideology. Any 'belittling of the Socialist ideology,' he wrote, '*any withdrawing* from it, means by the same token the strengthening of the bourgeois ideology ... the spontaneous development of the labour movement leads precisely to its subordination to the bourgeois ideology' (ibid., pp. 89-90). This is so, he explained, because of the enormous power of the ruling ideas: 'bourgeois ideology is 'far older in origin ... more completely developed, and ... possesses *immeasurably* greater means for being spread' (ibid., pp. 90-1). In opposition both to bourgeois ideology and to trade-union consciousness, socialist consciousness derives first of all from Marxist theory itself (ibid., p. 75); and, second, from those who create this theory, that is, from 'the educated representatives of the propertied classes - the intelligentsia' (ibid., p. 80). What had proved a source of much embarrassment for many socialists, the prominent role of middle-class intellectuals in their supposedly proletarian political organisations, would thus provide Lenin with the rationale for a political party 'of a *different kind*': an 'organization of revolutionaries ... people whose profession consists of revolutionary activity' (ibid., p. 156).

In the Soviet Union and elsewhere, both in culture and in politics, the Communist Parties claimed to provide precisely such intellectual leadership to the proletarian 'masses'. In short, they proclaimed themselves, at once, both political 'vanguard' and cultural avant-garde. Insofar as art and literature were concerned, this vanguard function would require both 'socialist realism' and 'revolutionary romanticism'. Following Stalin, Zhdanov preferred to introduce the latter notion through the metaphor of the engineer rather than the midwife:

> To be an engineer of human souls means standing with both feet firmly planted on the basis of real life. And this in its turn denotes a rupture with romanticism of the old type, which depicted a non-existent life and non-existent heroes ... Our literature ... must be a romanticism of a new type, revolutionary romanticism ... Soviet literature should be able to portray our heroes; it should be able to glimpse our tomorrow. This will be no utopian dream, for our tomorrow is already being prepared for today by dint of conscious planned work. (Zhdanov, 1977, pp. 21-2)

In the most literal of senses, then, Zhdanov envisaged the role of the writer as that of a social engineer. What both the Soviet authorities in general and Zhdanov in particular were increasingly to demand, and imperatively so, was an art that would be of directly political use to the new Soviet state. As the exiled Trotsky would dismissively argue: 'The official art of the Soviet Union - and there is no other over there - resembles totalitarian justice, that is to say, it is based on lies and deceit' (1970, p. 106).

But even at the Writers' Congress itself, a second and rather more defensible version of revolutionary romanticism had been suggested by Bukharin. 'Socialist realism dares to "dream"', Bukharin proposed:

> If socialist realism is distinguished by its active, operative character; if it does not give just a dry photograph of a process; if it projects the entire world of passion and struggle into the future; if it raises the heroic principle to the throne of history - then revolutionary romanticism is a component part of it ... In our circumstances romanticism is connected above all with heroic themes; its eyes are turned, not on the heaven of metaphysics, but on the earth, in all its senses - on triumph over the enemy and triumph over nature. (1977, pp. 253-4)

It is the future as freely chosen, heroic aspiration, rather than obligatory policy objective, which Bukharin hopes will inspire such 'revolutionary romanticism'. Though Bukharin himself would never have countenanced the thought, this is not really so very far from Blake or from Shelley.

While Bukharin's imminent disgrace would render him a non-person, whose ideas could be cited by Communists only as objects of disavowal, this much more properly Romantic version of revolutionary romanticism resonated powerfully within the ranks of the British Communist Party: Caudwell's highly regarded *Illusion and Reality* included bibliographical entries for Bukharin and Plekhanov, but for neither Zhdanov nor Radek (Caudwell, 1946, pp. 300, 308). Williams himself remembered Fox's *The Novel and the People* as a more 'central work' and doubted that he came across Caudwell during his time in the Party (Williams, 1979a, p. 44). But the latter's influence was to prove the more enduring, so much so that by 1958 Williams could single him out as 'the best-known' of the English Marxist critics (Williams, 1963, p. 268). Certainly, the subsequent publication record speaks for itself: *Illusion and Reality* was first published in 1937, only a few months after Caudwell had been killed in action with the International Brigade, it was republished in a new edition in 1946, and reprinted in 1947, 1950, 1955, 1958 and 1966; *The Novel and the People* was first published in the same year, again only months after its author's death in Spain, it was reprinted twice, in 1944 and 1948, and thereafter remained out of print until 1979.

For Caudwell, as for Communist Marxism more generally, the literary superstructures were essentially an effect of the developing material base. 'What is the basis of literary art?', he wrote, 'What is the inner contradiction which produces its own onward movement? Evidently it can only be a special form of the contradiction which produces the whole movement of society'. This contradiction, he proceeds to elaborate, is that of 'the endless struggle between man and Nature'

(Caudwell, 1946, p. 201), a struggle Caudwell himself defines simply as 'life', but which is in fact much closer to what Marx meant by 'mode of production'. Literature is thus essentially a by-product of economic activity: 'Poetry is clotted social history, the emotional sweat of man's struggle with Nature' (ibid., p. 130). In his opening, quasi-anthropological account of the historical origins of poetry, Caudwell writes that: 'the developing complex of society, in its struggle with the environment, secretes poetry as it secretes the technique of the harvest, as part of its non-biological and specifically human adaptation to existence' (ibid., pp. 29-30). His historical sociology defines poetry as in effect an 'expression' of one or another stage in the development of the mode of production. Cultural modernity is thus 'the superstructure of the bourgeois revolution in production' and modern poetry notoriously *'capitalist* poetry' (ibid., p. 55). In his historical survey of the development of modern English poetry, Caudwell sets out to establish strict correlations between specific periods in the development of capitalist society, the general characteristics of the equivalent literary-historical periods, and the technical characteristics of the corresponding poetic forms. The historical periodisation is specified precisely: 'Primitive Accumulation' runs from 1550-1600; 'The Industrial Revolution and the "Anti-Jacobin" Reaction' from 1750-1825; 'The Epoch of Imperialism' from 1900-1930. According to Caudwell, each of these (and there are nine in all) gives rise to certain quite specific general and technical characteristics in poetry. During the period of 'Primitive Accumulation', for instance, the general characteristic is that of the 'dynamic force of individuality', the technical characteristics lyrics suitable for group singing, on the one hand, and iambic rhythm, on the other. 'The iambic rhythm,' writes Caudwell, 'is allowed to flower luxuriantly and naturally; it indicates the free and boundless development of the personal will' (ibid., p. 117).

Like Plekhanov, Caudwell thought of culture as having an essentially adaptive function: 'The poem adapts the heart to a new purpose, without changing the eternal desires of men's hearts' (ibid., p. 30). In Caudwell's view, these eternal desires were fixed by the human 'genotype', that is, 'the more or less common set of instincts in each man' (ibid., p. 124). And for Caudwell, as for Plekhanov, a socio-functional explanation for the existence of art led easily to a valorisation of realist cultural forms. Art, he writes, 'remoulds external reality nearer to the likeness of the genotype's instincts ... Art becomes more socially and biologically valuable and greater art the more that remoulding is comprehensive and true to the nature of reality' (ibid., p. 261). During the 'Epoch of Imperialism', which in Caudwell's view had only recently come to an end, the central technical characteristic of bourgeois poetry had become the 'attempt entirely to separate the world of art from that of society', which culminated finally in 'the "completely free" word of *surréalisme'* (ibid., p. 121). Such art gives rise eventually to 'the spectacle of culture tragically perishing because its matrix, society, has become dispersed and sterile ... the pathos of art ... torn by insoluble conflicts and perplexed by all kinds of unreal phantasies' (ibid., p. 297). For Caudwell, 'The Final Capitalist Crisis', which he dates '1930-?', gives rise to the historically determined opportunity 'once again to give social value to all the technical resources, developed by the movement of the preceding stages' (ibid., p. 122). But, though the opportunity itself is historically determined, the capacity to avail oneself thereof remains a matter of political choice and political struggle. Hence, his concluding address to the bourgeois artist, made unselfconsciously in the name of 'the conscious proletariat':

> There is no neutral world of art, free from categories or determining causes. Art is a social activity ... You must choose between class art which is unconscious of its causality and is therefore to that extent false and unfree, and proletarian art which is becoming conscious of its causality and will therefore emerge as the truly free art of communism ... Our demand - that your art should be proletarian - is *not* a demand that you apply dogmatic categories and Marxist phrases to art ... We ask that you should *really* live in the new world and not leave your soul behind in the past ... We shall know that this transition has taken place when your art has become *living*; then it will be proletarian. Then we shall cease to criticise it for its deadness. (ibid., pp. 288-9)

Doubtless, there is much in Caudwell that is idiosyncratic, indeed original, his psychologism for instance. But both the general structure of Communist Marxism and the more specifically Romantic, as distinct from utilitarian, Bukharinite as distinct from Zhdanovite, conception of the role of the militant artist-intellectual recur throughout the British Communist cultural criticism of the 1930s. Alick West, for example, could move readily from the quasi-sociological proposition that the 'source of value in the work of literature is ... social energy and activity' (1975, p. 99), to a quasi-Romantic prescription that 'the criticism of our lives, by the test of whether we are helping to forward the most creative movement in our society, is the only effective foundation of the criticism of literature' (ibid., p. 102). This most creative movement, West spells out, 'is socialism', the function of criticism, therefore, 'to judge literature, both content and form, as a part of this movement'. And criticism 'can only fulfil this function', he adds, 'if it takes part in this movement on the side of the workers of the world' (ibid., pp. 102-3). A similarly quasi-sociological moment informs Fox's understanding of the role of the writer as 'winning the knowledge of truth, of reality'. Art, he continues, is a 'means by which man grapples with and assimilates reality' (Fox, 1979, p. 37). Such realism had been present in the early bourgeois novel, Fox explains, but in the twentieth century, in the age of 'philosophical decadence' and 'political counter-revolution', then 'no full and free expression of human personality is possible' (ibid., pp. 96-7). What is possible, however, is the 'new realism' that is socialist realism. Thence, once more, the quasi-Romantic call to arms: 'we must strain our inventive and creative faculties to the utmost ... let us go into the fight together encouraged by the thought that the fate of our language and the struggles to develop it, have ... always been ... closely bound up with the struggles of our country for national salvation' (ibid., p. 138).

In each case, determinist sociology and Romantic polemic are held in dynamic tension only by a near-apocalyptic understanding of the supposed 'general crisis of capitalism', in many respects startlingly reminiscent of Leavis's own. For it was the very urgency of the perceived crisis, the same urgency that compelled both Caudwell and Fox to volunteer for Spain, which conjured up the necessity of voluntarism. But when western capitalism settled into its long post-war boom, all of this began to seem hopelessly antiquated. As Williams himself was to recall:

> It may have seemed a natural response [to Leavisism] to retort that the point was not how to read a poem, but how to write one that meant something in the socio-political crisis of the time. But when the productive mood which was our way of replying by not replying faded away after the War, and we had to engage in literary criticism or history proper, we found we were left with nothing. (1979a, p. 45)

Under Which King, Bezonian?

Left with nothing by Communist Marxism, but increasingly distanced from Leavisism by virtue of its seemingly endemic political conservatism and cultural elitism, the more independently-minded left-wing British intellectuals of the 1950s slowly began to forge their own 'third way', both in politics and in cultural theory. The politics eventually became those of the 'New Left'; the theory what would be represented in structuralist restrospect as 'culturalism', but is perhaps more accurately described as 'left culturalism'. Quoting from Ibsen's *When We Dead Awaken*, Williams later described his own situation thus: 'coming "to a tight place where you stick fast. There is no going forward or backward". That was exactly my sensation ... this was how I saw the fate of the impulse of the late thirties ... It had been right, but it had been defeated; yet the defeat did not cancel it' (Williams, 1979a, pp. 62-3). The short-term solution, in the late 1940s, had been *Politics and Letters*; the longer-term, from 1956 on, the New Left. In the interim Williams produced his first four books: *Reading and Criticism*, a broadly Leavisite introduction to literary criticism aimed at adult education students (Williams, 1950); two books on drama, *Drama from Ibsen to*

Eliot (Williams, 1952) and *Drama in Performance* (Williams, 1954); and his first excursion into what would eventually become a routine part of the subject matter of Cultural Studies, the co-authored *Preface to Film* (Williams and Orrom, 1954). In each case, Williams attempted simultaneously to go beyond both Leavisism and Communist Marxism. This stage in the argument culminated in *Culture and Society*, which provides much of the subject matter for the chapter that immediately follows. Before we proceed, however, it might be as well to consider the more specific responses to Eliot, Leavis and Caudwell outlined in that book's closing chapters.

According to Williams himself, the initial stimulus toward the composition of *Culture and Society* had been provided by the publication in 1948 of Eliot's *Notes Towards the Definition of Culture*: he had planned 'to counter the appropriation of a long line of thinking about culture to what were by now decisively reactionary positions' (Williams, 1979a, p. 97). So when Eliot and Leavis enter his narrative, in the book's third part, there is an important sense in which the argument finally reaches its mark. And Eliot's was, of course, the most decisively reactionary of reactionary positions. Whether dealing with Eliot or with Leavis, Williams handles his opponents with that careful blend of respect and criticism, falling far short of polemic, which is characteristic of the entire work. So he is quick to admire Eliot's expanded sense of the term culture, but quick too to define its limitations: 'Eliot's categories are sport, food, and a little art - a characteristic observation of English leisure', rather than of 'a whole way of life' (Williams, 1963, p. 229). More seriously, Eliot's equation of class with function is 'narrow and misleading', his discussion of the different 'levels' of culture, theoretically 'illuminating' but practically 'misleading' (ibid., pp. 232-3). For Williams, however, the central problem in Eliot takes the form of an internal contradiction:

> a genuine theoretical objection to the principle and the effects of an 'atomized', individualist society is combined, and has to be combined, with adherence to the principles of an economic system which is based on just this 'atomized', individualist view. The 'free economy' ... not only contradicts the social principles which Eliot advances ..., but also, and this is the real confusion, is the only available method of ordering society to the maintenance of those interests and institutions on which Eliot believes his values to depend. (ibid., p. 237)

This is both right in itself and powerfully prescient. For in the late twentieth century, when conservative governments set out to privatise, commodify and individualise the entire social world, this theoretical flaw in Eliot's argument would emerge as the characteristic ideological contradiction within American Republicanism, British

Toryism and Australian Liberalism alike: in short, that between the claims of moral conservatism, on the one hand, and the demands of the market, on the other. Those who now inhabit the wasteland can see how little Eliot had understood of how it might be escaped.

Williams's treatment of Leavis and the Leavisites is similarly respectful. So the practical training outlined in *Culture and Environment* warrants 'major recognition', while Leavis's more general critical effort is itself 'a major achievement' (Williams, 1963, pp. 250, 255). But the achievement remains essentially 'defensive', Williams insists, and it does so, moreover, for reasons that are clearly immanent to the argument itself: first, too exclusively literary an understanding of culture; and secondly, too nostalgic an understanding of the pre-industrial past. Williams is quick to agree with Leavis that a society is 'poor indeed' with nothing but its own contemporary experience to live by, but quick too to insist that 'the ways in which we can draw on other experience are more various than literature alone.' To equate culture with literature, as Leavis does, is thus 'to expose a vital case to damaging misunderstanding' (ibid., pp. 248-9). Williams is quick to agree with Leavis as to the cultural significance of adaptation to the natural environment in rural communities, but quick too to condemn as 'foolish and dangerous' any indifference to 'the penury, the petty tyranny, the disease and mortality, the ignorance and frustrated intelligence' which also accompanied 'so-called organic society' (ibid., pp. 252-3). In each case, he insists, the Leavisites confuse the part with the whole: 'A valid detailed judgement grows too quickly into a persuasive outline' (ibid., p. 253). The remedy will lie in a more expanded conception of culture, understood as 'almost identical with our whole common life' (ibid., p. 249), rather than as the distinct possession of a literary 'minority'. Judged as a cultural pedagogy, the Leavisite version of practical criticism remained 'wholly valuable' for Williams. But the socio-historical 'myth' that accompanied it tended to produce 'a damaging arrogance and scepticism' and a 'denial of real social experience' (ibid., pp. 254-5). In short, Leavis was for the main part wrong about the society and the history, but right about the literature and the culture.

The obverse is true of Caudwell and the British Marxists: they are for the main part right about society and history, but wrong about literature and culture. So Williams describes Marx as having 'made the decisive contribution' to 'the vital lesson' of the nineteenth century, that 'the basic economic organization could not be separated and excluded from ... moral and intellectual concerns' (ibid., p. 271). By contrast, Williams's judgement on Caudwell's criticism seems peculiarly damning: 'for the most part his discussion is not even specific enough to be wrong' (ibid., p. 268); and 'it remains to be shown that "capitalist" is a relevant description of poetry at all' (ibid., p. 272). In its attempts to establish close correlations between economic and literary history, such Marxism seemed to Williams 'to involve both forcing and superficiality' (ibid., p. 272). Williams's more general indictment against British Marxism involved two main charges: firstly, that its practical recommendations were more complicit with Romanticism that its advocates commonly cared to allow; and secondly, that its accounts of the relation between culture and society were very often confused, oscillating between economic determinism and Romantic idealism simply 'as the need serves' (ibid., pp. 265-6). We should be clear that this is by no means an argument for Romanticism and against 'mechanical' materialism. On the contrary, it is in its more dogmatically prescriptive aspects that British Marxism is often at its most Romantic. Hence, the cruelly astute observation that, if existence determines consciousness, as Marx argued, then prescriptive criticism rests on the hubristic assumption that 'the prescribers ... somehow identify themselves with "existence"' (ibid., p. 274). At times, Williams even toys with the suggestion that his own position is the more properly Marxist. Certainly, such seems to be the implication of the casual observation that 'from their emphasis on ... interdependence ... and ... on movement and change, Marxists should logically use "culture" in the sense of a whole way of life' (Williams, 1965, p. 273). They do not, however, and for reasons that remain immanent to Marx's own Marxism: 'If one accepts "structure" and "superstructure", not as the terms of a suggestive analogy, but as descriptions of reality, the errors naturally follow ... if the terms are seen as ... analogy, they need ... amendment' (Williams, 1963, p. 273). Williams's amendments would be to Marx and to Lenin as well as to British Marxism; and they would be central to his own later work as well as to *Culture and Society*. Against Marx at his most deterministic, Williams insisted that: 'even if the economic element is determining, it determines a whole way of life, and it is to this, rather than to the economic system alone, that the literature has to be related' (ibid., p. 272). Against Lenin at his most voluntarist, he insisted that:

> if ... the working class cannot create a socialist ideology, Marx's account of the relation between ... existence and consciousness cannot easily be maintained; ... if the working people ... cannot go beyond 'trade-union consciousness' ... they can be regarded as 'masses' to be captured, the objects rather than the subjects of power. Almost anything can then be justified. (ibid., pp. 274-5)

The rival claims of politics and letters, Marxism and literature, had been aired, less dogmatically than in Zhdanov or Caudwell, by Trotsky in *Literature and Revolution* (Trotsky, 1960), written during the immediate aftermath of the Bolshevik Revolution, at a time when Communist cultural policy still retained a relatively pluralist character. In 1932 Leavis himself had published a forceful critique of this 'dangerously intelligent Marxist' (1932, p. 209), entitled 'Under Which King,

Bezonian?'. The title refers to *Henry IV Part II*, where Pistol brings Falstaff the news that Henry is dead and the young Prince Hal therefore now king. In the comic exchange that follows, Pistol confronts Shallow with a combination of meaningless choice and idle threat: 'Under which king, Bezonian? speak, or die.' This is more or less exactly how Leavis saw Marxism. 'The rigour of the Marxian dialectic ... is illusory, and the brave choice enjoined upon us the reverse of courageous, if courage has anything to do with thinking' (Leavis, 1932, p. 213). Trotsky's apparent sympathies for the claims of culture not withstanding, his Marxism had seemed to Leavis quite fundamentally disabling. The very culture that Trotsky professed to value was, in fact, threatened by mechanical civilisation, whether capitalist or communist, and any doctrine which sought to assert the priority of economics over art, methods of production over culture, politics over letters, base over superstructure, would inevitably become complicit with the logic of that civilisation. The choice Leavis refused was not that between politics and literature, however, at least not in any sense that most Marxists would have understood, but rather between Left and Right, proletarian and bourgeois, more precisely between Trotsky's dissident Marxism and Eliot's Anglo-Catholic Royalism. For Leavis, neither of these could even begin to grapple with the central problem of how to establish and maintain cultural continuity, a problem which could be adequately addressed only at the cultural level itself, as distinct from the political. Hence, his insistence that *Scrutiny*'s 'special educational interest ... is unprecedented and has already shown its strength' (Leavis, 1932, p. 214). As he would later restate the argument: 'the self-devotion of the intelligent may be more effectively enlisted than by an appeal to the Class-War' (Leavis, 1933, p. 323).

There is no mention of Leavis's essay (nor of Trotsky for that matter) in *Culture and Society*. And yet, in many respects, the one rehearses the other. For like Leavis, Williams had set out to address the central 'cultural' questions, from a standpoint deliberately distanced from the politics of the Left and of the Right. The obvious difference was that these latter were now represented by the Leavises as well as by Eliot. In 1979, the editors of the *New Left Review* suggested to Williams that: 'The book is entitled *Culture and Society*, and these two terms are the essential prisms through which all the individual figures in it are perceived ... there does appear to be a virtually systematic depreciation of the actual political dimension of all the figures whom you are discussing' (Williams, 1979a, p. 100). Insofar as this is true, Williams had in effect replicated what had been Leavis's own procedures. Williams himself resisted the suggestion, however, insisting that: 'It is not a general dismissal of politics' (ibid., p. 102). At the level of the text itself, if we can speak of such a thing, the balance of the evidence rests with the interviewers rather than the interviewee. Yet their suggestion radically underestimates the book's political effectivity in relation to its own immediate context. For at its most expressly political, as on

Eliot and 'atomised' society or Lenin and 'trade-union consciousness', it is difficult to imagine a discussion more directly suited to the new politics that enveloped the Left from 1956 on. By decentring the state in favour of 'civil society', *Culture and Society* had prefigured what would become one of the central preoccupations of the western Left in the late twentieth century. There would be later modifications both to its more general conclusions and to the particular criticism directed at Caudwell. Williams would even admit that he 'should have realized' that Caudwell's 'pressure was greater than mine ... I can now see what he was trying to do' (Williams, 1979a, pp. 127-8). Charity aside, however - and this is the word Williams actually uses - his central lines of argument, simultaneously with and against Leavisism, with and against Marxism, had now been clearly broached. They would find a ready audience in the New Left suddenly galvanised into existence by the coincidence of the Hungarian Revolution and the Suez Crisis.

Note

1 This is not to suggest that English was invented at Cambridge. On the contrary, there is a good argument to be made for its invention on the peripheries of Englishness (cf. Crawford, 1998). But it was Leavis and Leavisism that Williams himself encountered at Cambridge.

3

From Culture to Society

I see this cultural revolution as part of a great process of human liberation, comparable in importance with the industrial revolution and the struggle for democracy ... The essential values ... are common to the whole process: that men should grow in capacity and power to direct their own lives - by creating democratic institutions, by bringing new sources of energy to human work, and by extending the expression and exchange of experience on which understanding depends. (Williams, *Communications*)

In Chapter 4, I will attempt to argue a relatively strong case for the theoretical originality and importance of Williams's *Marxism and Literature* and of the various texts from the 1970s and early 1980s that provide its intellectual frame. However, there can be little doubt that his more general intellectual reputation rests substantially, not on these later 'cultural-materialist' writings, but on the two major works of the late 1950s and early 1960s, *Culture and Society 1780-1950* and *The Long Revolution*. As we have seen, the initial impetus toward *Culture and Society* had come as early as 1948. But Williams did not begin serious work on the book until 1950, when it bore the working title *The Idea of Culture*: an early version of the argument appeared in essay form under this title (Williams, 1953). The bulk of the work was written from 1954 on, however, with the final manuscript reaching the publisher in March 1956 (Inglis, 1995, p. 149). Its moment of composition was the early 1950s, a period Williams would later describe in the bleakest of terms: 'For the next ten years [after the closure of *Politics and Letters* - AM] I wrote in nearly complete isolation' (Williams, 1979a, p. 77).[1] The book was published in September 1958, selling out within a matter of months and going into its second printing in January of the following year. The moment of its initial reception was thus the late 1950s, a period Williams would recall with much greater enthusiasm (Williams, 1979a, pp. 361-2).[2] Between composition and reception lay the twin crises of 1956: on the one hand, the Anglo-French invasion of Egypt, and the crisis thereby occasioned within Britain itself; on the other, the Russian invasion of Hungary, and the subsequent crisis within the international Communist movement, not least within the ranks of the British Communist Party.

Culturalism and the First New Left

A little textbook history seems in order. In February 1956, Kruschev had made his so-called 'secret speech', indicting Stalin's legacy of 'the cult of personality', to a closed session of the 20th Congress of the Soviet Communist Party. Rumours of its content progressively leaked out to the Western Communist Parties, but were persistently denied by their leaderships. In June 1956, the US State Department published the full text, in more or less accurate translation, as we can now confirm. In July, the Egyptian Government of President Nasser nationalised the Anglo-French Suez Canal Company. In the same month, the Soviet Government forced the resignation of the hardline Stalinist First Secretary of the Hungarian Communist Party, in a move intended to placate calls for reform, which actually served only to encourage them further. On 23 October, the British, French and Israeli governments made secret speeches of their own in which they agreed to a joint military operation against Egypt. On the same day, mass demonstrations in Budapest were attacked by the police. On 24 October, the campaign for reform in Hungary finally reached insurrectionary proportions, when workers throughout the capital began to set up workers' councils. A new reformist government was formed under Imre Nagy, which within a matter of days had withdrawn Hungary from the Warsaw Pact. On 26 October, Israeli troops attacked Egypt across the Sinai; on 30 October, the British attacked Port Said; on 1 November, the Russians invaded Hungary, attacking Budapest on 4 November. The Russian Army would remain in Hungary until the collapse of the Soviet Union more than thirty years later. The Anglo-French invasion proved less successful: within days, the combined opposition of the United States, the Soviet Union and the United Nations forced a humiliating withdrawal, which effectively signalled the end of any residual British capacity to act independently of Washington.

The suppression of the Hungarian Revolution triggered widespread defections from the Western Communist Parties, very often leading to a wholesale capitulation to the political Right. In Britain and France, however, the fact of the imperialist adventure at Suez, compounded in part no doubt by its very failure, served so as to open up a political space for the New Left: the moral superiority of Western liberalism over Soviet Communism seemed less than self-evident in countries that had attempted their own invasion of an independent, sovereign nation-state. As David Widgery would later observe, the British New Left was 'formed by the collision and fusion of the two world-wide shock waves of Suez and Hungary' (1976, p. 25). In mid-1956, two Yorkshire Communists, E.P. Thompson and John Saville, both of them professional historians, began to publish *The Reasoner*, an internal Communist opposition newsletter. In an article dated 1 November 1956, published in what would be its final issue, Thompson resoundingly proclaimed that:

> The ... Hungarian people have written their critique of Stalinism upon their streets and squares. In doing so, they have brought back honour to the international Communist movement ... The socialism of free people, and not of secret speeches and police, will prove *more* dangerous to our own imperialism than any Stalinist state.
> (Thompson, 1976, pp. 71-2)

Within a year something like a third of the membership of the British Communist Party, Thompson and Saville included, had either resigned or been expelled. In March 1957, the first meeting of a non-party 'London Socialist Forum' was held at Holborn Hall. The Forum demanded the release of the philosopher, Georg Lukács, a member of Nagy's government still imprisoned in Rumania (Lukács was eventually freed, but Nagy himself was executed in June 1958). In April, a national conference of Socialist Forums, held at Wortley Hall in Sheffield, resolved to establish 'an organized movement of the Marxist anti-Stalinist left'. In May, Thompson and Saville began to publish *The New Reasoner*, as a journal of the 'ex-Communist Party', with an editorial board that included Doris Lessing, Mervyn Jones, Peter Worsley and John Rex. More or less simultaneously, Stuart Hall, Raphael Samuel, Alan Hall and Charles Taylor had begun to publish the *Universities and Left Review* with funds raised from the defunct Oxford Socialist Society (Phillips, 1976, p. 451; Inglis, 1995, pp. 153-4). On 17 February 1958, the Campaign for Nuclear Disarmament held its inaugural meeting at Methodist Central Hall in London. The first CND march to the Aldermaston Atomic Weapons Research Establishment mobilised some 10,000 people at Easter of that year (Phillips, 1976, p. 453). The New Left was in the process of being transformed into the political core of a wider mass movement.

This, then, was the milieu from which *Culture and Society* drew much of its initial audience. As Inglis astutely observes:

> The sacred texts of this unprecedented kind of new political movement, combining ... in its savoury brew old Popular Front and new popular culture, old political radicalism and even older Morrisian romanticism, new sympathetic internationalism and just-as-new social libertarianism, novels and wage-theory, sex and disarmament,

were *The Uses of Literacy* and *Culture and Society*. It was a strong and sat-isfying mixture exactly because it included so much that until recently had been counted out of culture as not decorous enough, not classy enough, not *old* enough ... Williams was quickly appoint-ed pole star in this new little universe. (1995, p. 157)

Though distant from the initial dissensions within the Communist Party, Williams threw himself with enthusiasm into the New Left. Invited to speak to the Universities and Left Review Club in London during 1959, he found it 'a very important experience'. 'These were well attended, lively meetings', he would recall:

which opened up quite new areas of discussion. There was a differ-ence of a whole generation between the group which had started pub-lishing *Universities and Left Review* from Oxford, and the group which separately created *The New Reasoner*, who had come out of the Communist Party over Hungary ... my paradoxical position ... was that I belonged by age to the group that had just left the Communist Party, but I was really rather nearer in preoccupation to the group which had started *Universities and Left Review*. (Williams, 1979a, pp. 361-2)

In the course of 1959 the editors of the two magazines were involved in merger negotiations, which eventually led to the formation of the combined *New Left Review*, the first issue of which was published early in 1960. By his own account, Williams was uninvolved in the pre-merger negotiations, but was 'brought into the planning stage of the new review, once the merger had been agreed' (Williams, 1979a, p. 363). A founder member of the combined editorial board, Inglis insists that 'Raymond *always* turned up to the Board meetings' (1995, p. 156).

The founding theoretical moment of left culturalism can be located fairly precisely in the early writings of three 'key' figures: Williams, Thompson and Hoggart. Both Williams and Hoggart were by origin working-class 'scholarship boys', both Williams and Thompson were ex-Communists; all three had been trained as undergraduates in English Literature, Thompson and Williams at Cambridge, Hoggart at Leeds; all three had seen active service in the British Army during the Second World War; all three had worked in adult education, Thompson in the Extra-Mural Department at Leeds University, Hoggart in the Department of Adult Education at Hull, Williams in Extra-Mural Studies at Oxford. All three would come to occupy promi-nent positions in the intellectual landscape of the 1960s. It was Thompson, however, who stood at the political centre of the move-ment of '1956', initially as the dissident Communist co-editor of *The Reasoner*, later the ex-Communist co-editor of *The New Reasoner*, later still one of the founding editors of the *New Left Review*. In retrospect, it seems clear that Thompson's own political and intellectual evolution was quite decisively formed by the crisis in western Communism occasioned by the Hungarian Revolution: over twenty years later he would still loyally beat 'the bounds of "1956"' (Thompson, 1978, p. 384). Moreover, something at least of what would become 'left culturalism' had begun to be explored in the first edition of his *William Morris* (Thompson, 1955); rather more in the remarkable *New Reasoner* essay, 'Socialist Humanism' (Thompson, 1957); and eventually a great deal more in the magisterial *The Making of the English Working Class* (Thompson, 1963). *William Morris* had opened the way with its deeply appreciative study of a writer hitherto excluded from the canonical wisdom both of Leavisism and of official Communist Marxism. If Thompson here reclaimed Morris for Marxism, then he also, and simultaneously, discovered in Morris much of the strength of the earlier Romantic critique of utilitarianism. As Thompson would later recall, 'the book ... is, in a central respect, an argument about the Romantic tradition ... Morris, by 1955, had claimed me. My book was then ... already a work of muffled "revisionism"' (1977, pp. 769, 810). That revisionism became explicit during the often bitter controversies of the following years, which culminated in the famous essay on 'Socialist Humanism'. Here Thompson quite deliberately set out to repudiate the base/superstructure formula as 'belittling ... conscious human agency in the making of history' and sought, equally deliberately, to explain the criminality of Stalinist politics as itself an effect of the economic determinism of official, orthodox Marxism.

In 1963, Thompson published *The Making of the English Working Class*, much of which had been researched from Leeds, some in John Nelson's study in my own home-village of Birstall. The book built on the theoretical and political legacy of socialist humanism, and on an extraordinary richness of empirical detail, so as to produce what Thompson termed 'a biography of the English working class from its adolescence until its early manhood' (1963, p. 11). The base/superstructure model is here not so much discarded as transcended, or at least definitively outflanked, and on Communist Marxism's own preferred terrain, moreover, that of the working class and working-class consciousness, by a history of political struggle and popular culture, trade unionism and religion, community and conflict, in which class is understood as a cultural process as much as an economic phenomenon. The book's opening lines explain it to be 'a study in an active process, which owes as much to agency as to conditioning. The working class did not rise like the sun at an appointed time. It was present at its own making' (ibid., p. 9). It is also a testament to the 'heroic culture' of a working class which 'nourished, for fifty years, and with incomparable fortitude, the Liberty Tree' (ibid., p. 832). That culture was clearly, for Thompson, something of very considerable value in itself. In the book's closing lines, he harkens back to Morris, if only obliquely, when he draws attention to the elements in common between this working-class resistance to utilitarianism, which provided much of his subject matter, and that other tradition of Romantic anti-utilitarianism:

> Such men met Utilitarianism in their daily lives, and they sought to throw it back, not blindly, but with intelligence and moral passion ... In these same years, the great Romantic criticism of Utilitarianism was running its parallel but altogether separate course. After William Blake, no mind was at home in both cultures, nor had the genius to interpret the two traditions to each other. In the failure of the two traditions to come to a point of junction, something was lost. How much we cannot be sure, for we are among the losers. (ibid., p. 832)

Whatever the eventual importance of Thompson's scholarly writings, the theoretical moment of 1956 registered much more immediately and much more visibly in the work of dissident ex-Leavisites than in that of dissident ex-Communists. The key texts here are, as Inglis rightly observes, Hoggart's *The Uses of Literacy* (1958), first published in 1957 by Leavis's own publisher, Chatto and Windus, and Williams's *Culture and Society*, published the following year, again by Chatto. It should come as little surprise, then, that a discussion between Williams and Hoggart, around the theme of working-class culture, should have figured in the first issue of the *New Left Review* (Hoggart and Williams, 1960). *The Uses of Literacy* was extremely well received: the paperback edition, first published in 1958, was reprinted in 1959, 1960, 1962, 1963, 1965, 1966, 1968 and 1969 (and many times thereafter, we might add). It marked the initial point at which post-Leavisite culturalism decisively shifted emphasis away from 'literature' and towards 'culture'. The book is divided into two parts, the first of which, 'An "Older" Order', provides what is in effect an ethnographic account of the North of England working-class culture within which Hoggart had been nurtured. This culture, that of the inter-war years, is assessed positively, as is the extent to which some of its elements still persist. But Hoggart's central theme, outlined in the book's second part, 'Yielding Place to New', is that of the damage done the older culture by the newer mass arts, newspapers, books, magazines, and so on. Here, Hoggart uses the techniques of Leavisite practical criticism to analyse popular texts. He summarises his own argument thus: 'The old forms of class culture are in danger of being replaced by a poorer kind of classless ... culture ... and this is to be regretted' (Hoggart, 1958, p. 343). Like the Leavises, Hoggart was arguing a theory of cultural decline; like the Leavises, he attached major responsibility for this state of affairs to the commercial mass media. For Hoggart, however, it was the culture of the working class itself, rather than that of the 'sensitive minority' that needed to be valorised, if only so as, in turn, to be elegised. He remained particularly acute, moreover, on the ways in which 'competitive commerce' had been able to undermine the older order, precisely by manipulating that order's own resources against itself, thus learning 'to express our habitual moral assumptions but in such a way that they weaken the moral code they evoke; to say the right things for the wrong reasons' (ibid., p. 244).

Hoggart's achievement had been to divest Leavisism of something at least of its cultural elitism, if not perhaps of its nostalgia, Thompson's to divest Marxism of its economic determinism, and to make explicit what had previously been an implicit, and often unacknowledged, Romanticism. But the achievement is in each case both reactive and contained: Hoggart reacts against, but nonetheless within, Leavisism; Thompson against, but nonetheless within, the then received version of Marxism. In Williams, by contrast, we find something much closer to a proper synthesis between idealism and materialism, Leavisism and Marxism. He had inherited from Leavis a commitment to holistic conceptions of culture and methods of analysis, a strong sense of the importance of the particular, whether in art or in 'life', and an insistence on the absolute centrality of culture. He rejected its cultural elitism, however, especially as displayed in the 'mass civilization versus minority culture' topos. From Communist Marxism, he had inherited a radically socialistic critique of the 'materiality' of ruling class political, economic and cultural power, while rejecting the barely disguised economic determinism of the base/superstructure model. All of this would come together into something like a coherent intellectual position in the pages of *Culture and Society* and *The Long Revolution*.

From Culture to Society

The central procedure of *Culture and Society* could not be more Leavisite: to move, by way of close readings of a series of particular texts, to the account of a distinctively 'English' national 'tradition'. Moreover, Williams's sense of the intellectual content of this tradition has much in common with that of Leavis or Eliot. And for Williams, as for Leavis, the tradition is seen as developing in more or less explicit antagonism to utilitarianism (though this remains in many respects a surprisingly underdeveloped theme). Williams's strategic purpose was nonetheless radically opposed to the explicit cultural and political conservatism displayed by Eliot, and increasingly by the Leavises too. For Williams sought to demonstrate that, in its very complexity, the 'culture and society' tradition remained not only finally unassimilable to any obvious conservatism, but also often openly amenable to radical, indeed socialistic, interpretation. This is not to suggest that Williams retained anything more than an entirely residual sympathy for Communist Marxism: both the particular judgement on Caudwell and the more general conclusions on Marxism attest to the considerable distance he had travelled since leaving the Party. But, like Thompson, Williams sees in Morris a 'pivotal figure', whose attempt to reconcile Romantic anti-utilitarianism and working-class opposition to capitalism suggest 'directions which ... have become part of a general social movement' (Williams, 1963, p. 165). 'The significance of Morris in this tradition', he would write, 'is that he sought to attach its general values to an actual and growing social force: that of the organized working class. This was the most remarkable attempt that had so far been made to break the general deadlock' (ibid., p. 153). Like Thompson, Williams would aspire to renew this attempt in his own work.

The book's declared subject was the 'idea of culture', as it had developed in English intellectual life from the late eighteenth to the mid-twentieth century; its declared analytical strategy to trace the changing usage of five 'keywords': 'industry', 'democracy', 'class', 'art' and 'culture' itself. These changes, Williams explains, 'bear witness to a general change in our characteristic ways of thinking about our common life' (ibid., pp. 11, 13). Culture had a certain priority over the other keywords, nonetheless, because the issues concentrated in its meanings are those raised by the changes in meaning of each of the others. 'The development of the word culture', Williams insisted, 'may be seen ... as a special kind of map by means of which the nature of the changes can be explored' (ibid., p. 16). It was here that Williams identified the four kinds of meaning of the word 'culture', ranging from an individual habit of mind through to the whole way of life of a people (ibid., p. 16), that we noted in Chapter 1; here too that he charts its emergence as 'an abstract and an absolute', simultaneously separated out from, and yet also a 'mitigating and rallying alternative' to 'the driven impetus of a new kind of society' (ibid., p. 17). All this is sketched out in the book's Introduction, which concludes with the warning that he expected 'the book to be controversial ... for I am inquiring into our common language, on matters of common interest, and when we consider how matters now stand, our continuing interest and language could hardly be too lively' (ibid., p. 19). This is itself a nicely representative instance of one of the book's more obviously defining characteristics: its combination of a magisterially authoritative tone, performatively 'summing up' the national intellectual tradition, with a partisanly controversial argument for a qualitatively different account of what that tradition might be. The rhetoric is worthy of Eliot; the substance of Marx.

Culture and Society is divided into three parts, dealing respectively with the years 1790 to 1870, 1870 to 1914, and 1914 to 1950. Williams's version of the 'Nineteenth-Century Tradition', which runs from Burke and Cobbett, through Romanticism, utilitarianism and the 'industrial novelists', to Newman and Arnold, Ruskin and Morris, establishes the central organising framework for his analysis. The turn-of-the-century

'Interregnum', which includes Wilde and Gissing, Shaw and Hulme, clearly interested Williams the least of his three periods: 'we shall not find ... anything very new: a working out, rather, of unfinished lines' (ibid., p. 165). But the account of 'Twentieth Century Opinions', which runs from Lawrence and Tawney to Orwell, and includes Eliot, Leavis and the British Marxists as we have seen, once again seems to command Williams's respect and engagement. He summarises the book's general argument thus in the 'Conclusion':

> In the first period ... we find the long effort to compose a general attitude towards the new forces of industrialism and democracy ... in this period ... the major opinions and descriptions emerge. Then ... there is a breaking-down in to narrower fronts, marked by a particular specialism in attitudes to art, and, in the general field, by a pre-occupation with direct politics. After 1914 these definitions continue, but there is a growing preoccupation, reaching a climax after 1945, with the issues raised not only by the inherited problems but by new problems arising from the development of mass media of communication and the general growth of large-scale organizations. (ibid., pp. 286-7)

In retrospect and with the benefit of theoretical hindsight, it is easy to indict Williams's tradition for sins of omission and commission. He would himself concede that T.H. Green should have been included and that Wordsworth clearly warranted more extensive consideration (Williams, 1979a, p. 98). These individual instances aside, there are also obvious structural limitations to the range and scope of what Williams meant by the tradition. Most obvious to a twenty-first century reader, is the relative absence of women on the one hand, sexual radicalism on the other. Only two of the forty writers Williams discusses were female: Elizabeth Gaskell and George Eliot (Williams, 1963, pp. 99-104, 112-19). We know that Williams's first draft had included a chapter on William Godwin (Williams, 1979a, p. 99). But why not on Mary Wollstonecraft, one is tempted to ask? Why not on their daughter, Mary Shelley? For that matter, why not on the Brontës? Why not the Pankhursts? Why not Virginia Woolf? Why not Q.D. Leavis, who rates only one passing mention in the entire book (Williams, 1963, p. 247)? Why wasn't 'gender' or 'sexuality' one of Williams's keywords? Why does the chapter on John Stuart Mill make mention neither of *The Subjection of Women* nor of Harriet Taylor (cf. Mill, 1970; Mill and Taylor Mill, 1970)? The answer is in each case fairly obvious: if not explicitly patriarchal, Williams's version of the 'culture and society' tradition was, at the very least, heavily gendered as masculine, more so in fact than Leavis's 'great tradition'. And, if not explicitly homophobic, Williams's treatment of Wilde, as a latter-day Romantic saved from aestheticism only by the 'general humanity' of his socialism (Williams, 1963, pp. 174-5), was, at the very least, strangely blind to a queer sexual politics which would resonate powerfully with late twentieth-century sexual radicalism (Sinfield, 1994).

Just as striking, and perhaps more surprising - given Williams's other political and scholarly interests - are the historical and geographical limits to his tradition. Historically, it dates only from the late eighteenth century and thus tends to follow Leavis, rather than Eliot, in stressing the long-term cultural consequences of the Industrial Revolution, rather than those of the seventeenth-century English Revolution. Geographically, it is also an overwhelmingly English affair, more or less indifferent both to other European traditions and to the subordinate national cultures of the British Isles. Here, too, it tends to follow Leavis, rather than Eliot. The lack of interest in the seventeenth century would prompt Williams to a 1963 'Postscript' on Milton (Williams, 1963, pp. 324-5) and, later still, to a more general admission that 'my historical perception ... made it difficult to see the real connections with the Civil War' (Williams, 1979a, p. 131). Williams is not at all clear as to where the fault lay in this perception, but one might hazard the observation that an emphasis on the long revolutions of economics and culture will tend to detract from the significance of political 'short revolutions', such as that of 1649. It is a strange omission, nonetheless, for a theorist impressed in any way by either Eliot or Caudwell. The geographical limits seem stranger still and for a number of reasons. They are belied by Williams's own interest in comparative, as distinct from 'national', approaches to drama studies, even in the early work which pre-dates *Culture and Society* (Williams, 1952). They are belied, too, by his own Welshness, which makes it doubly problematic that a Scotsman like Carlyle or Irishmen like Burke, Wilde and Shaw should be casually assimilated to this 'English' tradition, without any sense of their possible place in other, different national traditions. Wilde, after all, was not only gay, but also an Irish nationalist, and could as easily be discussed in relation to Joyce and Yeats as to Pater and Whistler.[3] They are belied, finally, by the obvious debt owed to German thought both by English Romanticism in general and by Coleridge and Carlyle in particular, which remains powerfully suggestive of the fruitful lines of inquiry available to a more properly comparatist approach, such as that eventually pursued in Hartman (1997). That Williams was also a declared 'internationalist', even an anti-imperialist, in politics serves only to compound the problem.

Taken to task by the *New Left Review* some twenty years later, for the book's lack of engagement with problems of 'British imperial hegemony and oppression abroad', Williams explained that 'the Welsh experience' of 'subjection to English expansion', which ought to have enabled him 'to think much more closely and critically', was 'at that time very much in abeyance' (Williams, 1979a, p. 118). One waits in vain either for any further elaboration on his own part or for the interviewers to pursue the matter further. The answer is less than satisfactory, nonetheless, if only because Williams's Welshness was by no means entirely 'in abeyance' at 'that time': *Culture and Society* had been dedicated to his three children, Merryn, Ederyn and Gwydion Madawc, the last born during the book's long gestation, and these are by no means conventionally English names; *Border Country*, the first novel in his Welsh trilogy, had been written and rewritten, originally as *Brynllwyd*, later still as *Village on the Border*, between 1947 and 1958, that is, precisely during the period in which he wrote *Culture and Society*. Seven years later, during a conference at the University of London's Institute of Education, Edward Said would refer to this exchange and quietly take Williams to task for the over-identification with Anglo-Britishness. 'Certainly if you read *Culture and Society* again,' Said says, addressing both Williams and their shared audience:

> and take almost without exception all the major statements on cul-
> ture in the nineteenth century by the great sages and novelists, they
> refer to 'our' culture as opposed to 'theirs', 'theirs' being defined and
> marginalized essentially ... by virtue of race ... there is this tradition
> which you are required to understand and learn ..., but you cannot
> really be of it; you can be in it but you are not *of* it. (Williams and
> Said, 1989, p. 196)

Once again, one wants to know how Williams will reply; once again, the conversation breaks off just as it is about to get interesting. The issue is raised a third time, and much more trenchantly, by a younger postcolonial critic a few years after Williams's death: 'Williams's con-fidence in traveling/comparatist method is entirely devoid of the kind of skepticism that comes out of serious self-reflexivity. This is particu-larly unfortunate since Williams's subject position is contradictory. For, it is both oppositional-marginal and dominant-central' (Radhakrishnan, 1993, p. 289). Indeed, it is: as Welsh, working-class and socialist, it is 'oppositional-marginal'; as Western, middle-class and Cambridge Professor, it is of necessity also 'dominant-central'. For Radhakrishnan, however, as for postcolonial criticism more generally, the force of 'dominant-central' falls overwhelmingly on 'Western'; and conversely, it is in Williams's Welshness, rather than his status as a working-class organic intellectual, that his speaking position becomes 'oppositional-marginal'. But this surely misses the point - as Aijaz Ahmad, for example, does not (Ahmad, 1992, pp. 92-3) - of the 'classed' nature of academic literary discourse, both in the West and elsewhere. This is particularly unfortunate, to borrow a phrase, since a proper recognition of Williams's achievement in *Culture and Society* requires above all that we understand precisely the class content of the English literary tradition.

For this was Williams's achievement: that, despite all these retro-spectively apparent limitations, whether of gender, sexuality, historical periodisation, nationality or colonialism, he nonetheless succeeded in wresting the very idea of the tradition out of the hands of Eliot's and Leavis's cultural conservatism. This was, of course, his conscious, seriously self-reflexive, intent. He had set out 'to refute the ... use of the concept of culture against democracy, socialism, the working class or popular education' and to do so, moreover, by way of a kind of prototypical deconstruction, by discovering within the tradition the repressed legacy 'of the tradition itself' (Williams, 1979a, pp. 97-98). There is an important sense, then, in which Williams is simultaneously (re)constructing and deconstructing the literary tradition. As he would explain to the *New Left Review* editors:

> One now finds constant reference to the 'culture and society tradition' as if it was something I had been taught at Cambridge and then critically assessed ... it is a curious effect of the style of the book that it reads like somebody selecting and redisposing something which is already a common property. Whereas what the book was really doing was making it one. (Williams, 1979a, p. 99)

It is this 'curious effect' - that of borrowing from Eliot and Leavis their sense of the common intellectual property, so as to turn it against their own class prejudices - which most clearly characterises the book's achievement as a (re)'making' of the tradition. If for Williams himself this was overwhelmingly a matter of social class and of labour and socialist politics, by the same token the book also established the theoretical space for other remakings, be they feminist, queer or postcolonial. The concept Williams coined to describe this process was that of the 'selective tradition'.

Culture and Society ends with a 'personal conclusion' (Williams, 1963, p. 287) that is perhaps the most remarkable, and certainly at the time the most controversial, section in the book. Quite fundamentally, Williams begins by rejecting the Leavisite notion of 'mass civilization', and with it the notion of 'masses': 'There are in fact no masses; there are only ways of seeing people as masses' (ibid., p. 289). He rejects also the Leavisite notion of a distinctively valuable minority culture, but does so nonetheless in distinctly Leavisite terms. A culture, he writes, 'is not only a body of intellectual and imaginative work; it is also and essentially a whole way of life' (ibid., p. 311). In principle this is little different from Leavis's, or indeed Eliot's, sense of the connectedness of culture as art, and culture as way of life. But in the practical application of the principle, Williams so expands its range as to include within 'culture' the 'collective democratic institution', by which he means, primarily, the trade union, the co-operative, and the working-class political party. 'Working-class culture,' he continues: 'is primarily social (in that it has created institutions) rather than individual (in particular intellectual or imaginative work). When it is considered in context, it can be seen as a very remarkable creative achievement' (ibid., p. 313). Or, as he would later write: 'Culture is ordinary, in every society and in every mind' (Williams, 1989a, p. 4).

Thus redefined, Eliot's and Leavis's notions of a single common culture become supplemented, and importantly qualified, by that of a plurality of class cultures. Yet, despite such qualification, the normative ideal of a common culture remains central: 'We need a common culture, not for the sake of an abstraction, but because we shall not survive without it' (Williams, 1963, p. 304). A common culture may not yet properly exist, but it remains desirable nonetheless, and moreover, it provided for Williams, as it had for Leavis, the essential theoretical ground from which to mount an organicist critique of utilitarian individualism. A common culture could never be properly such, Williams argues, if established on the basis of the kind of vicarious participation which Leavis and Eliot had sanctioned. 'The distinction of a culture in common', he writes in the book's closing pages, 'is that ... selection is freely and commonly made and remade. The tending is a common process, based on a common decision' (ibid., p. 322). In a characteristically leftist move, Williams thus relocates the common culture from the idealised historical past it had occupied in Leavis and Eliot, to the not too distant, still to be made, democratically socialist future. And it is in the working-class 'idea of solidarity', that Williams finds 'potentially the real basis of a society' (ibid., p. 318). But, even as he insisted on the class determinations of culture, he was careful also to note the extent to which such distinctions of class are complicated, especially in the field of intellectual and imaginative work, by 'the common elements resting on a common language' (ibid., p. 311). For Williams, any direct reduction of art to class, such as had clearly been canvassed by Caudwell, remained entirely unacceptable: 'The area of culture', he observes, 'is usually proportionate to the area of a language rather than to the area of a class' (ibid., p. 307).

The idea of a common culture is now a distinctly unfashionable notion, except perhaps amongst American conservatives. For, of course, multicultural identity politics, which powerfully shaped the radical agenda over the last two decades of the twentieth century, have tended to valorise difference and subordinate identity over commonality and community. Hartman makes essentially the same point, citing Blake against Williams, albeit with aesthetic rather than political intent, when he asks of *Culture and Society*: 'what should we do with our surplus imagination, its *uncommon* culture, which is playful, extravagant, dangerous, often sublime and a bit crazy?' (Hartman, 1997, p. 62). Little wonder that Williams's admirers have often been ill at ease with the notion: for Jardine and Swindells, it was a 'minefield' (1989, p. 115); for Brenkman, multiculturalism sounded its 'death knell' (1995, p. 253). In 1986, even Williams himself had relegated the question of the common culture 'to the fifties and very early sixties' (Williams and Said, 1989, p. 193). The context in which Williams makes this remark is interesting, however. Asked whether the concept of a common culture marginalises the kind of subordinate voice to which his work has been addressed, he replies that this earlier 'very particular phase' of the debate had been characterised by a complex 'overlap', where 'on the one hand, you use the notion of an extending and participating common culture against the notion of a reserved or elite culture; on the other hand, you argue ... that the very idea ... challenges these divisions, separations and conflicts, which are yet rooted in real historical situations'. His own work, however, is no longer situated within this overlap, he suggests:

> What I have mostly been writing about since that time has been divisions, problems, inside the culture; things which *prevent* the assumption of a common culture as a thing which now exists ... So, if one says, does the use of this idea create problems ... , it *is* the problem; this is what the analysis has been about.

But then he adds:

> Certainly, the project is something 'common' in that sense, something in the sense of a shared culture includes diversity. But the moment the notion of community is appropriated for a version which is going to be dominant, and to which variations are going to be subordinate, then the same value has turned in an opposite direction. (Williams and Said, 1989, p. 194)

This is not Williams at his most lucid. But it is clear that there are few fundamental differences between the position of the 1950s and that of the 1980s. The positive content of the idea of a common culture is, in each case, an argument for extension and inclusion; the negative, an argument for domination and subordination. Williams had shifted his own emphases as the wider debate itself had shifted, but to much less effect, nonetheless, than he wished to suggest. This would be deeply problematic, if by common culture we meant a shared body of beliefs, texts and practices, as Williams's extempore answer to what was a spoken question almost suggests he did. For, as all good postmodernists rightly insist, any one set of beliefs, texts and practices can only be some group's preference, as against some other's. But, as Eagleton has recently reminded us, Williams's sense of a common culture was primarily a matter of institutions rather than of texts. Here, Eagleton distinguishes between what he terms 'cultural politics', in the sense of a politics internal to culture, and 'the politics of culture', in the sense of culture's extra-cultural political preconditions. He stresses that, while postmodern identity politics have been mainly about the former, Williams's own work was much more interested in the latter

(Eagleton, 2000, p. 122). In short, Williams was concerned with the problem of how to establish democratic socialism as the political pre-condition for a common culture, rather than with the attempt to identify the specific content of any such culture. This distinction of Eagleton's - which is in some ways analogous to that in Benjamin between politicised aesthetics and aestheticised politics (Benjamin, 1973a, pp. 243-4) - is surely extraordinarily helpful both in itself and as a way into an understanding of what most clearly distinguished Williams's work from the contemporary 'postmodern' left.

The Long Revolution

The institutional focus, prefigured in *Culture and Society*, becomes central to *The Long Revolution*, first published in 1961 and 'planned and written as a continuation' of the earlier book (Williams, 1965, p. 9). Here, Williams sought to chart the long history of the emergence of modernity, and of the interrelationships, within British society, between the democratic revolution, the industrial revolution, and the 'cultural revolution' embodied in the extension and actual or potential democratisation of communications (ibid., pp. 10-12). As he would later recall, the book elicited an extremely hostile immediate response:

> There was a full-scale attack of the most bitter kind in certain key organs ...*Culture and Society* soon acquired the reputation of being a decent and honourable sort of book, whereas this was a scandalous work. It was a standard complaint that I had been corrupted by sociology, that I had got into theory ... it was perceived as ... much more dangerous. (Williams, 1979a, pp. 133-4)

The central novelty of *The Long Revolution*, and the source of much this hostility, lies in its form, in its peculiar combination of an extensive opening theoretical discussion, with an essentially 'sociological' substantive second part, and an expressly political third part. There is much that must have been offensively innovative in each. The three, apparently disparate, parts of the book are held together, however, by a very strong, underlying sense of the materiality of culture, at once a restatement and a transcendence of the position originally outlined in *Culture and Society*.

The opening theoretical discussions are dense, original and distinctly 'unEnglish'. The book's first chapter uses the history of the idea of the individual creative mind as a foil against which to develop Williams's own theory of art as a form of social communication. Steering between romantic idealism, on the one hand, and social reductionism, on the other, he argues that art is, at once, both creative and social. Art and culture are indeed ordinary, he insists yet again, but neither is thereby diminished. To the contrary: 'Art is ratified ... by the fact of creativity in all our living ... We create our human world as we have thought of art being created. Art is a major means of precisely this creation' (Williams, 1965, p. 54). In the second chapter, Williams outlines a prospectus for what would soon become a thoroughgoing cultural materialism. 'It was certainly an error', he wrote against Leavisite humanism, 'to suppose that values or art-works could be adequately studied without reference to the particular society within which they were expressed'. But, 'it is equally an error', he wrote against Communist Marxism, 'to suppose that the social explanation is determining, or that the values and works are mere by-products' (Williams, 1965, p. 61). He moves thence to what might well be the book's central set of propositions:

> If the art is part of the society, there is no solid whole, outside it, to which ... we concede priority. The art is there, as an activity, with the production, the trading, the politics, the raising of families ... It is ... not a question of relating the art to the society, but of studying all the activities and their interrelations, without any concession of priority to any one of them we may choose to abstract ... I would define the theory of culture as the study of relationships between elements in a whole way of life. The analysis of culture is the attempt to discover the nature of the organization which is the complex of these relationships. Analysis of particular works or institutions is, in this context, analysis of their essential kind of organization, the relationships which works or institutions embody as parts of the organization of a whole. (Williams, 1965, pp. 61-3)

The third chapter resumes the critique of the false antithesis between individual and society, but at the socio-political level, rather than the artistic. This leads to an expressly political conclusion, which strongly echoes the more generally libertarian preoccupations of the early New Left. 'If man [sic] is essentially a learning, creating and communicating being,' Williams argues, 'the only social organization adequate to his [sic] nature is a participatory democracy, in which all of us, as unique individuals, learn, communicate and control' (ibid., p. 118). The fourth and final chapter of this opening theoretical section develops a critique of the falsely abstract nature of the various images of society available to our culture. 'The truth about a society', he writes:

> is to be found in the actual relations, always exceptionally complicated, between the system of decision, the system of communication and learning, the system of maintenance and the system of generation and nurture ... The formula that matters is that which, first, makes the essential connexions between what are never really separable systems, and second, shows the historical variability of these systems. (ibid., p. 136)

This is a much more structured sense of the social than anything in Leavis, but also a much more experiential (or 'actual') sense than anything in Marxism. Its gesture toward the 'system of generation and nurture' is interestingly suggestive of what would become a matter of central concern, only a few years later, for 'second wave feminism'. The suggestion is hurriedly passed over, however. For, even if the truth about society concerns each of these four 'systems', when Williams comes to define the long revolution, only a few pages later, then it is as a process concerning only three: the political, cultural and economic, but nonetheless not the familial (ibid., p. 141). Taken to task for this omission by the *New Left Review's* editors, Williams embarrassedly admitted that: 'I had such a comparatively unproblematic experience both in my own home and in my own family ... that I was not as intensely aware of disorder and crisis in the family as ... in other areas' (Williams, 1979a, p. 150). This is disingenuous, for, as Williams himself knew, experience always entails interpretation and is therefore never truly unproblematic. He was able to read the experience thus, in part, because this was precisely how the 'culture and society tradition' had read it, through 'the late nineteenth-century ideology of work and ... of the domestic/the family' (Jardine and Swindells, 1989, p. 110). This is not an isolated instance in Williams, moreover, but rather a characteristic, almost systematic, weakness. But the weakness is in the particular content of the ideology and not, as Jardine and Swindells themselves argue, in the form of the 'literary' itself. We shall return to this matter in Chapter 7.

In the book's second part, Williams moves to supplement the more conventional procedures of Leavisite textual criticism, deployed in *Culture and Society*, with a directly material analysis of the historical development of a number of major British cultural institutions. There are pioneering analyses of the education system and the growth of the reading public, the popular press and the development of 'Standard English'; these are followed, in turn, by chapters on the social backgrounds of a selection of canonical English writers, on the social history of dramatic forms and on the contemporary novel, all of which remain distinctly 'sociological' in their general import. There are weaknesses, of course, for example, the lack of interest in the seventeenth century, which is carried over from *Culture and Society* into the account of the popular press in *The Long Revolution*. Williams is thus quite mistaken to describe the newspaper as a 'creation of the commercial middle class, mainly in the eighteenth century' (Williams, 1965, p. 197). For, as he would later himself acknowledge, its origins are much earlier, dating from the collapse of official censorship during the opening stages of the English Revolution (Williams, 1979a, p. 131).[4] Whatever the particular weaknesses, however, both the range of the analysis and the wealth of the empirical detail remain enormously impressive. And its more radically democratic political implications are often spelt out with some determination. So, Williams is clear that the education system's commitment to 'sorting and grading' serves the needs of 'a class society' rather than those of its pupils (Williams, 1965, p. 168). Similarly, the chapter on the reading public is clearly intended as a rejoinder to the Leavises' pessimistic reading of cultural modernity. As against their cultural elitism, Williams insists: first, that 'quality' is by no means identical to tradition; and, second, that 'inferior' literature is itself valuable in certain circumstances. If there is indeed a problem, he adds, then it will best be explained, not by the cultural weaknesses of individual readers, but by 'deep reasons in our social organization' (ibid., p. 193).

At times, the book becomes positively pathbreaking, as for example in the chapter on the social history of English writers, based on a long-range study of 350 canonical writers, drawn from the *Oxford Introduction to English Literature*, for the period 1470-1920. Williams divides the writers into nine main sub-periods and compares their educational and social-class backgrounds. This leads him to a series of suggestive conclusions: that the relative popularity of Elizabethan drama is correlated with the relatively diverse class background of its writers; that the more socially limited drama of the period 1580-1680 and the class-based Restoration theatre are correlated with a corresponding narrowing of social-class backgrounds; that, in the eighteenth century, there is an apparent correlation between the new middle-class literature and new middle-class writers; and that the late nineteenth century witnesses a social and imaginative narrowing of the literary mainstream, partly offset by the special importance of 'minority' groups, such as women and foreigners (ibid., pp. 264-5). Richard Altick would later contrast Williams's chapter unfavourably with his own survey of 1,100 writers over the period 1800-1935 (Altick, 1978, p. 49). For all the additional detail, however, Altick's evidence does little more than confirm different aspects of Williams's account. If there is an obvious weakness in Williams, it is one he shares with Altick: a dependence on retrospective canonisation for the definition of the sample. The total number of published writers was clearly very much larger than that in either sample,[5] so that, if canonisation is the effect of traditions as selective as Williams himself suspected, then there would be good reason to question their representative quality.

The book's concluding third part, on 'Britain in the 1960s', is an exploratory inquiry into the 'structures of feeling' of the early 1960s, which critically addresses the politico-cultural problems of the moral decline of the labour movement. Each of the movement's institutions, party, union and co-operative, is now, Williams observes, 'discovering that the place in existing society proposed for it ... is essentially subordinate' (Williams, 1965, p. 329). This subordination will be to ideas, especially the 'concepts of the organised market and the consumer', he insists, as much as to the capitalist class. In their substance, moreover, these concepts are profoundly anti-democratic: 'we have many of the forms of democracy', he continues, 'but find these continually con-fused by the tactics of those who do not really believe in it, who are genuinely afraid of common decisions openly arrived at, and who ... partly succeed in weakening the patterns of feeling of democracy which alone could substantiate the institutions' (ibid., p. 334). In these circumstances, he concludes, the much vaunted 'classlessness' of the affluent 1960s is 'simply a failure of consciousness' (ibid., p. 352). The analysis is extraordinarily prescient, serving to remind us very force-fully of the very real continuities between the conservatisms and labourisms of the 1960s and those of today, the rhetoric of Thatcherism notwithstanding. As Williams had understood, the 1960s marked 'a very critical phase in the long revolution', where dissent itself could move either toward the need to frame new expectations or toward 'being capitalized, as a new kind of distraction' (ibid., p. 382). In short, this was already what we have since come to know as postmodernity. Williams himself still held out the hope for a distinctly New Leftist renewal of the promise of the long revolution:

> Here, if meaning communicates, is the ratifying sense of movement, and the necessary sense of direction. The nature of the process indi-cates a perhaps unusual revolutionary activity: open discussion, extending relationships, the practical shaping of institutions. But it indicates also a necessary strength: against arbitrary power whether of arms or of money, against all conscious confusion and weakening of this long and difficult human effort, and for and with the people who in many different ways are keeping the revolution going. (ibid., p. 383)

The combination of a sharply analytical intelligence and an at times near-utopian radical vision, which culminates in this closing invoca-tion, must have spoken powerfully and provocatively to a society still slowly shrugging off the moral and political torpor of the 1950s.

Selective Tradition

The second chapter of *The Long Revolution* is devoted to a theoretical elaboration of two of Williams's key concepts, respectively 'selective tradition' and 'structure of feeling'. These are central ideas in Williams, both of which had appeared in his earlier work, both of which would persist into the later cultural materialism. They are given extensive articulation in *The Long Revolution*, however, and it therefore seems appropriate to subject them each, by turn, to relatively detailed analysis at this juncture. The notion of the selective tradition had been first canvassed in *Culture and Society*. If the common culture is not yet fully common, as we have seen Williams insist, then it tends to follow

that the literary and cultural tradition cannot be the objective unfold-
ing of the consciousness of a people, as the Leavisites had argued, but
must rather be the outcome, in part, of a set of interested selections
made in the present. So Williams argues that: 'a tradition is always
selective, and ... there will always be a tendency for this process of
selection to be related to and even governed by the interests of the
class that is dominant' (1963, pp. 307-8). Where Leavis had revered the
'great tradition', Williams would thus discover a selective tradition.
But nonetheless, the tradition cannot be reduced to class. 'If we are to
understand the process of a selective tradition,' writes Williams: 'we
shall not think of exclusive areas of culture but of degrees of shifting
attachment and interaction, which a crude theory either of class or of
standards is incompetent to interpret' (Williams, 1963, p. 310).
Once again, we observe the double distancing, both from Marxism's
crude theories of class, and from Leavisism's apparently equally crude
theory of standards.[6]

The argument is repeated, and significantly elaborated upon, in the
opening theoretical chapters of *The Long Revolution*. Culture exists at
three levels, Williams observes: first, that of the lived culture of a particular time and place, which is only fully accessible to those who were
part of it; second, the recorded culture of deposited texts, artefacts and
knowledges; and third, the culture of the selective tradition (Williams,
1965, p. 66). In one sense, Williams's point is simply obvious: the historical record is so large that only a 'selective process, of a quite drastic kind' can make it available to subsequent generations. The argument has a less obvious corollary, however: 'Theoretically, a
period is recorded; in practice, this record is absorbed into a selective
tradition; and both are different from the culture as lived' (ibid.,
pp. 66-7). Such selections begin within the period itself, but are continued by subsequent generations, and are always necessarily matters
of evaluation: 'from the whole body of activities, certain things are
selected for value and emphasis' (ibid., p. 67). The traditions thus
formed are what we tend to mean by our culture, but they are nonetheless both more and less than that: 'The selective tradition ... creates, at
one level, a general human culture; at another level, the historical
record of a particular society; at a third level ... a rejection of considerable areas of what was once a living culture' (ibid., p. 68). Selection is
a retrospective process, Williams continues, made and remade, not by
the past, but in and for a sequence of successive 'presents': 'the cultural tradition can be seen as a continual selection and re-selection of
ancestors' (ibid., p. 69). It is thus motivated above all by contemporary
interests and values: 'selection will be governed by many kinds of special interest, including class interest ... The traditional culture of a society will always tend to correspond to its *contemporary* system of interests and values' (ibid., p. 68). As in *Culture and Society*, the stress falls
once again on selection according to class-specific criteria, but once
again, also, on the reality of a truly general human culture. To illus-

trate and test the point, Williams cites as an example the England of the 1840s. If we are to understand the culture of the period, he argues, we should begin with the Sunday newspapers, which were by far the most widely read, rather than with the daily *Times*, as most histories tended to do. If the literature, then we need to consider the 'most widely read writers', Lytton, Maryatt, James and Grant, as well as Dickens, Thackeray and the Brontës; the pornographic, the philosophical, historical, religious and poetic writing as well as the prose fictions (ibid., pp. 70-2). This will lead us, in turn, into a 'social history' of the period's institutions (ibid., p. 72). 'This is the reality', Williams concludes, 'that various strands of the selective tradition tend to reduce, seeking always a single line of development' (ibid., p. 74). It is tempting to read this as if Williams were a proto-postmodern cultural relativist, but it would be a misreading nonetheless. For, at this stage, at any rate, he was still willing to use the language of literary evaluation to sift 'the good from the less good and the bad'; still willing to concede that: 'To a considerable extent ... the work we know from the 1840s is the best work of the period' (ibid., p. 75).

The real theoretical novelty of the argument lies, not so much in the turn from evaluation, as in its postponement and careful qualification and, more importantly, in the analytical shift from the content of the canon toward the processes of institutionalised canon-formation. In this second aspect, Williams's work runs interestingly parallel to some of the variously postmodern and post-structuralist thematics which remain influential in contemporary Cultural Studies. In their discovery that all knowledge is social and all meaning plural, more recent post-structuralisms have discovered the futility of structuralist aspirations to scientificity. Practically, this led to an emergent preoccupation with reader response, reception, the role of the reader, and similar, related concepts. In his formulation of the concept of a selective tradition, Williams had made an essentially analogous theoretical move. Previously, culturalisms had typically subscribed to a kind of 'objective idealism' in which truth was seen as inhering in the cultural tradition itself. Williams's deconstruction of this notion, through the idea of the selective tradition, had effected a relativising turn similar to that of post-structuralism in relation to structuralism, by virtue of what was, in effect, an appeal to the role of the (collective) reader. This stress on the selectivity of the tradition is suggestive of Williams's developing sense of the materiality, historicity and social arbitrariness of the linguistic sign, all of which can be seen as loosely analogous to similar thematics in Foucault and Derrida. In the reference to contemporary class interests, moreover, Williams more than gestures toward a recognition of the intricate nature of power within discourse such as one finds in both Foucault and Bourdieu. The contrast with Leavis and Eliot should be obvious: there was indeed something distinctly unEnglish about this Welshman's theorising.

Structures of Feeling

Williams's first attempt at a theorisation of the concept of 'structure of feeling' is in the early *Preface to Film*. His initial use of the term warrants quotation at some length:

> I use the phrase *structure of feeling* because it seems to me more accurate ... than *ideas or general life* ... while we may, in the study of a past period, separate out particular aspects of life, ... this is only how they may be studied, not how they were experienced. We examine each element as a precipitate, but in the living experience of the time every element was in solution, an inseparable part of a complex whole ... it is from such a totality that the artist draws; it is in art, primarily, that the effect of the totality, the dominant structure of feeling, is expressed and embodied ... To relate a work of art to any part of that observed totality may, in varying degrees, be useful; but it is a common experience, in analysis, to realize that when one has measured the work against the separable parts, there yet remains some element for which there is no external counterpart. This element ... is what I have named the *structure of feeling* of a period and it is only realizable through experience of the work of art itself, as a whole. (Williams, 2001, p. 33)

As Higgins rightly notes, Williams quoted only selectively from these pages, during the 1979 *Politics and Letters* interviews, with the effect that the earlier argument was represented as more compatible with Marxism than had actually been the case (Higgins, 1999, pp. 38, 40-1; Williams, 1979a, pp. 158-9). Higgins seems to me mistaken, nonetheless, to insist that this first use of the concept is intended 'as a conscious alternative and direct challenge' to Marxism (Higgins, 1999, p. 41). When Higgins writes that Williams's '*ideas* or *general life*' refers directly to 'the Marxist structure and superstructure paradigm', quoting from Marx a line in which neither term is used, he surely forces the argument (ibid., p. 40). The point, rather, is that Williams was developing his own distinctive line of thinking, in creative tension with both Marxism and Leavisism. Structure of feeling is one of a series of related concepts - discourse, ideology, world vision are obvious alternatives - used in literary and cultural studies to denote the patterned 'articulation' of different texts and sign-systems. As Williams himself glossed the term:

> The point of the deliberately contradictory phrase ... is that it was a structure in the sense that you could perceive it operating in one work after another which weren't otherwise connected - people weren't learning it from each other; yet it was one of feeling much

more than of thought - a pattern of impulses, restraints, tones, for
which the best evidence was often the actual conventions of literary
or dramatic writing. (Williams, 1979a, p. 159)

Some such concept seems essential to contemporary Cultural Studies;
the only question is which. Superstructure clearly doesn't belong in
this series, insofar as it appears to suggest merely epiphenomenal relations to a primary reality located elsewhere, that is, in the economic
'base'. Nor does tradition, in either Eliot's or Leavis's sense, since it
denotes a relation of historical sequence, rather than contemporaneous
sets of relations. Which is only to say that Williams's formulation of
the concept of 'structure of feeling' is itself part of a much broader
movement away from both idealism and materialism and toward the
newly 'synthetic' paradigms of the late twentieth century.

The term is used only sparingly, and in relatively untheorised fashion, in *Culture and Society* (Williams, 1963, pp. 56, 100). But it seems
clear that Williams intends it to refer to a more generally common possession than the specifically intellectual content of the tradition itself
(ibid., p. 119). Moreover, there is also an important sense in which the
book performatively illustrates the practical workings of the concept.
The novelty of the more general argument in *Culture and Society* is
clearly foreshadowed in its initial unlikely pairing of Burke and
Cobbett, the one a reactionary opponent of the French Revolution, the
other a radical critic of the new industrial class system. Williams's
point, however, is that 'we can only understand this tradition of criticism of the new industrial society if we recognize that it is compounded of very different and at times even directly contradictory elements'
(ibid., p. 38). At issue, then, are not only a series of individual opinions
- though these certainly matter - but also, and more centrally, the 'historical formation' of a 'structure of meanings, ... a wide and general
movement in thought and feeling' (ibid., p. 17); that is, in short, more
or less exactly what Williams would mean by 'structure of feeling'.

In *The Long Revolution*, Williams proposes a further theoretical elaboration of the concept. Once again, he uses the analogy with solution
and precipitate, where the former is the whole lived experience, the
latter an aspect of the whole subsequently recovered only abstractly.
'The most difficult thing to get hold of', he writes, 'is this felt sense of
the quality of life at a particular place and time: a sense of the ways in
which the particular activities combined into a way of thinking and
living' (Williams, 1965, p. 63). He cites Erich Fromm's notion of 'social
character' and Ruth Benedict's 'pattern of culture' as helpful, but concludes that each of these is too 'abstract' for his own purposes. To get
the sense of the lived 'experience', he continues, we need the sense of
'a further common element', 'a particular community of experience
hardly needing expression, through which the characteristics of our
way of life ... are in some way passed, giving them a particular and

characteristic colour' (ibid., pp. 63-4). This further common element is the structure of feeling: 'as firm and definite as "structure" suggests, yet it operates in the most delicate and least tangible parts of our activity' (ibid., p. 64). 'In one sense', Williams writes:

> this structure of feeling is the culture of a period: it is the particular living result of all the elements in the general organization. And it is in this respect that the arts of a period ... are of major importance. For here, if anywhere, this characteristic is likely to be expressed: often not consciously, but by the fact that here ... the actual living sense, the deep community that makes the communication possible, is naturally drawn upon. (ibid., pp. 64-5)

A structure of feeling, he makes clear, is neither universal nor class specific, though it is 'a very deep and wide possession'. Nor is it formally learned, he speculates, and thence follows its often peculiarly generational character: 'the new generation will have its own structure of feeling, which will not appear to have come "from" anywhere' (ibid., p. 65).

The concept has been criticised by Williams's comrades on the Left, most obviously by the young Eagleton, who at his most Althusserian, would insist that what structure of feeling 'designates, in effect, is ideology'. The notion had been put to 'superb use' by Williams, he conceded, but nonetheless marked a 'limit' in the latter's thought. For, even though it reached beyond Hoggart's notion of a 'feeling-*complex*' towards 'feeling-*structure*', Williams still lacked 'the theoretical terms which might specify the precise articulations of that structure.' In short, for Williams 'structure' had been reduced to mere 'pattern' (Eagleton, 1976, pp. 33-4).[7] But Williams had been very clear that structure of feeling designated something other than ideology, if by ideology we mean, as most Marxists did, a relatively formalised belief system, where the belief system of the dominant class becomes the dominant ideology. In *The Long Revolution*, he had used the term 'social character' in preference to ideology but he was clear nonetheless as to the distinction he intended to make: 'structure of feeling ... is different from any of the distinguishable social characters, for it has to deal not only with public ideals but with their omissions and consequences, as lived' (Williams, 1965, p. 80).

In *Marxism and Literature*, Williams would later repeat this argument, in more or less exactly these terms, but in opposition to the more explicitly Marxist concepts of 'world-view' and 'ideology' (Williams, 1977a, p. 132). In both cases, it is clear that he intended 'structure of feeling' to include a strong sense of the experiential specifically excluded from most conceptions of ideology. One might wish to insist that the experiential is a matter of no consequence - although I cannot quite see why - but one cannot reasonably accuse Williams of confusion between this concept intended for these purposes and others designed for quite different purposes. Furthermore, what applies to ideology, applies almost equally to other parallel concepts available to contemporary Cultural Studies. The crucial difference, moreover, between structure of feeling and these other variously available French or German theoretical conceptions lies precisely in Williams's debt to Leavisism. As he would explain to the *New Left Review*, '"experience" was a term I took over from *Scrutiny* ... Leavis's strength was in reproducing and interpreting what he called "the living content of a work"' (Williams, 1979a, pp. 163-4).

Something of very real theoretical significance had been achieved in this synthesis between Marxism and Leavisism, even in these early formulations. Certainly, Williams himself would use the concept of structure of feeling to great effect in his work on the novel and on the drama. Later, it would occupy a commanding position in his cultural materialism. Later still, it would be taken up by writers as influential as Eagleton himself, Jameson and Said (Eagleton, 1984; Jameson, 1991; Said, 1993). Hartman observes of *The Long Revolution* that 'Williams thinks of culture instrumentally, as a very special means of social education and progress', much as had Communist Marxism; but adds that this 'instrumentalism' is combined with an idealist sense of culture as a 'tending of natural growth' (1997, p. 63). Hence, his description of Williams's prose as 'in the verbal orbit of idealism', despite its 'understanding of the "material community"' (ibid., p. 85). This may be precisely Williams's strength, however: that he learnt to combine a Leavisite sense of experience, or 'feeling', with a Marxist sense of 'structure'. In *The Long Revolution* itself, the achievement was still not yet fully synthetic - for that we have to await the mature cultural materialism - but it was a provisional solution of very substantial proportions and one, moreover, which would powerfully inspire the early history of British Cultural Studies.

Materialising Culture

In the interim between the first publication of *The Long Revolution* in 1961 and that of *Marxism and Literature* in 1977, Williams's work proceeded by way of a series of, often radically innovative, encounters with an extremely diverse set of substantive issues, ranging across the whole field of literary and cultural studies: two books on the mass media, *Communications* (Williams, 1962) and *Television: Technology and Cultural Form* (Williams, 1974b); three on drama, the entirely new *Modern Tragedy* (Williams, 1966) and extensively reworked and revised versions of two earlier books, *Drama from Ibsen to Brecht* (Williams, 1973a) and the second edition of *Drama in Performance* (Williams, 1968a); three studies in what might conventionally be considered literary criticism, *The English Novel: From Dickens to Lawrence* (Williams,

1974a), *George Orwell* (Williams, 1971a) and *The Country and the City* (Williams, 1973b); and an introductory study in socio-historical philology, *Keywords* (Williams, 1976a). The latter work represented an obvious continuation of the keywords motif in *Culture and Society*: neither a dictionary nor a glossary, it was, as Williams explained, 'the record of an inquiry into a *vocabulary*' (Williams, 1976a, p. 13), tracing the political history of the meanings of 110 words he deemed significantly connected to 'culture' and 'society'. The book is still widely used in higher education and has proven immensely valuable as a guide to teachers and students, myself included. But it is hardly the 'entirely original venture ... akin to that of the Marxist critique of political economy' hailed by the *New Left Review* (Williams, 1979a, pp. 175-7). There are obvious omissions from its list of keywords: no entries for 'experience' or 'feeling', which seems strange given Williams's own interests; no attempt to rectify the absence of 'gender' and 'sexuality' or 'feminism' from *Culture and Society*;[8] nothing on 'race' or even 'ethnicity'. More seriously, the book remains locked into the theoretical moment of *Culture and Society*. As Inglis rightly observes, by the time Williams published *Keywords* 'his own thinking had gone well beyond its method' (Inglis, 1995, p. 247; cf. Williams, 1973c; Williams, 1980b). In short, the book is an after-effect of *Culture and Society* rather than an anticipation of *Marxism and Literature*.

The two studies of the mass media were also extensions from Williams's earlier work, but they are much more theoretically innovative than their apparently 'popular' presentation might suggest. Taken together, they come very close to defining the subject matter of what is now conventionally regarded as 'media studies'. Williams himself described *Communications* as an introduction to the study of 'the institutions and forms in which ideas, information, and attitudes are transmitted and received' (Williams, 1976b, p. 9), which is as good a definition of Cultural Studies as any. The emphasis on the connectedness of forms and institutions, and also of technologies, was to prove an enduring theme in his work, by no means confined to these particular studies of the press and television. But here it occupied a peculiar saliency: our 'communication models', Williams explains, that is, our forms, can 'become embodied in institutions which are then very powerful in social effect.' The central 'crisis in modern communications', he continues - in effect, that of the contradiction between commodification and democratisation - 'has been caused by the speed of invention and by the difficulty of finding the right institutions in which these technical means are to be used' (Williams, 1976b, p. 12). Both books sought to develop a critique of media institutions and texts which would avoid the disabling cultural elitism characteristic, not only of Leavisism, but also of much available Marxist commentary. Both sought thereby to identify the institutional structures which might sustain a properly democratic communications system.

The prospectus for a non-elitist common culture is canvassed in

Williams's insistence that these communications technologies 'are the contemporary tools of the long revolution towards an educated and participatory democracy' (Williams, 1974b, p. 151). That for a non-elitist Cultural Studies is spelt out in his stress on the fundamental commonality of all culture. 'Our real purpose', he writes:

> should be to bring all cultural work within the same world of discourse: to see the connections between Elia and the manufactured television personality as well as the difference in value between *Lord Jim* and *Captain Condor*. We have to learn confidence in our own real opinions, and this depends on a kind of openness and flexibility ... which much that is called 'criticism' does nothing to help. (Williams, 1976b, p. 147)

The particular insights for which both books are still remembered[9] tend to follow from this overall framework. They are often very acute, nonetheless: for example, the realisation that advertising was concerned, not so much with information about particular products, as with the creation of 'a whole style of life, centred largely in fantasy ... not clarifying experience but deliberately confusing it' (Williams, 1976b, pp. 83-4); or that the development of radio and television had been crucially connected to 'mobile privatisation' (Williams, 1974b, p. 26), that is, to an at once mobile and home-centred way of life, where the home 'might appear private and "self-sufficient", but could be maintained only ... from external sources', a relationship creating both 'the need and the form' of the new kind of communication (Williams, 1974b, p. 27). Williams's approach to televisual form also famously prompted an entirely novel treatment of programming as total broadcasting 'flow', rather than a sequence of discrete programmes (ibid., p. 90). Viewing, he observed, is 'planned, by providers and then by viewers, *as a whole*'; the 'central television experience', he argued, is 'the fact of flow' (ibid., pp. 93, 95). The approach has remained influential in television studies (cf. Jameson, 1991, pp. 70-1), though not without its critics (Laing, 1991, pp. 166-7).

In the work on literature and drama, as in that on the press and television, Williams continued to insist on the 'ordinariness' of culture. Against the weight of contemporary academic opinion, he argued in *Modern Tragedy* for the significance of the everyday 'modern experiences that most of us call tragic' (Williams, 1979b, p. 14). Once again against the weight of contemporary academic interpretation, he argued in *The Country and the City* for a critique based on 'questions of historical fact' (Williams, 1973b, p. 12) of such mythologising misrepresentations of rural life as those in the tradition of English country-house poetry. In both books the relevant experience is understood as essentially social and historical. Hence, for example, the judgement on Jonson and Carew that: 'It is what the poems are: not country life but social compliment; the familiar hyperboles of the aristocracy and its attendants' (ibid., p. 33). The work on literature and drama also enabled a further refinement of the notion of 'structure of feeling'. In *The English Novel* Williams attempted to show how, from Dickens to Lawrence, the novel had become one medium amongst many by which people sought to master and absorb new experience, through the articulation of a structure of feeling the key problem of which was that of the 'knowable community' (Williams, 1974a, pp. 14-15). In *Drama from Ibsen to Brecht* he produced an account of the development of naturalism and of expressionism in the modern theatre, organised around precisely 'the history and significance of the main dramatic forms - the conventions and structures of feeling' (Williams, 1973a, p. 14). In Modern Tragedy he would insist on 'the connections between revolution and tragedy', on the ways in which the 'social fact' of revolution can become the 'structure of feeling' of tragedy (Williams, 1979b, pp. 64-5).

In the work on drama, moreover, as in that on television, a new awareness of the social conventionality of form, and of the interrelationship between technology and form, was increasingly brought to bear. Dramatic convention, Williams wrote, 'is, ... often, just this question of a relation between form and performance ... to put the matter in this way is to realize also that it is a question of audiences; it is there, in the theatre as a social institution, that conventions are really made' (Williams, 1973a, p. 398). Williams's coupling of the problem of cultural form to that of cultural technology clearly drew attention, in the case of both television studies and drama studies, to the materiality of what were, in orthodoxly Marxist terms, 'ideal' superstructures. This led him, in turn, to a simultaneous rejection both of 'technological determinism' and of the notion of 'symptomatic technology', that is, the argument that technology is symptomatic of other socio-cultural developments (Williams, 1974b, p. 13). Neither view is entirely adequate, he argues: because technologies are sought with intent, rather than simply developing as an autonomous dynamic in their own right; and because they meet known social needs, to which they are central, not marginal. His conclusion warrants repetition:

> When there has been such heavy investment in a particular model of social communications, there is a restraining complex of financial institutions, of cultural expectations and of specific technical developments, which though it can be seen, superficially, as the effect of a technology is in fact a social complex of a new and central kind. (Williams, 1974b, p. 31).[10]

The chronological overlap between Williams's work in theatre studies and that on the mass media was thus by no means merely 'coincidental'. Disparate though the work might appear, it had proceeded along clearly connected lines of inquiry. And these connections were empirical and substantive as well as theoretical and methodological. As Williams had already noted in the 'Conclusion' to *Drama from Ibsen to Brecht*: 'drama is no longer coexistent with theatre ... The largest audience for drama, in our own world, is in the cinema and on television' (Williams, 1973a, p. 399).

Notes

1 This does something of a disservice to Williams's adult education colleagues and students (cf. McIlroy and Westwood, 1993).

2 It remained in print more or less continuously thereafter and, by 1979, had sold some 160,000 copies (Williams, 1979a, p. 7n).

3 When set beside the chapters on Lawrence and T.S. Eliot, Joyce's absence seems very telling. He cannot have been excluded on the grounds that he was Irish, since so many Irishmen already inhabited Williams's tradition. I am tempted to treat this as yet another legacy from Leavis, who had been very clear that Lawrence and Eliot were the more significant writers (Leavis, 1962b, p. 36).

4 There were four newspapers in 1641, 167 in 1642, 722 in 1645. As Hill concludes, 'newspapers were of crucial importance in the struggle for men's minds' during the 1640s (1985, pp. 39-40). The radical Levellers published a weekly newspaper, the *Moderate*, which ran for sixty-three weeks (Brailsford, 1961, p. 570).

5 From a comparison between census data and the number of new titles, Nigel Cross has calculated that 'there were about 20,000 persistent nineteenth-century writers' in England (1985, p. 3).

6 Note Williams's own recollections of Leavis himself at examiners' meetings: 'The common pursuit, the collaborative spirit, I would think, looking across at Leavis and expecting some shared sense of the problem: the marking had to be done, while the system was there, but was this mood necessary to it? It was a shock when I ... saw him going along ... with the cold distance of the exercise. Standards, standards' (Williams, 1984a, p. 116).

7 If structure of feeling was indeed ideology, then the theoretical terms which might specify the precise articulations of its structure were, of course, those of Althusser's theory of ideology. Hence, Eagleton's own elaborately acronymic 'categories for a materialist criticism', which ranged from 'General Mode of Production (GMP)' through to 'Aesthetic Ideology (AI)' (1976, p. 44).

8 Morag Shiach has nominated twenty-two additional keywords, listed alphabetically from 'body' to 'wife', for inclusion in a 'feminist version' of *Keywords* (1995, p. 68).

9 Inglis describes *Communications* as the 'first, and forever essential textbook' for media studies (1995, p. 173).

10 Rehearsing the argument much later, in circumstances increasingly perceived as fraught with intellectual and political danger, Williams would insist that: 'a technical invention as such has comparatively little social sig-

nificance. It is only when it is selected for investment toward production, and when it is consciously developed for particular social uses - that is, when it moves from being a technical invention to what can properly be called an available *technology* - that the general significance begins' (Williams, 1989a, p. 120).

4

Theorising Culture

Theory we certainly need, for all sorts of reasons that would be too tedious to rehearse ... What we need over and above theory, however, is the critical recognition that there is no theory capable of covering, closing off, predicting all the situations in which it might be useful. This is another way of saying, as Williams does, that no social or intellectual system can be so dominant as to be unlimited in its strength. (Said, *The World, the Text and the Critic*)

In his work of the late 1960s and early 1970s, Williams had sought to explore the imbrication of form, technology and ideology, by turn, in literature, drama and the mass media. The cumulative effect of these apparently quite diverse lines of inquiry would eventually be registered in *Marxism and Literature* and *Culture*, his two most obviously 'theoretical' works. Ironically, both were published as textbooks, *Marxism and Literature* by Oxford University Press as the first in a series of 'Marxist Introductions', *Culture* by Collins in the 'Fontana New Sociology' series. There is hardly anything, however, of the textbook about *Marxism and Literature*: 'almost wholly theoretical' in form, to borrow Williams's own description, the book 'is not a summary; it is both a critique and an argument' (Williams, 1977a, pp. 6, 1). The critique, directed simultaneously at Marxism and at Literature, is both powerful and instructive; the argument difficult and original. *Culture* stays closer to the template of the textbook, but functions, nonetheless, primarily as an introduction to, and empirical extension from, the argument outlined in *Marxism and Literature*. The densely theoretical character of this particular moment in Williams renders it quite unrepresentative of his broader critical effort. As a result, *Marxism and Literature* tends to be read as an exceptional text, an aberrant excursion into Theory by a writer whose proper business lies elsewhere. So Inglis

dismisses it as 'his unreadable book ... fearsomely jargon-heavy ...,
solemn, abstract and opaque' (1995, pp. 249-52); while Turner praises
it as an 'extraordinary theoretical "coming out"', where 'Williams
finally admits the usefulness of Marxism' (1996, p. 60); and both are
agreed as to the book's exceptionality. Both also seem to me mistaken.
Much more appropriate is O'Connor's emphasis on 'a *fundamental*
theoretical continuity although there were shifts and changes' (1989,
p. 103). But even this underestimates the extent to which the theoretical argument for cultural materialism arises directly from Williams's
earlier work in literary and cultural studies. As he explains in the
book's Introduction: 'every position in it was developed from the
detailed practical work that I have previously undertaken, and from
the consequent interaction with other ... modes of theoretical assumption and argument'. Williams adds that 'anyone who wants to know
what I "really, practically" mean by certain concepts' should look to
his other books, citing eight of them by name (Williams, 1977a, p. 6).
One might perhaps substitute 'developments' for 'shifts and changes'
in O'Connor's formulation, for there *are* real developments between
The Long Revolution and *Marxism and Literature*: in the conceptualisation of structure of feeling, in the stress on the materiality of form, and
in that on the interconnectedness of form and technology. These arise,
furthermore, within what was very obviously a rapidly changing intellectual and political context, that of what might loosely be termed 'the
Sixties'. And it is this changing context, as much as any immanent theoretical development, which most clearly marks the difference
between *The Long Revolution* and *Marxism and Literature*.

Writing on the British New Left, Peter Sedgwick distinguished
between what he termed the 'Old New Left', which formed out of the
political crises of 1956, and the 'New New Left', for whom the central
political experience was that of 1968 (Sedgwick, 1976). Williams had
belonged to the first formation, of course, and had played a central
role in its evolution. In a number of important respects, his work both
echoed and helped to form the sensibility of that early New Left: for
example, his interest in culture as creative rather than merely epiphenomenal; in the particularities of the British experience, as distinct
from the abstract 'internationalism' of the Russophile Communists; in
the complex realities of contemporary working-class life understood
by neither Leavisite nor Communist dogma; and in the potential for a
socialism that would be, at once, both popular and democratic. The
New New Left, by contrast, found its inspiration in the May '68 Events
in Paris, in the Vietnam Solidarity Campaign, the Prague Spring and
the revolt on the campuses. Where the Old New Left had attempted to
preserve the particularities of the British national experience from
Stalinist internationalism, this New New Left spurned nationalism in
general, and the peculiarities of the English especially, in favour of an
uncompromising internationalism which took as its primary political
responsibility solidarity with the Vietnamese Revolution. Where the

Old New Left had situated itself somewhere in the political space between the left-wing of the Labour Party and the liberalising wing of the Communist Party, this New New Left rejected both Labourism and Communism in favour of various 'ultra-leftisms', Guevarism, Maoism, Trotskyism. Where the Old New Left had sought to counterpose 'experience' and 'culture' to Communist dogmatism, this New New Left discovered in the various continental European 'Western Marxisms' a type of 'Theory' that could be counterposed both to the empiricism of English bourgeois culture and to the pragmatism of the British Labour Party.

Theory and the British New Left

At this point, it might be as well to elaborate a little both on the history of Western Marxism and on that of its British and Anglophone receptions. As we noted in Chapter 1, the term 'Western Marxism' was coined by Merleau-Ponty, to distinguish Western European 'critical' Marxism from official Communist, 'scientific' Marxism. This was an intellectual tradition, the characteristic thematics of which were philosophical 'totality', human agency and subjective consciousness. At its point of origin in the early 1920s, in the work of Georg Lukács, Karl Korsch and Antonio Gramsci, this stress on agency and consciousness had served to underwrite a leftist rejection of political fatalism. But as that moment of revolutionary optimism failed, then so the emphasis had shifted towards an analysis of the system-supportive nature of cultural legitimations. Such motifs are present from the very beginning, for example in Lukács's theory of reification (Lukács, 1971a, pp. 83-110) and, by some readings, in Gramsci's theory of hegemony (Gramsci, 1971, pp. 210-76). But they become much more apparent in later formulations, perhaps most strikingly so in the critique of the Enlightenment and of the capitalist 'culture industry' developed by Adorno and Horkheimer (Adorno and Horkheimer, 1979, pp. 120-67). This shift from an initial celebration of the emancipatory potential of culture as human self-activity, to a subsequent recognition of the debilitating and disabling power of culture as 'ideology', marks the historical trajectory of Western Marxist thought from the early 1920s to the 1960s. But it continues also as a recurrent tension within Western Marxism. In the work of Lukács's disciple, Lucien Goldmann, for example, the tension runs between a sociology of the world vision, which stresses the intellectual creativity of social classes and groups, and a sociology of the novel, which stresses the rigorous homology between the historical development of the novel form and that of the commodity market (Goldmann, 1964, pp. 89-102; Goldmann, 1975, p. 7). In the existential Marxism of Jean-Paul Sartre, there is an analogous tension between a determination to vindicate the rationality of praxis, by demonstrating that human history can be understood entirely in terms of human projects, and a substantive emphasis on the ways in which real popular revolutions, confronted by scarcity, collapse into 'seriality' (Sartre, 1976, pp. 43-7; Sartre, 1976/1977, p. 162).

Much of this work was unavailable in English translation until well into 'the sixties'. Some of Lukács's later 'socialist realist' writings had been translated in the early 1960s (Lukács, 1962, Lukács, 1963), Sartre's *Qu'est-ce que la littérature?* very promptly in 1950 (Sartre, 1950), and Goldmann's *Le Dieu caché* reasonably so in 1964 (Goldmann, 1964). But it was not until 1971 that substantial translations of the two 'key texts' in the Western Marxist tradition, Lukács's *Geschichte und Klassenbewusstsein* and Gramsci's *Quaderni del carcere*, were finally published (Gramsci, 1971; Lukács, 1971a). Goldmann's book on Kant and Lukács's *Die Theorie des Romans* followed in the same year (Goldmann, 1971; Lukács, 1971b), Adorno and Horkheimer's *Die Dialektik der Aufklärung* a year later (Adorno and Horkheimer, 1972), the first volume of Sartre's *Critique de la raison dialectique* not until 1976 (Sartre, 1976). For the New New Left of the 1960s the lure of 'Theory' reached its apogee, however, not in any of these earlier 'humanist' Western Marxisms, but in the 'structural Marxism' of the French philosopher, Louis Althusser. Althusser's *Pour Marx*, first published in French in 1966, had been very rapidly translated into English in 1969 (Althusser, 1969); an abridged edition of the co-authored *Lire le Capital*, first published in 1965, appeared in English in 1970 (Althusser and Balibar, 1970); *Lenin and Philosophy*, a collection of essays published separately in France during 1968 and 1969, followed a year later (Althusser, 1971). The *New Left Review* and its associated publishing house, New Left Books, came to provide an important conduit for these various Western Marxisms into British intellectual life. As the *Review*'s editor would later explain: 'NLR set out from the mid-sixties onwards to introduce the major intellectual systems of continental socialism in the post-classical epoch into the culture of the British Left' (Anderson, 1980, p. 149). In itself this contributed an important service not only to the British Left, but to British, and indeed Anglophone, intellectual life in general. If the tone was often far too reverential - Thompson would later refer to the *Review*'s 'theoretical heavy breathing' (Thompson, 1978, p. 405) - then the intent, to criticise 'calmly and systematically, every one of the theoretical schools within "Western Marxism"' (Anderson, 1980, p. 149) was entirely honourable. That said, we need also note that, for much of the late 1960s and early 1970s, the *Review*'s theoretical interests and sympathies were defined primarily in relation, not so much to Western Marxism *per se*, but rather to Althusserian 'theoretical practice'.

In Althusser's work, the characteristically Western Marxist tension between culture as praxis and culture as domination finally attained the unhappiest of all possible resolutions: neither abolished nor transcended, it was in effect repressed. Althusser's distinctive contribution was to read Marxism as if it were a structuralism - much as his friend and colleague, Jacques Lacan, had read Freudian psychoanalysis - so that the older Western Marxist prioritisation of agency and *praxis* was altogether subsumed into a general theory of structural determination. In Althusser, culture is neither a superstructural effect nor the expression of the truth of a social totality, but rather an autonomous structure of 'ideology', with its own specific effectivity, located within and in relation to a wider structure of structures. In a much quoted essay on 'Ideology and Ideological State Apparatuses', he argued that ideology is necessarily embedded in institutions, or 'state apparatuses' as he termed them, and that its social function is that of the reproduction of the relations of production. Culture comes to be understood, then, in essentially structuralist terms, as '*"constituting" concrete individuals as subjects*' (Althusser, 1971, p. 171). Ideology thereby represents, for Althusser, 'the imaginary relationship of individuals to their real conditions of existence' (ibid., p. 162). It was this peculiar hybrid of Marxism and structuralism that would excite the most extreme of New New Left enthusiasms, and yet simultaneously propel many of the Old New Left towards the most vehement of animosities toward 'continental Theory'. Moreover, Althusserianism appeared to have some peculiar purchase on the field of literary and cultural studies. Since art, though not itself an ideology according to Althusser, is nonetheless an allusion to ideology (ibid., p. 122), it becomes possible to read literature 'ideologically'. Althusser himself had developed a theory of symptomatic reading, which sought to reconstruct the 'problematic' of the text (Althusser and Balibar, 1970, pp. 30-4), that is, the structure of determinate absences and presences which occasion it. For the major Althusserian literary critics, Pierre Macherey in France (Macherey, 1978) and Eagleton in England (Eagleton, 1976), the new literary science would be directed at analogous readings of literary texts, thereby revealing ideology itself as the real object of literary studies. It was a project which would inspire nothing but contempt in Thompson: 'to suppose this to advance a "science" of materialist aesthetics is to calumniate both science and materialism' (Thompson, 1978, p. 358).

The shift between the two New Left formations had been prefigured by the distinctly acrimonious transfer of the editorship of the *New Left Review* from Stuart Hall to Perry Anderson during 1962. Williams's own role at this time is interesting: he chose to act as a mediator between the two groups and thus, in effect, helped to secure the succession for the group around Anderson (Williams, 1979a, p. 365). It was not that Williams positively endorsed the changes in style and content proposed by Anderson and his collaborators. It was rather 'a survival strategy that I mainly argued' (ibid., p. 366). For many on the Old New Left, however, this new political generation remained incorrigibly alien. For Thompson, settling old and not so old scores in the wonderfully vindictive 'Foreword' to *The Poverty of Theory*, the ten years after 1968 had been 'a time for reason to sulk in its tent', a time when 'Every pharisee was being more revolutionary than the next; some of them have made such hideous faces that they are likely to be stuck like that for life' (Thompson, 1978, p. ii). It had also been a time when he had quietly joined the Labour Party. There is, no doubt, much to be admired in Thompson's polemic against Anderson's *New Left Review*, and by extension against the entire generation of '68'. Doubtless, the *Review*'s encounter with Western Marxism had produced an at times hair-raising theoreticism; doubtless, third-world guerrilla movements had provided a bizarrely improbable model for radical politics in an advanced capitalist society; doubtless, much of what Thompson had to say about Althusserian 'structural Marxism' contained more than a grain of truth. But the depth of Thompson's disdain for 'those barrels of enclosed Marxisms which stand, row upon row, in the corridors of Polytechnics and Universities' (Thompson, 1978, p. 383) suggested a distinct lack of political charity and intellectual generosity.

While Thompson continued to beat 'the bounds of "1956"' (ibid., p. 384), Williams's own political evolution followed a rather different route. As early as 1965 he had joined the Vietnam Solidarity Campaign, by far the more 'militant' of the main bodies organising in opposition to American involvement in Vietnam. That Williams's political sympathies, from 1968 on, lay with the second generation of New Left intellectuals became increasingly apparent. He shared much of the *New Left Review*'s interest in Western Marxism, as essays on Goldmann, Gramsci and Sebastiano Timpanero, published in the *Review* in 1971, 1973 and 1978 respectively, clearly attest (Williams, 1971b; Williams, 1973c; Williams, 1978a). Indeed, in the Introduction to *Marxism and Literature* he would recall that 'I felt the excitement of contact with ... new Marxist work ... As all this came in, during the sixties and early seventies ... an argument that had drifted into deadlock ... in the late thirties and forties, was being vigorously and significantly reopened' (Williams, 1977a, p. 4). Williams shared, too, the New New Left's deep and growing hostility to the Labour Party. Writing in the 'Retrospect and Prospect' to the third edition of *Communications*, he would conclude with some bitterness, of the experience of Labour governments, that 'most of the serious proposals were contemptuously pushed aside ... The most plausible formation for intermediate reform has thus ... not only defaulted on its own best purposes but ... has shown itself ... to be an active part of the very system which it has appeared to oppose' (Williams, 1976b, pp. 181-2). The contrast between Williams's *Marxism and Literature* and Thompson's *The Poverty of Theory*, published within a year of each other, is especially telling: in their relations with this younger generation of radical intellectuals, it was, paradoxically, Thompson, the self-proclaimed scourge of sectaries, whose habits both of style and of thought remained by far the more sectarian. But for all Williams's 'leftism', his is a movement in relation to an already established position, an evolution rather than a sudden 'coming out', and one that had been well under way long before 1977. It had been actively prefigured in *Modern Tragedy* and in *The Country and the City*, both of which were written in deliberate reaction against the predominant conservatism of Cambridge English studies (Williams, 1979b, pp. 243-4, 304) and in active solidarity with the 'third world' revolutionary movements. In *Modern Tragedy*, these are invoked in such a fashion as to call into question the ultimate validity even of the long revolution itself: 'Our interpretation of revolution as a slow and peaceful growth ... is at best a local experience ..., at worst a sustained false consciousness' (Williams, 1979b, p. 79). In *The Country and the City*, their successes provide the book with its concluding vindication: 'the "rural idiots" and the "barbarians and semi-barbarians" have been, for the last forty years, the main revolutionary force in the world' (Williams, 1973b, p. 304).

Turning to Gramsci: Hegemony, Culture and Ideology

In Williams's earlier, 'left culturalist' writings, the 'deep community' that is culture simultaneously transcends class and yet is irredeemably marked by it. For all the eloquence with which this position is argued, it remains quite fundamentally incoherent: the competing claims of commonality and difference, culture and class, Leavisism and Marxism, form a circle which stubbornly refuses to be squared. But in the later, 'cultural materialist', phase of his work, it finally became possible for Williams to explain, to his own satisfaction at least, how it could be that structures of feeling are common to different classes, and yet nonetheless represent the interests of some particular class. In this later phase, Williams's engagement with Western Marxism, and with various forms of Third Worldist 'ultra-leftism', parallels, but nonetheless neither reduplicates nor inspires, that of Anderson's New New Left. Initially, this engagement meant little more than a recognition that not all Marxisms were necessarily economically determinist, and a corollary discovery of theoretical preoccupations similar to his own in the work of individual Western Marxist writers: the obviously important instance here is Goldmann. Later, however, it came to entail a much more positive redefinition of Williams's own theoretical stance: here, the encounter with Gramsci becomes absolutely central. As Williams would insist in *Marxism and Literature*: 'Gramsci's ... work is one of the major turning-points in Marxist cultural theory' (Williams, 1977a, p. 108). Let us consider each in turn, both in their own right and by way of their influence over Williams.

Goldmann's 'sociology of literature' had been widely translated into English, Goldmann himself had visited Britain on more than one occasion, and his work had come to command a considerable respect on the British intellectual left. Very much under the influence of the early Lukács, Goldmann had sought to substitute a 'social totality' model for the orthodoxly Marxist base/superstructure model. Hence, for Goldmann: 'It is when he (*sic*) replaces the work in a historical evolution which he (*sic*) studies as a whole, and when he (*sic*) relates it to the social life of the time at which it was written - which he (*sic*) also looks upon as a whole - that the enquirer can bring out the work's objective meaning' (Goldmann, 1964, p. 8). In his earlier writings at least, Goldmann conceives of this relationship between literature and society, text and context, as essentially one of 'homology', and one typically 'mediated', moreover, through the 'world vision' of a social class or group. By the term 'world vision', Goldmann refers to 'the whole complex of ideas, aspirations and feelings which links together the members of a social group' (ibid., p. 17). Such world visions, he insists, can exist on two different planes: 'that of the *real* consciousness of the group, ... or that of their *coherent* exceptional expression in great works of philosophy or art' (Goldmann, 1969, p. 130). Goldmann's coupling of coherence with exceptionality is fundamental to his argument: the coherent 'expression' in art, of what is in quotidian life only ever incoherent, thereby represents the *'maximum of potential consciousness'* (Goldmann, 1969, p. 103) of the group or class to which the artist belongs. This notion of the world vision is employed by Goldmann in his early study of Kant, and with considerable erudition in his major work on Pascal and Racine, *The Hidden God*. The efficacy with which Goldmann had been able to elucidate the internal structures of the Jansenist 'tragic vision', at work in both Pascal's *Pensées* and Racine's drama, suggested the value of this concept of the world vision not only to Williams, but to many others on the British intellectual left.

Williams's own interest in Goldmann is acknowledged most clearly in the obituary he wrote for the *New Left Review*. His fundamental response had been a recognition of affinity: he and Goldmann were 'exploring many of the same areas with many of the same concepts' (Williams, 1980c, p. 20). So, Williams points to the similarities between his and Goldmann's conceptions of structure (ibid., pp. 22-3), between the notion of structure of feeling and that of the world vision. Insofar as there is a difference between them, however, Williams concedes very little to Goldmann: certainly, there are concepts, such as that of the 'collective subject', which we ought 'to test in practice' (ibid., p. 28); but the approach is nonetheless 'in some ways static', 'too large in its categories' (ibid., p. 26) to come very close to actual literature. For Williams, Goldmann's concept of the 'world vision' is too often 'a summary of doctrines' and, as such, 'often some distance from the real structures and processes of literature' (ibid., p. 24). In *Marxism and Literature* the response is much the same: Goldmann's work is 'very important' (Williams, 1977a, p. 106), his analysis of the collective subject 'most interesting' (ibid., p. 195); but explanation in terms of homology suffers from 'an extreme selectivity' (ibid., p. 106); and abstracted notions of coherence or integration obscure the reality of 'radical tension and disturbance, even actual and irresolvable contradiction' (ibid., p. 197). What Williams discovers in Goldmann (and in

Lukács) is something much more akin to likemindedness than to inspiration: his own theoretical position, independently arrived at, and very much in isolation from continental European Marxism, is not so much challenged as confirmed, both by their insights and by what he perceives to be their deficiencies. The response to Gramsci, however, is of an altogether different order.

A single, slim volume of Gramsci's political writings had been translated into English during the 1950s (Gramsci, 1957), a limited critical debate had followed during the 1960s (cf. Merrington, 1968), and an English translation of Fiori's biography of Gramsci had been published in 1970 (Fiori, 1970). But there had been nothing even remotely equivalent to the positive avalanche of Gramsci scholarship, and Gramsci polemic, witnessed over the next twenty years. The first English publication of selections from Gramsci's *Prison Notebooks* was a major intellectual event, then, and was certainly taken as such by Williams. As is now well known, Gramsci had substituted for the more orthodoxly Marxist base/superstructure model a civil society/political society model, where the latter term refers to the coercive elements within the wider social totality, the former to the non-coercive. Hence the famous formula: 'State = political society + civil society, in other words hegemony protected by the armour of coercion' (Gramsci, 1971, p. 263). The term hegemony here refers to the processes by which a system of values and beliefs supportive of the existing ruling class becomes permeated throughout the whole of society. Hegemony is thus a value consensus, and one very often embodied in common sense, but constructed, nonetheless, in the interests of the ruling class. Every state, Gramsci argues, 'is ethical in as much as one of its most important functions is to raise the great mass of the population to a particular cultural and moral level, ... which corresponds ... to the interests of the ruling class'. The schools, the courts, but also 'a multitude of other so-called private initiatives and activities', together form what Gramsci terms 'the apparatus of the political and cultural hegemony of the ruling classes' (Gramsci, 1971, p. 258). The functioning of this apparatus is essentially the work of intellectuals, whom Gramsci characterises as 'the dominant group's "deputies" exercising the subaltern functions of social hegemony and political government' (ibid., p. 12). Gramsci distinguishes between 'organic' intellectuals, that is, the type of intellectual which each major social class creates for itself so as to 'give it homogeneity and an awareness of its own function' (ibid., p. 5); and traditional intellectuals, that is, 'categories of intellectuals already in existence ... which seem to represent ... historical continuity' (ibid., p. 7). Hegemony is never in principle either uncontested or absolute, but is only ever an unstable equilibrium, ultimately open to contestation by alternative social forces. For Gramsci, the central political problem therefore becomes that of the creation of a layer of organic working-class intellectuals capable of leading their own class in this battle for counter-hegemony.

Williams was impressed both by Gramsci's work on intellectuals, which seemed to him an 'encouraging' and 'experimental' model for work in the sociology of culture (Williams, 1977a, p. 138), and by the wider implications of the theory of hegemony itself. The significance of the latter had registered initially in an essay written for the *New Left Review* in 1973, entitled 'Base and Superstructure in Marxist Cultural Theory' (Williams, 1980b, p. 37). But in *Marxism and Literature*, the argument is elaborated upon at much greater length. The first and last chapters respectively of the book's first part are devoted to two key concepts, and two keywords, deriving respectively from Leavisism and Marxism: 'Culture' and 'Ideology'. In a subsequent chapter, Williams argues for the theoretical superiority over each of these of the Gramscian notion of hegemony:

> 'Hegemony' goes beyond 'culture' ... in its insistence on relating the 'whole social process' to specific distributions of power and influence ... Gramsci therefore introduces the necessary recognition of dominance and subordination in what has still, however, to be recognized as a whole process. It is in just this recognition of the *wholeness* of the process that the concept of 'hegemony' goes beyond 'ideology'. What is decisive is not only the conscious system of ideas and beliefs, but the whole lived social process as practically organized by specific and dominant meanings and values. (Williams, 1977a, pp. 108-9)

For Williams, Gramsci's central achievement consists in the articulation of a culturalist sense of the wholeness of culture with a more typically Marxist sense of the interestedness of ideology. Thus hegemony is 'in the strongest sense a "culture", but a culture which has to be seen as the lived dominance and subordination of particular classes' (ibid., p. 110). Understood thus, culture is no longer either 'superstructural', as the term had normally been defined in the Maxist tradition, or 'ideological', in the more generally Marxist or more specifically Althusserian definition. On the contrary, 'cultural tradition and practice ... are among the basic processes', which need to be seen 'as they are ... without the characteristic straining to fit them ... to other and determining ... economic and political relationships' (ibid., p. 111). Whether all of this remains exactly faithful to Gramsci's own intent seems open to some doubt. Gramsci himself repeatedly deploys the distinction between 'structure' and 'superstructure', and, while recognising the 'complex, contradictory or discordant' qualities of the latter, nonetheless insists that the *'ensemble* of the superstructures is the reflection of the *ensemble* of the social relations of production' (Gramsci, 1971, p. 366). But as Stuart Hall has somewhat cynically observed of the *Prison Notebooks*: 'What was undoubtedly a limitation from a textual point of view - namely, the fragmentary nature of his writings - was ... a positive advantage' (1991, p. 8) for subsequent Gramscian theory. Whatever the original authorial intention (and this is by no means self-evident), Williams's appropriation of Gramsci finally delivered that resolution of culturalist and Marxist thematics hitherto denied him.

Traditions, Institutions and Formations

The dominant or hegemonic culture, Williams reminds us, 'is always an active process', an organisation of often quite disparate meanings, 'which it specifically incorporates in a significant culture'. Rehearsing an argument first broached in *Culture and Society*, he points once again to the decisive importance of selective tradition in the effective operation of processes of incorporation:

> tradition is ... always more than an inert historicized segment; indeed it is the most powerful practical means of incorporation. What we have to see is ... a *selective tradition*: an intentionally selective version of a shaping past and a pre-shaped present, which is then powerfully operative in the process of social and cultural definition and identification. (Williams, 1977a, p. 115)

Once again, he stresses the full extent to which such tradition is a product of contemporary culture: 'It is a version of the past', he writes, 'which is intended to connect with and ratify the present. What it offers ... is a sense of *predisposed continuity*' (ibid., p. 116). In *Marxism and Literature*, however, tradition is seen, not only as selective, but also as necessarily dependent upon 'identifiable institutions', on the one hand, and what Williams terms 'formations', on the other, that is: 'those effective movements and tendencies, in intellectual and artistic life, which have significant and sometimes decisive influence on the active development of a culture' (ibid., p. 117). The issue is explored at greater length in *Culture*, where Williams advances a preliminary historical typology of institutions and formations. Here he distinguishes four main types of 'authorial' institution, each of which provides a distinctive 'solution' to the sociological problem of how to maintain the artist: respectively, the 'instituted artist', 'patronage', the 'market' and, finally, what he terms 'post-market institutions' (Williams, 1981, pp. 36-56).

By the first of these, Williams refers to a communally-sponsored, particular social role, typically that of the prophet-seer, often found in tribal societies, whether pre-literate or literate: his own example is that of the Celtic bards. Here the role of the 'artist' is 'instituted' as such, as an official part of the central organisation of the society. Williams identifies five different kinds of patronage, though only three seem especially important, those he terms, respectively, 'retainer and commission', 'protection and support' and 'sponsorship' (Williams, 1981, pp. 39-43). In the first, the court or the aristocratic household officially recognises and retains the individual cultural producer in a relatively close and permanent relationship with the patron. In the second, an enduring but less intimate relationship is established between patron and artist: his example is that of the Elizabethan theatre companies. In the third, artworks are commodities for general sale, but a particular sponsor nonetheless provides initial financial support so as to make their production possible. Market institutions proper are those where artworks are produced as commodities for sale on the market. Discussing writing in particular, Williams identifies four main types of market production: 'artisanal', where the individual writer sells the artwork directly in the market; 'post-artisanal', where the writer sells to a bookseller; 'market professional', where increasingly professionalised writers sell literary properties to increasingly capitalised publishers; and 'corporate professional', where the writer works as a salaried employee of large media corporations, for example in television, radio, journalism and advertising (ibid., pp. 44-54). The central matter at issue here is not so much the employment contract itself as the point of origin of the production. As Williams notes, the corporate structure is increasingly characterised by 'a highly organized and fully capitalized market in which the direct commissioning of planned saleable products has become a normal mode' (ibid., p. 52). In retrospect, Williams's tentative understanding of government arts funding, both direct and indirect, as a fourth set of distinctively 'post-market' institutions, seems sadly optimistic. For it must have become apparent, under Thatcherism if not before, that state sponsorship is normally the reward for patriotism, loyalty and respectability and, as such, tends to reproduce and complement the socio-cultural effects of the market. It seems unhelpful, then, to attempt to analyse its operation in this way. Which is not to suggest, however, that post-market relations are unimaginable nor that they can never come into existence. On the contrary, the attempt to define, understand and, most importantly, actively produce precisely such post-market institutions will almost certainly be of quite fundamental importance to any attempt to create a truly common culture.

Turning to formations, Williams is insistent that these 'have a variable and often oblique relation to formal institutions' (Williams, 1977a, p. 117). The stress falls here on the necessary non-correspondence between selective tradition, dominant institutions and artistic formations. Within any apparent hegemony, he writes: 'there are not only alternative and oppositional formations ... but, within what can be recognized as the dominant, effectively varying formations which resist any simple reduction to some generalized hegemonic function' (ibid., p. 119). In *Culture*, Williams identifies three main kinds of pre-capitalist formation: 'bardic orders', that is, organisations of instituted artists; 'craft guilds', which were common in late medieval cultural production; and 'academies', which eventually separated out from the guilds as 'art' began to distinguish itself from 'craft' (Williams, 1981, pp. 58-61). Successor institutions to both guilds and academies persist into modernity, respectively, the craft union and the academy as educational institution. But Williams also identifies two further kinds of formation distinct to the capitalist mode of cultural production, the 'professional society' and the artistic 'movement'. Professional societies are organisations of market professionals, sometimes augmented by corporate professionals, which aim to further their collective economic interests in the cultural market place. Movements, by contrast, are organised around essentially non-economic objectives; this is 'a quite different type of cultural formation, in which artists come together in pursuit of some specific artistic aim' (ibid., p. 62). As Williams notes, movements of this type - circles, schools, 'isms' of various kinds - have been of central importance to the recent history of the arts. He develops a relatively sophisticated theoretical framework for their analysis and applies it to three concrete instances, the circle around William Godwin, the Pre-Raphaelite Brotherhood and the Bloomsbury Group. The detail need not detain us here, but we should note his conclusion that:

> No sociological analysis of formations can replace either general history or more specific individual studies. Yet it is still an indispensable kind of analysis, since there is normally a very wide gap between, on the one hand, general history and the associated general history of particular arts, and, on the other hand, individual studies. (ibid., p. 86).

The Alternatives to Hegemony

In one respect, at least, Williams's reading of Gramsci is unusually faithful to its object: for both the Italian revolutionary and his Welsh interpreter, it was the counter-hegemonic moment that was especially significant. Hence, Williams's attempt to distinguish between those practices, experiences, meanings and values that are part of the effectively dominant culture and those that are not. For all his attention to hegemonic traditions, institutions and formations, Williams remains insistent that, at the level of 'historical' as distinct from 'epochal' analysis, that is, at the level of movement rather than system, there is much in any lived culture that cannot be reduced to the dominant (Williams, 1977a, p. 121). Here, Williams dissented sharply from the implied consensualism of both Althusserian theories of ideology and the then current sociological versions of 'the dominant ideology thesis': *'no mode and therefore no dominant social order'*, he writes *'and therefore no dominant culture ever in reality includes or exhausts all human*

practice, human energy, and human intention' (ibid., p. 125). Williams's
initial theorisation of the alternatives to hegemony had been broached
in the 1973 *New Left Review* essay, where he had sought to distinguish
between 'alternative' and 'oppositional', 'residual' and 'emergent' cultural elements (Williams, 1980b, pp. 39-42). The terminology recurs
both in *Marxism and Literature* and in *Culture*. By 'residual' Williams
means, not so much the simply 'archaic', defined as 'that which is
wholly recognized as an element of the past', but rather those cultural
elements, external to the dominant culture, which nonetheless continue to be lived and practised as an active part of the present 'on the
basis of the residue ... of some previous social and cultural institution
or formation' (Williams, 1977a, p. 122). Unlike the archaic, the residual
may be oppositional or, at least, alternative in character. Thus Williams
distinguishes organised religion and the idea of rural community,
which are each predominantly residual, from monarchy, which is
merely archaic.

But it is the properly 'emergent', that is, those genuinely new meanings and values, practices, relationships and kinds of relationship,
which are substantially alternative or oppositional to the dominant
culture (Williams, 1977a, p. 123), that most interest Williams. For
Williams, as for Gramsci, the primary source of an emergent culture is
likely to be the formation of a new social class. But there is also a second source of emergence: 'alternative perceptions of others, in immediate relationships; new perceptions and practices of the material
world' (ibid., p. 126). For Williams, as for Gramsci, the exemplary contemporary instance of a new social class is that of the development of
the modern working class. At the second level, however, which
Williams terms 'the excluded social [human] area', a level which often
remains peculiarly pertinent to the analysis of artistic and intellectual
movements, the situation is much less clear. As Williams writes in
Culture: 'No analysis is more difficult than that which, faced by new
forms, has to try to determine whether these are new forms of the
dominant or are genuinely emergent' (Williams, 1981, p. 205). This tes-
timony to complexity is no mere rhetorical gesture on Williams's part.
Quite the contrary: his work both in drama studies and in media studies, that is, in each of the two areas of substantive cultural analysis
which had come most to concern him, had made Williams all too
aware of the difficulties entailed in distinguishing the properly emergent from the merely novel.

Theoretically at least, Williams is able, in *Marxism and Literature*, to
offer an unusually interesting formulation of the problem itself, if not
necessarily of how it might be resolved. Here, he redeploys and significantly redefines his earlier notion of 'structure of feeling'. An emergent culture, he argues, unlike either the dominant or the residual,
requires not only distinct kinds of immediate cultural practice, but also
and crucially 'new forms or adaptations of forms'. Such innovation at
the level of form, he continues, 'is in effect a *pre-emergence*, active

and pressing but not yet fully articulated, rather than the evident emergence which could be more confidently named' (Williams, 1977a, p. 126). And it is precisely at this level of the pre-emergent that the concept of structure of feeling is brought back into play. From *The Long Revolution* onwards, as we have seen, Williams had used the term to denote both the immediately experiential and the generationally specific aspects of artistic process. In *Marxism and Literature*, both emphases are retained, but are conjoined to a quite new stress on cultural pre-emergence. In this reformulation, the experiential remains at odds with official, 'formal' culture precisely insofar as it is indeed genuinely new: 'practical consciousness is what is actually being lived, ... not only what it is thought is being lived' (ibid., pp. 130-1). And similarly, the generationally specific remains different from the experience of previous generations precisely insofar as it too is indeed genuinely new. Structures of feeling, writes Williams - again turning to the solution/precipitate metaphor, but here significantly reworking it:

> can be defined as social experiences *in solution*, as distinct from other social semantic formations which have been *precipitated* and are more evidently and more immediately available ... The effective formations of most actual art relate to already manifest social formations, dominant or residual, and it is primarily to emergent formations ... that the structure of feeling, *as solution*, relates. (ibid., pp. 133-4)

Structures of feeling are no longer, then, in any sense 'the culture' of a period: they are, rather, precisely those particular elements within the more general culture which most actively anticipate subsequent mutations in the general culture itself; in short, they are quite specifically counter-hegemonic.

At one level, this distinctly Gramscian reformulation of the notion of 'structure of feeling' merely recaptures something of what Williams had intended all along: the problem of the knowable community in the English novel, and the naturalistic revolution in the modern theatre, each delimit a distinct structure of feeling only insofar as they are indeed genuinely innovatory. But in each case, these respectively pre-emergent qualities are never fully theorised. It is as if the concept itself is still pre-emergent and requires the encounter with Gramsci for precipitation. Moreover, the substantive question of the precise interplay between the emergent or pre-emergent, on the one hand, and novelty within the dominant, on the other, in both mass media and modernist avant-garde forms, was to become especially pressing for Williams in his later works. The issue is broached very clearly in *Culture*. But it becomes absolutely central to the two major works of the 1980s, the 1983 reworking of the long revolution analysis, *Towards 2000* (Williams, 1983), and the posthumously published and sadly unfinished *The Politics of Modernism* (Williams, 1989a). Both attempt to reformulate the earlier aspiration to community and to culture as a whole way of life, by way of a critique of 'postmodern' appropriations of modernism and the mass media, a critique which rejects, in principle, in theory, and in practice, the antithesis between mass civilisation and minority culture, without thereby becoming trapped in the cultural logic of commodification.

In *Towards 2000*, Williams shows how postmodernism effectively collapses the distinction between minority and mass arts: 'There are very few absolute contrasts left between a "minority culture" and "mass communications"', he writes, 'many minority institutions and forms have adapted, ... with enthusiasm, to modern corporate capitalist culture' (Williams, 1983, pp. 134, 140). The older modernisms, which had once threatened to destabilise the certainties of bourgeois life, have been transformed, he argues, into a new '"post-modernist" establishment', which 'takes human inadequacy ... as self-evident' (ibid., p. 141). The deep structures of this now dominant post-modernism are present, moreover, in effectively popular cultural forms, such as film, television and fiction: 'these debased forms of an anguished sense of human debasement ... have become a widely distributed "popular" culture that is meant to confirm both its own and the world's destructive inevitablities' (ibid., pp. 141-2). If the dominant culture had indeed so mutated, Williams was still able to detect resistance to it from within popular life, in the 'very general area of jokes and gossip, of everyday singing and dancing, of occasional dressing-up and extravagant outbursts of colour' (ibid., p. 146). Moreover, a second site of cultural resistance continues to be provided by the radical intelligentsia. Hence, the identification of a more properly innovatory, pre-emergent 'structure of feeling' - though the term itself is not actually used - in the politics of the contemporary new social movements (ibid., p. 250). But these pre-emergences are quite different from the 'pseudo-radicalism' of 'the negative structures of post-modernist art' (ibid., p. 145), which are themselves neither pre-emergent nor emergent, but rather a moment of novelty, indeed perhaps the institutionalisation of novelty itself, within the already dominant culture.

In *The Politics of Modernism* Williams would state the case much more forcefully:

> Are we now informed enough, hard enough, to look for our own double edges? Should we not look, implacably, at those many formations, their works and their theories, which are based practically only on their negations and forms of enclosure, against an undifferentiated culture and society beyond them? ... Are we not obliged to distinguish these reductive and contemptuous forms, these assayers of ugliness and violence, which in the very sweep of their negations can pass as radical art, from ... very different forms of relating or common exploration, articulation, discovery of identities, in ... con-

sciously extending and affiliating groups ...? Can theory not help in its refusal of the rationalizations which sustain the negations, and in its determination to probe actual forms, actual structures of feeling, actually lived and desired relationships, beyond the easy labels of radicalism which even the dominant institutions now incorporate or impose? (Williams, 1989a, pp. 175-6)

To affirm as much, it is clear, would be to break decisively with the predominantly postmodernist cultural forms, and their variously post-structuralist, post-Marxist, and post-feminist theoretical legitimations, which still construct much of the erstwhile radical intelligentsia in the image of Williams's 'New Conformists'.

Theorising Culture: Deconstructing Base and Superstructure

Williams's 'Base and Superstructure' essay had signalled not only a new reading of Gramsci, but also an attempt to recast the base/superstructure formula itself. He had argued for a 'revaluation' of each of the three terms in the formula, 'base', 'superstructure' and 'determination', so that: the first would now denote the primary production of society itself and of people themselves, rather than the merely 'economic'; the second, the whole range of cultural practices, rather than a merely secondary and dependent 'content'; and the third, the 'setting of limits and exertion of pressures', rather than predetermined causation (Williams, 1980b, pp. 34-5). The latter proposition is very much the same as that advanced the following year in *Television: Technology and Cultural Form*. In *Marxism and Literature*, however, the argument is taken further, but in a direction that leads, perhaps paradoxically, very much away from, rather than toward, the more classically Marxist formulations of the problem. Once again, determination is taken to mean the setting of limits and exertion of pressures (Williams, 1977a, p. 87); once again, production is understood as applying to a much wider realm than the merely economic, so that the 'productive forces' are 'all and any activities in the social process as a whole' (ibid., p. 93). But the notions of 'base' and 'superstructure', which had acquired an entirely temporary and very much conditional legitimacy in the 1973 essay, are here consigned to a theoretical oblivion much akin to that in *Culture and Society*: 'contrary to the development in Marxism, it is not "the base" and "the superstructure" that need to be studied, but specific and indissoluble real processes' (ibid., p. 82). Ironically, Williams is very much concerned to invoke Marx himself against subsequent Marxism on precisely this point. 'Marx's original criticism', he insists, 'had been mainly directed against the *separation* of "areas" of thought and activity ... The common abstraction of "the base" and "the superstructure" is thus a radical persistence of the modes of thought which he attacked' (ibid., p. 78). It is difficult to avoid the suspicion that here, at least, Williams protests too much. And yet there is a strong sense in which his position is indeed 'Marxist'. For this is no simple return to the argument of *Culture and Society*, but rather the development of an entirely new argument, by which Williams seeks to convict Marxism of, in the telling phrase of his 1979 *New Left Review* interlocutors, 'not so much ... an excess but ... a deficit of materialism' (Williams, 1979a, p. 350). What the base/superstructure formula fails to acknowledge, he charges, is precisely the materiality of the superstructures themselves. Hence, the characteristically ruthless judgement that: 'The concept of "superstructure" was ... not a reduction but an evasion' (Williams, 1977a, p. 93).

Superstructure, Williams concludes, and other, related usages within Marxist discourse, such as 'ideology' or 'the realm of art and ideas', each misrepresent what are in fact real and material activities as somehow unreal and immaterial. None of these activities can then be grasped as they are: 'as real practices, elements of a whole material social process; not a realm or a world or a superstructure, but many and variable productive practices, with specific conditions and intentions'. The way forward, he insists, is 'to look at our actual productive activities without assuming in advance that only some of them are material' (Williams, 1977a, p. 94). If Williams retains a concept of determination, then, as he certainly does, it is nonetheless a concept of multiple determination, more akin to the culturalist sense of a whole way of life than to the Marxist notion of a determining base and a determined superstructure. But that whole way of life is now both thoroughly material and thoroughly marked by the impress of power and domination, in all its particular aspects. This stress on the materiality of cultural production had been a recurrent theme in Williams's work from *The Long Revolution* onwards, most especially so in his writing on drama and on the mass media. But in *Marxism and Literature*, it attains a much more explicit formulation than any hitherto. In *Culture*, and in a 1978 essay published by the Yugoslav journal, *Prilozi: Drustvenost Komunikacije*, the process would be taken even further, as Williams would seek to analyse means of communication as in themselves means of production (Williams, 1980d, pp. 50-63; Williams, 1981, pp. 87-118). In *Marxism and Literature*, however, the argument leads immediately towards what is in effect a 'deconstruction' of probably the most sacred of all Leavisite categories, that of 'Literature' itself. The specialising concept of 'Literature', Williams recognises, is an important instance of 'the aesthetic' (Williams, 1977a, p. 150), and the aesthetic itself a specifically bourgeois evasion, by which art and thinking about art 'separate themselves ... from the social processes within which they are ... contained' (ibid., p. 154).

To such evasions, and to their often transparently elitist ideological functions, Williams seeks to counterpose a stress on 'the multiplicity of writing' (ibid., p. 146), and on 'the variability, the relativity, and the multiplicity of actual cultural practice' (ibid., p. 153). In the third and final part of *Marxism and Literature*, and again in *Culture*, this leads to an extended theorisation of the social processes of art and literature themselves. Here the account is premised upon what is clearly the distinguishing proposition of cultural materialism, that of the materiality of cultural production. Drawing extensively on the work of the Russian Marxist semiotician, V.N. Vološinov (Vološinov, 1973), Williams argues for a theory of 'language as activity, as practical consciousness' (Williams, 1977a, p. 36). Whether spoken or written, language is, for Williams, not a 'medium', in the sense of an intermediate communicative substance, mediating between thought and expression, but rather a constitutive element of material social practice (ibid., pp. 158-9, 165). More particularly: 'Language is in fact a special kind of material practice: that of human socialilty' (ibid., p. 165). Linguistic signification is then, for Williams as much as for any structuralist, a 'real and demonstrable activity' (ibid., p. 167), with its own distinctively material, and in a sense 'formal', properties. But signs are not thereby 'arbitrary', as structuralism and post-structuralism tend to claim. Quite the contrary, they function within 'lived and living relationships', and it is these relationships, sociologically determinate rather than arbitrary in character, which in Williams's view *make all formal meanings significant and substantial*' (ibid., p. 168). Moreover, he continues, the structuralist concept of the sign significantly occludes the distinction between speech and writing: 'Spoken words are a process of human activity using only immediate, constitutive, physical resources. Written words ... are a form of material production, adapting non-human resources to a human end' (ibid., p. 169).

Writing, Williams argues, is better understood as 'notation' than as 'sign', since, unlike speech, it is at once both materially objectified and reproducible, and this reproducibility is itself necessarily dependent on the socio-cultural system within which the notation is operative (ibid., pp. 146, 170). Such dependence is in fact much more characteristic of writing than of many other cultural techniques, such as dance, song and speech. As Williams observes in *Culture*: 'Writing ... is wholly dependent on forms of specialized training, not only ... for producers but also, and crucially, for receivers' (1981, p. 93). Derrida famously charged the western philosophical tradition with adherence to a falsely 'logocentric' notion of language as 'voice', and of writing as the expression of speech, insisting to the contrary that the true nature of language is more clearly revealed in writing than in speech (Derrida, 1973, p. 92; Derrida, 1982, p. 316). Derrida's critique of logocentrism runs interestingly parallel to Williams's own critique of 'expressivism' (Williams, 1977a, p. 165). But where Derrida, the prophet of *différance*, chooses to privilege writing over speech, it is Williams, ironically enough, who proves able to register this distinction, between speech and writing, word and notation, as quite simply difference. For

Williams, moreover, though writing is not speech, and notation not expression, expression is nonetheless not thereby excluded from a 'fully social' theory of literature: 'the notations are relationships, expressed, offered, tested, and amended in a whole social process, in which device, expression, and the substance of expression are in the end inseparable' (ibid., p. 172).

Theorising Culture: Towards a Social Theory of Literature

Central to Williams's understanding of what any fully social theory of literature might be is the concept of form. At the most basic of levels, form means no more than the rules and conventions specific to particular 'kinds' of art. If these conventions are always necessarily constraining, then they are simultaneously also enabling: they typically entail a complex combination of prohibitions on what may not be done, recommendations as to what can be done and prescriptions as to what should be done. In this latter respect, they can be considered forces of production, that is, cultural technologies for the production of art. In conventionally literary-critical terms, notions of 'form' or 'genre' are used precisely to classify literature and literary history 'not by time or place ... but by specifically literary types of organisation or structure' (Wellek and Warren, 1976, p. 226). They are thus deemed to possess an essential immutability, which renders their character fundamentally ahistorical. Confronted by the possibility of 'a sociology of form', Wellek and Warren remained unconvinced that 'the social determination of genres ... could be shown conclusively' (ibid., p. 109). But it is difficult, nonetheless, to imagine how form could be constructed other than by people in interaction with other people, that is socially. Indeed, there is a plausible case to be made that it is at this level of form that the social enters most profoundly into the constitutive nature of art itself. Williams's own sense of the social conventionality of form, and of the interdependence of form, technique and technology, had emerged as much from his work in drama studies and television studies as anywhere. In *Marxism and Literature*, Williams argues for the theoretical superiority of notions of form over mere 'genre-classification' (Williams, 1977a, pp. 185-6). For Williams, the problem of form is: first, that of the historically variable relations between social modes and individual projects, and, second, that of the specifiable material practices within which those relations are enacted (ibid., p. 187). Form, then, is not so much a matter of classification as of social relationship: 'it is ... a social process which ... becomes a social product. Forms are ... the common property ... of writers and audiences or readers, before any communicative composition can occur' (ibid., pp. 187-8). Here, Williams's argument is primarily theoretical in character. In *Culture*, however, such theorisation is supplemented by a fairly lengthy and nuanced socio-formal analysis of the history of the drama (Williams, 1981, pp. 148-80); and by an attempt to distinguish three different 'levels of form', denoted, respectively, as 'modes', 'genres' and 'types'.

Williams reserves the term 'mode' for those very general conventions, at the deepest level of form, for example, the dramatic, the lyrical and the narrative, which, though socially and historically created, nonetheless persist through very different social orders. The level of relations involved, Williams writes, 'can be more accurately referred to an anthropological or societal dimension than to the sociological in the ordinary sense ... they are very general, and their reproduction is at least relatively autonomous' (1981, p. 194). He rehabilitates the term 'genre' to refer to that level of form which, though certainly enduring, has some definite dependence on epochal change between social orders, for example the genres of tragedy or comedy within the dramatic mode, or of epic and romance within the narrative. Such genres are 'significantly more subject to variation between different epochs and different social orders', he observes, noting that neither the epic nor romance survived into the modern, bourgeois epoch 'at least without radical redefinition' (ibid., p. 195). Finally, he defines as 'types' those effective general forms which, in their characteristic distributions of interest, are typical only of a particular social order, as, for example, in the case of bourgeois drama or the realist novel (ibid., p. 196). At each of these levels, form is, of course, by definition reproducible; and for Williams, as for Althusser, culture is thereby necessarily reproductive (ibid., p. 184). Williams distinguishes two main kinds of meaning attaching to the term 'reproduction': on the one hand, uniform copying by processes of mechanical reproduction; on the other, genetic reproduction, 'where typically forms - species - are prolonged, but in intrinsically variable individual examples' (ibid., p. 185). Clearly, the reproduction of literary and cultural form is analogous to reproduction in this second sense of the term. But for Williams, as not for Althusser, culture is also necessarily productive as well as reproductive: 'social orders and cultural orders must be seen as being actively made ... unless there is ... production and innovation, most orders are at risk' (ibid., p. 201). And at their furthest reach, as we have seen, such innovations in form will signify what is for Williams perhaps the most important of all cultural possibilities, that of an emergent structure of feeling. For Williams, a proper attention to the typical, the modal, the characteristic, should thus also enable us to recognise 'innovation in process ... one of the very few elements of cultural production to which the stock adjective, "creative", is wholly appropriate.' (ibid., p. 200).

For Williams, form is essentially an aspect of textuality, which inheres within a designated group of texts as their common textual property. By contrast, much recent post-structuralist theory has evinced a thoroughgoing scepticism as to the possibility of discovering any definitive meaning inherent within a text, preferring rather to focus on the indefinite plurality of possible readings to which a text might give rise. And what applies to a text in particular applies to the form in general. This line of argument can be prosecuted by way of either Derridean or Foucauldian argument. If the former, as with Anne Freadman for example, then the problem becomes that of how to deconstruct the intricate nature of the text 'in the systems deployed to classify it' (Freadman, 1988, p. 95); if the latter, as with John Frow, then that of how to understand such systems as institutional arrangements through which networks of intertextuality are socially 'constructed ... maintained or shifted' (Frow, 1986, p. 187). On either view a sociology of form, such as Williams envisaged, becomes simply inoperable. As Tony Bennett - yet another Foucauldian - puts it, 'the concept of genre is more usefully interpreted when used as a means for analysing historically and culturally variable systems for the regulation of reading and writing practices than as a kind of writing amenable to socio-genetic explanation' (Bennett, 1990, p. 81). Like Williams, Bennett and Frow freely acknowledge the necessarily social nature of literary relations. Like Williams, they each set out to sidestep such ontological dualisms as those between 'real' history and 'less real' literature, base and superstructure, 'real' content and 'less real' form. This may be achieved in one of two ways, however, either by historicising literature, as does Williams, or by narrativising history, as do Bennett and Frow.

Frow and Bennett are much more interested in the socio-discursive institutionalisation of 'literary history', as a contemporary academic discipline, than in literary 'history', in the sense of 'the past' as real object. Thus, Frow: 'The gestural appeal to the "materiality" of history, and its definition as "the real" ... are indicative of the theological function the concept plays ... The absolute existence of the referent outside any semiotic framework is the tautological guarantee of a truth which transcends ideology' (1986, pp. 27-8). And Bennett: 'history ... is most appropriately regarded as a specific discursive regime, governed by distinctive procedures, through which the maintenance/transformation of the past as a set of currently existing realities is regulated' (1990, p. 50). When followed through to their logical conclusions, such conceptions point toward an epistemological relativism such as could effectively free literary-historical research from almost any (extra-discursive) empirical controls. The fundamental problem here is a radical over-emphasis on reading as against writing, consumption as against production, the present as against the past, in short, almost the obverse of the vices characteristic to Leavisism. No doubt, the past can only ever be understood in the present. No doubt, texts and forms (or genres) repeatedly acquire new meanings, which often function, in turn, so as to systematically organise and reorganise present understandings both of the present and of the past, both of those texts and forms and of others. But this need not imply that the historical past is in principle either unknowable or unrecoverable. And, insofar as the past is recoverable, there is nothing to preclude an at least proximate understanding of the generic conventions operative at the time when a text was written or composed, as also those governing later moments in the subsequent histories of its reception. Nor is there any good reason to suppose that such conventions are never transmitted through time and space. Which means that certain forms might well recur, in some at least of their significant aspects, in geo-historical contexts quite different from those of their origin. As Williams knew well, form is not simply a matter of retrospective academic classification, as post-structuralism suggests, but also a prospectively productive force within the mode of cultural production.

What for Leavis had been a 'Literature', a canon of exemplary creative works, expressive of a national tradition, and what for Marxism had been an ideological superstructure of the economic system, becomes in Williams's cultural materialism a distinctive subset of socially specific, materially determinate, forms and practices. It is only a subset because the category, 'Literature', denotes for Williams only a particular, socially valorised selection from the whole body of socially available writing, and writing in turn only one amongst many forms of cultural practice. Bereft of canon and national tradition alike, the obvious question arises as to what will become of authorship, in Leavisism the ultimate guarantee, in principle at least, of the authoritative meaning of the literary work. In its own assault on literary humanism, structuralism and post-structuralism had prosecuted a vigorous campaign against the notion of authorship. Arguing that literary texts should be understood in terms of intertextuality rather than supposed authorial intentions, Barthes had polemically announced 'the death of the Author' (Barthes, 1977, p. 148). Less polemically, but equally determinedly, Foucault had elaborated upon this notion so as to explain authorship as a function of its various institutional uses (Foucault, 1977a, pp. 113-38). Such 'decentring' of the author is very obviously anticipated in Williams's own chapter on 'The Social History of English Writers', in *The Long Revolution* (Williams, 1965, pp. 254-70). In *Marxism and Literature* Williams readily concedes the problematic status of the figure of the author (Williams, 1977a, p. 192). But for Williams authorship cannot be reduced to an effect either of textuality or of the institutionalised processing of texts. Rather, the central question remains, much as argued by Goldmann, that of the dynamic interrelationship between social formation, individual development and cultural creation: 'Taken together', he concludes, 'these ... allow a fully constitutive definition of authorship' (ibid., p. 197). For Williams, then, the author as writer, though not as authoritative source or origin, remains, if not central, then at least not yet radically decentred. It is too easy to dismiss this as residual humanism: what matters here is Williams's refusal to reduce the moment of literary production to that of consumption.

Where Barthes inaugurated the French section of what would later become, in Eagleton's rather nice joke, the 'Readers' Liberation Movement' (Eagleton, 1986, p. 181), Williams continued to hold firmly to the irreducibility of authorship and readership, either to each other or to an amorphous 'textuality', and to the necessarily material sociality of each, both in themselves and in relation to each other. 'In this at once social and historical perspective,' he writes, 'the abstract figure of "the author" is ... returned to these varying *and in principle variable* situations, relationships, and responses' (Williams, 1977a, p. 198).

Beyond Marxism, Beyond Literature

In the 'Base and Superstructure' essay, Williams had worried that the Lukácsian concept of totality might too easily be emptied of any Marxist content, that is, of any notion of determination (Williams, 1980b, p. 36), thereby becoming almost trivially circular in effect. The obvious question arises as to whether or not his own cultural materialism might provide occasion for similar concern. Such concerns very obviously inspire Eagleton's view, to which we referred in Chapter 1, that Williams's position is essentially pre-Marxist. Writing in defence of the base/superstructure model, Eagleton insists that the classically Marxist version of that model is not, as Williams supposed, an ontological proposition about the materiality or immateriality of superstructures, but rather a historical proposition as to the way in which some material activities, those denoted as 'the base', are more fundamentally determining within the social process than those other, equally material but nonetheless less causally effective, activities, denoted as 'the superstructure' (Eagleton, 1989b, pp. 168-9). Insofar as Williams's cultural materialism rejects the base/superstructure model, then, Eagleton argues, it 'does indeed hold to a "circular" theory of the social formation, one in this respect little changed from his earlier work ... Essentially Marxist concepts ... were transplanted into the cultural realm to "materialize" cultural processes, ... so *intensifying* Williams's pre-Marxian "circularity"' (Eagleton, 1989b, pp. 171-2). There is a certain disingenuousness, nonetheless, to Eagleton's defence of 'classical Marxism': as he himself concedes, the 'vulgar Marxism' of Marx's own *The German Ideology* had in fact dematerialised the superstructure; so, too, did the kind of Communist Marxism against which Williams had been obliged to define his own argument. Insofar as cultural materialism does perhaps re-invent the wheel, as Eagleton charges (ibid., p. 168), then this suggests only the much greater propensity to collective amnesia amongst cultural theorists than amongst wheelwrights. But Eagleton is right, nonetheless, to point to the circularity, indeed the deliberate circularity, of Williams's later position. In the 1973 essay itself, Williams had attempted to circumvent any such fate through the invocation of class intentionality, so that social structure comes to be understood as ordered by 'the rule of a particular class' (Williams, 1980b, p. 36). By *Marxism and Literature*, however, even this latter, residual notion of the 'base' had finally been abandoned.

When the editors of the *New Left Review* raised with Williams exactly this question of circularity, he was quick to concede 'warm agreement' to the historical priority of some determinations over others; but quick also to reformulate the matter at issue in terms of 'the specificity of capitalism' (Williams, 1979a, p. 140). In *Marxism and Literature*, he had pointed to Marx's own distinction between 'production in general', that is, the human historical process by which we produce ourselves and our societies; and 'capitalist production', that is, commodity production on the basis of wage labour and capital (Williams, 1977a, pp. 90-1). It is the social reality of capitalism itself, Williams insists, which progressively reduces production in general to commodity production in particular; the base/superstructure formula in Marxism merely reproduces and replicates that reduction at the level of theory (ibid., p. 92). He repeats this argument in the *New Left Review* interview:

> in the 20th century the exponents of capitalism have been the most insistent theorists of the causal primacy of economic production. If you want to be told that our whole existence is governed by the economy, go to the city pages of the bourgeois press - that is really how they see life. (Williams, 1979a, p. 141)

Elsewhere, he adds a distinctly 'postmodern' inflection to this sense of the specificities of capitalism. For if capitalism begins by extruding cultural production, as also other forms of non-commodity production, from the economic 'base', it eventually proceeds, in the late twentieth century, to an effective reincorporation of much of our culture back into that 'base', but on terms very much dictated by the economy. This is, of course, the commodity culture of postmodernism. And it is a culture which, in Williams's view, remains radically unamenable to analysis in terms of any base/superstructure metaphor. For Williams, cultural materialism is itself at one level a specific theoretical response to the cultural specificities of postmodern, late capitalism: 'cultural theory was not reworked as a critique within a theoretical tradition', he writes, 'but as a response to radical changes in the social relations of cultural process'. At a time when broadcasting and publishing, advertising and the press had already been transformed into major industries, it had simply become impossible, he continues, 'to see cultural questions as practically separable from political and economic questions, or to posit either second-order or dependent relations between them' (Williams, 1980a, p. 245).

In the *Politics and Letters* interviews, Williams credits Lukács as the original proponent of this view that the priority of the economic is not so much a general feature of human social life as a distinguishing peculiarity of capitalism. But there are more obvious sources much closer to hand, surely, in that very same culturalist tradition which inspired *Culture and Society*. When Williams points - rightly in my view - to the complicity between Marxist theoretical reductionism on the one hand, and the real reductions of bourgeois reality on the other, he echoes something of Leavis's own judgement that Communism aims 'at completing the work of capitalism and its products'. And behind Leavis there stands the whole tradition of Romantic and post-Romantic anti-utilitarianism. This tradition and its legacy in Williams's own early formulations - of 'structure of feeling', of the 'selective tradition', of the inadequacies of the base/superstructure thesis - remain much more actively present in the later cultural materialism than is often supposed. Indeed, Turner's judgement on *Marxism and Literature*, that Williams 'accepted his place within a Marxist tradition only to disappear into it' (1996, p. 62), is in fact perilously close to the opposite of the truth. What disappears in Williams's 'Marxism' is precisely the central but false tenet of virtually all hitherto existing Marxist cultural theory, that of a determining base and a determined superstructure; what appears in its place is a radically novel theoretical position, selectively appropriating both Marxist and culturalist traditions, so as to theorise not only its own distinctive subject matter, that is, the socio-semiotic systems of late capitalist society, but also the very conditions of its own theoretical novelty. The squared circle of Williams's own 'circularity' is thus a profoundly historicist response to his own historicity. Insofar as Williams became a Marxist, then, it was only ever as a 'heretic in truth' - to borrow Eagleton's borrowing from Milton - whose return to the fold can only ever ensure that 'the fold will never be the same again' (Eagleton, 1989b, 175). This is not so much Marxism, then, as post-Marxism; not so much culturalism as what I have elsewhere termed 'post-culturalism' (Milner, 1994, p. 70).

Williams's entire intellectual effort was organised around a continuing political project, that of a radically democratic, popular socialism, in which the idea of a common culture, truly made in common, might finally be realised. It was organised also around an enduring 'structure of feeling', the main categories of which were: the centrality of culture, as both textual artefact and lived experience; the fundamental importance of serious intellectual work; and the persistent significance of class and community. Thus 'culture' came to mediate between intellectual work on the one hand, and class and community on the other, in Williams's own structure of feeling as surely as it had in his personal biography. Within the broad contours of this continuing political project and this continuing structure of feeling, Williams's work was to prove remarkably innovative. In his more general formulations of the theory of cultural materialism and in his later substantive work on postmodernity, he moved beyond both the left culturalisms of the Old New Left and the theoreticist Marxisms of the New New Left into what was surely a properly post-Marxist, post-culturalist theoretical terrain. The achievement is remarkable, but somehow unsurprising, for, of course, Williams *valued* change. This capacity for change, described by Eagleton as an 'almost intuitive "prevention" of ... new births' (Eagleton, 1976, p. 35), was not simply a particular, contingent, personal strength. It was something which arose directly from his understanding of cultural analysis as the 'study of patterns and relationships, in a whole process' (Williams, 1965, p. 119), with the stress placed equally on each of the latter two terms.

An imagination such as Williams's could not settle for beating the bounds, whether between disciplines or between generations, as Thompson's unfortunately had. Which is why, to engage in a comparison that is unavoidably invidious, Williams really was by far the most intellectually and politically significant figure to write about literature and culture in the English language during the twentieth century. As he himself observed: 'Marxism in Britain ... in this field has not been an offshore island but a major contributor' (Williams, 1980a, p. 246). That this is so was in large part Williams's own personal accomplishment. He had intended *Marxism and Literature* as 'a starting-point for new work', to be done by himself and by others (Williams, 1977a, p. 6). Reflecting back some twenty years later, Hartman would conclude that: 'the full possibilities of the concept of culture as a constitutive social process' have 'not been achieved', while nonetheless readily conceding that *Marxism and Literature* 'shows what progress has been made, as well as delineating the scope of the problem' (Hartman, 1997, p. 210). The extent to which Williams's intentions have been realised, the extent of the progress already made and the scope of the problems still to be addressed will be explored in the chapters that follow.

5

Rethinking Mass Civilization

To take a meaning from experience, and to try to make it active, is in fact our process of growth. Some of these meanings we receive and re-create. Others we must make for ourselves, and try to communicate. The human crisis is always a crisis of understanding: what we genuinely understand we can do. I have written this book because I believe the tradition it records is a major contribution to our common understanding, and a major incentive to its necessary extensions. There are ideas, and ways of thinking, with the seeds of life in them, and there are others, perhaps deep in our minds, with the seeds of a general death. Our measure of success in recognizing these kinds, and in naming them making possible their common recognition, may be literally the measure of our future. (Williams, *Culture and Society*)

Williams's cultural materialism emerged from a sustained encounter between Leavisite literary criticism and socialist politics. It was never, however, merely an attempt either to politicise literature or to 'enculture' politics. Insofar as such tendencies were present in his work, as indeed they were, they indicate not so much its particularity as its more generally representative quality. For, the elision of politics and letters was, in fact, quite fundamentally constitutive, not only of post-war British left intellectualism, but also in some respects of the entire post-war British social-democratic settlement. As Alan Sinfield has interestingly observed:

The hopes that have been placed in literature have been surprisingly close to the centre of the postwar settlement. The idea was that the benefits that the upper-class had customarily arranged for itself would now be generally available ... So what had hitherto been ... the culture of the leisure class was proclaimed ... as a universal culture. (1997, p. 2)

It would be surprising if Williams's work were not implicated in this more general culture of which it formed a part: as he himself once explained, his was 'an ordinary life, spanning the middle years of the twentieth century' (Williams, 1979b, p. 13). But the originality of both the life and the work consisted not in this elision between literature and politics, but in something close to its obverse: in the way he ultimately chose to 'deconstruct' both left politics and literary criticism, both Marxism and Literature. This was a 'deconstruction', however, which clearly predated Derridean deconstruction proper. Williams's work had in practice long sought to problematise the socio-discursive boundaries of both political radicalism and cultural work: hence, his support for a 'New Left', rather than the old left of the Communist and Labour parties; hence, too, his enthusiasm for the new proto-disciplines of Cultural Studies and media studies, rather than simply 'Marxist literary criticism'. In each of these areas, his contribution was to prove formative, sometimes quite decisively so. In this chapter, we move to an account of the influence of cultural materialism on Cultural Studies and media studies; in the next, to that on what had once been 'literary studies'.

Cultural Materialism, Structuralism, Post-Structuralism

We have referred to Williams's work as in some sense a 'deconstruction', a reference which serves to remind us yet again of the wider intellectual context within which cultural materialism had evolved. For, if Williams's work represented the central instance of an indigenously British critique of more traditional literary humanisms, then structuralism and post-structuralism performed analogous functions within French intellectual life. We have had occasion to refer to this French tradition: partly because of the obvious parallelism between British and French developments; but also partly because French theory came to exercise a considerable fascination for British intellectual radicalism from the mid-1960s onwards, that is, in precisely the period in which Williams was working towards a mature cultural materialism. Before proceeding, it might be as well to entertain a brief digression on the subject of French (post-) structuralism and its Anglophone reception. There were many different versions of structuralism, both in general and as applied to literature and culture in particular. But for our purposes, it might best be defined as an approach to the study of human culture, centred on the search for constraining patterns or structures, very often using methods borrowed from structural linguistics (Robey, 1973, pp. 1-2). Durkheim's work on 'primitive' religion and Saussure's on language (Durkheim, 1976; Saussure, 1974), first published in 1915 and 1916 respectively, directly anticipated the subsequent histories of the two academic disciplines most implicated in structuralism, anthropology and semiology. During the late 1950s and the early 1960s, a continuing tradition of post-Durkheimian anthropology came to coincide with a revival of Saussurean semiology, initiated in the first place by Barthes, and with the translation of a series of texts from the Russian Formalist school of literary criticism, so as to generate what became the theoretical moment of French high structuralism. This was, above all, the moment of Barthes himself, but also that of Lévi-Strauss's structural anthropology, Foucault's archaeology of knowledge and Althusserian structural Marxism.

Each of these structuralisms displayed a recurrent aspiration to scientificity. At the end of *The Archaeology of Knowledge*, however, Foucault confessed uncomfortably that his discourse was 'avoiding the ground on which it could find support' (1972a, p. 205). The embarrassment was distinctive, but not the problem. For Barthes, for Lévi-Strauss, for Althusser, as for Foucault, the central repressed problem had been throughout that of how to guarantee the scientificity of a knowledge that was, according to the logic of its own argument, either socially or intra-discursively located. No solution to this problem appeared possible from within structuralism. Hence, the move by both Barthes and Foucault, during the 1970s, toward different versions of 'post-structuralism'. Hence, too, Derrida's meteoric rise to intellectual pre-eminence during the same period. Each of these various post-structuralisms insisted that meaning could never finally be pinned down, not even by structuralism itself. Three main versions of post-structuralism thus emerged: the type of literary deconstruction practised by the later Barthes, and more influentially by Derrida; Foucault's middle period writings on the theme of knowledge/power relations, which he himself denoted by the term 'genealogy'; and the various semiotic reconstructions of Freudian psychoanalysis developed initially by Lacan, and further pursued, perhaps even more influentially so, by Julia Kristeva and Luce Irigaray. The ten years after 1974 witnessed the translation into English of a series of key post-structuralist texts. Derrida's *De la grammatologie* and *L'écriture et la différance*, both originally published in 1967, first appeared in English translation in 1974 and 1978 respectively (Derrida, 1974; Derrida, 1978); Barthes's *S/Z* (1970) was first published in English in 1974, *Le plaisir du texte* (1973) in 1975, *Sade, Fourier, Loyola* (1971) in 1976 (Barthes, 1974; Barthes, 1975; Barthes, 1976); collections of Foucault's essays dating from 1962-1972 and from 1972-1977 appeared in English in 1977 and 1980 respectively (Foucault, 1977a; Foucault, 1980); 1977 also saw the first English translation of *Surveiller et punir* (1975), 1978 that of the first volume of the *Histoire de la sexualité* (1976) (Foucault, 1977b; Foucault, 1978); selections from Lacan's 1966 collection of *Écrits* appeared in English in 1977, Kristeva's *La Révolution du langage poétique* (1974) in 1984, Irigaray's *Speculum de l'autre femme* (1974) and *Ce sexe qui n'en est pas un* (1977) both in 1985 (Lacan, 1977; Kristeva, 1984; Irigaray, 1985a; Irigaray, 1985b). Whatever their respective theoretical merits and demerits there can be little doubt that in France itself these various points of departure from structuralism bore the dual impress of the initial political disillusionments of the immediate post-1968 period and, subsequently, an emergent postmodernisation of the French intelligentsia.

For much of the British intelligentsia, however, Althusserianism had provided an initial introduction not only to Marxism, but also to structuralism, and to what would eventually become significantly post-structuralist thematics. Althusserianism thus established a continuing identification between structuralist theory and radical politics, which would later secure a disproportionately leftist audience for the subsequent importations of French post-structuralism proper. Moreover, until well into the 1980s the conservative intellectual establishment in Britain, and the literary establishment in particular, sustained an implacable hostility to 'structuralism', a term which came to signify not only structuralism proper, but also the various post-structuralist successor doctrines, and indeed, all manner of alien 'isms'. During the late 1970s and the early 1980s, Williams's cultural materialism thus evolved within an intellectual and political milieu which clearly overlapped with that of a certain kind of 'deconstruction'. This was certainly not deconstruction as it was then developing in North America, most especially at Yale (Bloom et al., 1979), nor even exactly as pursued by Derrida himself. It was, as Easthope pointed out, a post-structuralism much more indebted to Marxism in general, and to Althusserianism in particular, than that available either in France or in the United States (Easthope, 1988, pp. 21-2, 161-4). Despite considerable initial antipathy, Williams himself clearly recognised the developing affinity between his own cultural materialism and this kind of 'radical semiotics' (Williams, 1984b, p. 210). Such interpenetrations and interconnections, between cultural materialism, structuralism and post-structuralism, and between each of these and the continuing legacies of more traditional Marxisms and culturalisms, powerfully shaped the development of Cultural Studies and literary studies, and also that of the more general intellectual culture of the Left.

Williams and Hall

Leavisite literary criticism had constructed popular culture, not as part of the subject matter of 'English', but rather as the discipline's excluded antithetical other. The sheer volume of attention paid to working-class culture by both Hoggart and Williams, quite apart from the often positive valorisations attached thereto, clearly transgressed those disciplinary boundaries. But whatever Williams's and Hoggart's own personal intentions, English itself proved quite unamenable to the kind of disciplinary reconstruction implied by *The Uses of Literacy* and *The Long Revolution*. Almost by default, then, 'the popular' became the subject matter of the new proto-discipline of 'Cultural Studies'. In 1962

Hoggart was appointed Professor of Modern English Literature at Birmingham University. Two years later, largely at his instigation, the University established a Centre for Contemporary Cultural Studies, with Hoggart as its first Director. When Hoggart left to take up a position with UNESCO in 1968, he was succeeded by Hall. From the very beginning, Hoggart had acknowledged Williams's 'interesting work' in *Culture and Society* as a source of intellectual inspiration (1970, p. 255). Subsequent commentary has continued to emphasise that the new sub-discipline owed its initial theoretical foundations at least as much to Williams as to Hoggart (Green, 1978, p. 211; Hall, 1980a, p. 58; Jones, 1982, p. 111). Certainly, Williams himself regarded the Centre as 'an excellent pioneering example' (Williams, 1976a/b, p. 149) of needed institutional innovation. During Hall's term of office, moreover, the Centre became, in effect, the intellectually pre-eminent institutional location for Cultural Studies, not only in Britain but throughout much of the English-speaking world. As Lawrence Grossberg, editor of *Cultural Studies* and a leading figure in the making of American Cultural Studies, observed in a 1988 lecture: 'there remains something like a center - to be precise, the tradition of British cultural studies, especially the work of the Centre for Contemporary Cultural Studies' (Grossberg et al., 1988, p. 8). Graeme Turner, a founding editor of the *Australian Journal of Cultural Studies* and a key figure in the development of Cultural Studies in Australia, put it even more succinctly: 'the Birmingham Centre ... can justifiably claim to be the key institution in the history of the field' (Turner, 1996, p. 70).

As Director, Hall displayed a remarkable flair for academic entrepreneurship. He established a house journal for the Centre, *Working Papers in Cultural Studies*, eleven issues of which were published during the 1970s. The 1975 double issue, Nos 7/8, and the 1977 issue, No. 10, were each republished in book form by Hutchinson (Hall and Jefferson, 1976; Centre for Contemporary Cultural Studies, 1978), as was a subsequent retrospective overview of the Centre's work during the period of Hall's Directorship (Hall et al., 1980). All three volumes included contributions by Hall himself. In 1978, Hall co-authored, with a number of colleagues from the Centre, a highly acclaimed 'Cultural Studies' account of 'mugging', which sought to analyse the ways in which media constructions of black criminality had functioned so as to confer popular legitimacy on a developing state authoritarianism (Hall et al., 1978a). Though Hall moved from Birmingham in 1979, to take up the chair of sociology at the Open University, his influence over the Centre's intellectual evolution had proven decisive. At the Open University, moreover, he was involved in the co-production of U203, 'Popular Culture', an interdisciplinary undergraduate course, convened by his eventual successor, Tony Bennett, which ran from 1982 to 1987, and which in its first year attracted over 1000 students (Bennett, 1986, p. vii). As Easthope observed, U203 was 'the most ambitious, serious and comprehensive intervention in cultural studies in Britain, and, apart from the work of the Birmingham Centre, the most important' (1988, p. 74). The course generated three commercially published, edited collections (Bennett et al., 1981; Waites et al., 1982; Bennett et al., 1986), two of which included important essays by Hall (Hall, 1981; Hall 1986).

More than any other single figure, then, Hall can claim credit for the successful institutionalisation of academic Cultural Studies in Britain. There is, no doubt, an unavoidable reductionism about any attempt to construct a particular career as fully representative of a collective intellectual project: the Birmingham Centre had two distinguished Directors after Hall, Richard Johnson and Jorge Larrain; interesting work continued to emanate from Birmingham even after the Centre's dissolution into a combined Department of Cultural Studies and Sociology (Webster, 2000); even under Hall's Directorship CCCS had produced work much less clearly marked by his direct influence (Women's Studies Group, 1978; Clarke et al., 1979); and there were 'centres' other than Birmingham, for example, the Centre for Cultural Studies at Leeds University and the Centre for Mass Communication Research at Leicester, or the Institute for Cultural Policy Studies at Griffith University in Brisbane. But, for all this necessary qualification, Hall's career does in fact enjoy an unusually representative quality, sufficiently such at least as to justify an initial approach to the question of the relationship between Cultural Studies and cultural materialism by way of an examination of that between his work and that of Williams. Williams and Hall had worked together on the founding, Old New Left, editorial board of the *New Left Review*; they had co-authored with Thompson the Old New Left's major political manifesto; and, as Hall himself would later recall, 'we have found ourselves shaping up to the same issues, or crises: and shaping up ... from the same directions' (Hall, 1989a, p. 54). These affinities were not merely political. As Easthope observed: 'Cultural studies, media studies, work on television and film, the teaching of communication - all these in Britain bear the imprint of the work of Raymond Williams. That work has been widely promoted by the Birmingham Centre ... led ... by Stuart Hall' (1988, p. 71). There is an element of exaggeration here: the Centre's commitment to ethnographic research, for example, clearly owed more to Hoggart than to Williams. But it is certainly true that, for much of the 1970s at least, there was an unusually close parallelism between Williams's and Hall's respective intellectual evolutions: both very clearly moved from an essentially left-Leavisite culturalism toward a more properly Gramscian perspective. The 'concept of "hegemony"', Hall observed in 1980, 'has played a seminal role in Cultural Studies' (Hall, 1980b, p. 35). And as late as 1976, Hall and his colleagues in the Centre had paired the concept of hegemony with that of culture, in ways which simultaneously echoed the argument of Williams's (1973c) 'Base and Superstructure' essay and anticipated that of *Marxism and Literature*. itself (Clarke et al., 1976, pp. 10-13).

There were few doubts here as to the centrality of class in cultural analysis: 'In modern societies', wrote Hall and his collaborators, 'the most fundamental groups are the social classes, and the major cultural configurations ... "class cultures"' (Clarke et al., 1976, p. 13).

Hall, however, had proved much more responsive than Williams to the lure both of Althusserianism in particular and of structuralism in general. Indeed, his early much-cited essay on 'Encoding and Decoding in Television Discourse', originally published as a CCCS Stencilled Paper in 1973, had drawn heavily on French and Italian semiotic theory so as to mount a very effective critique of American mass-communications theory (Hall, 1980c). More pointedly, the Centre's 1978 volume, *On Ideology*, chose to situate Gramsci in relation to Althusser rather than to Williams; and what was true of the volume as a whole was true also of Hall's own particular contributions (Hall, 1978; Hall et al., 1978b). The precise point at which these divergences finally come to constitute a difference is difficult to document. By 1980, however, when Hall first published his seminal sketch of the current state of the theoretical art in Cultural Studies (Hall, 1980a), Williams's 'culturalism' was no longer the obviously available starting point for the would-be discipline, but rather only one of two competing paradigms, each with its attendant strengths and weaknesses. The 'Cultural studies: two paradigms' essay was included as a set text for U203, republished in one of the Open University readers (Bennett et al., 1981, pp. 19-37), and again in a later collection of articles from *Media, Culture and Society* (Collins et al., 1986a, pp. 33-48), and soon came to provide a central organising device for theoretical debate in the field. It rehearsed much that had previously been argued by Richard Johnson, including the distinction itself between 'culturalism' and 'structuralism' (Johnson, 1979), but was nonetheless much more preoccupied with the theoretical status of Williams's own work. Furthermore, it was published very nearly simultaneously with an extended commentary by Hall on the *Politics and Letters* interviews (Hall, 1980d), later included in Eagleton's 1989 *Festschrift*. Together, the two pieces provided a fairly concise statement of Hall's reactions, not only to Williams's earlier left culturalism, but also to his mature cultural materialism.

Hall himself actually registered no such distinction in Williams's work, but rather, 'a striking continuity of basic position ... even in his more acceptable recent formulations' (Hall, 1989a, p. 62). In the 'Cultural studies: two paradigms' essay, Williams's work was closely identified with that of Thompson, as parallel instances of a similar culturalism: here, the continuity ran, not only between *Culture and Society* and *The Making of the English Working Class*, but also, and more surprisingly, between *Marxism and Literature* and *The Poverty of Theory*. For Hall, 'culture' in Williams and 'experience' in Thompson performed fundamentally analogous theoretical functions, simultaneously denoting, and thereby improperly eliding the distinction between, active consciousness and relatively 'given', determinate conditions. The result was a theoretical humanism, with two distinguishing characteristics: first, a general 'experiential pull', and second, an 'emphasis on the creative' (Hall, 1980a, p. 63). For both Thompson and Williams, then, the 'authenticating test', in Hall's view, was that provided by 'experience'. His response to such empiricism was almost conventionally structuralist:

> Analysis must deconstruct ... 'lived wholeness' in order to be able to think its determinate conditions ... this confusion, which persists even in Williams's later work, ... continues to have disabling theoretical effects ... so long as 'experience' continues to play this all-embracing role, there will be an inevitable theoretical pull towards reading all structures as if they expressively correlated with one another. (Hall, 1989a, p. 62)

The scene was set, then, for the structuralist 'interruption' as theoretical salvation. And so it emerged: structuralism recognised the presence of constraining relations of structure; it acknowledged the importance of different levels of theoretical abstraction; it conceived of the social whole as an adequately complex unity-in-difference; it successfully replaced the category of experience with that of ideology (Hall, 1980a, pp. 67-9). Formally, of course, Hall aspired, not to any thoroughgoing structuralism, but to a Gramscian synthesis of the two paradigms: 'between them ... they address what must be the *core problem* of Cultural Studies' (ibid., p. 72). The developmental logic of the argument, however, actually left culturalism with remarkably little to do. Its strengths, we learn, 'can almost be derived from the weaknesses of the structuralist position' (ibid., p. 69), as backhanded a compliment as they come; and these belong, in any case, quite specifically to Gramsci rather than to Williams or to Thompson. In truth, Hall's was an anti-culturalist argument, its effects all the more damaging both for its professed evenhandedness and for the quasi-filial respect it accorded the 'culturalists': to become a 'founding father' is to become, perhaps unavoidably, just a little *passé*.

To some extent, Hall caricatured both Williams and Thompson. Neither was quite so unaware of structural determinacy as Hall suggested: indeed, Williams's notion of determination as the setting of limits and exertion of pressures, though certainly not structuralist, was nonetheless fully compatible with a strong sense of structure. Nor were they quite so empiricist: Williams's own work was in many respects intensely theoretical, as Hall himself had cause to remark (Hall, 1980b, p. 19); and, its title not withstanding, Thompson's *The Poverty of Theory* actually developed a highly nuanced account of the dialogue between theory and evidence in historical research (Thompson, 1978, pp. 197-242). If Williams preferred the concept of hegemony to that of ideology, this was for reasons that were both the-oretically articulate in their own right, and theoretically defensible in terms of a broadly 'Gramscian' aproach to cultural analysis. The point, however, is that Hall's Gramsci was not Williams's. The difference between their respective readings of Gramsci takes us to what was actually the theoretical heart of the matter: that of whether to under-stand hegemony as culture or as structure, and of what relative weights to attach to the hegemonic and counter-hegemonic respectively. If hegemony is a culture, then it is materially produced by the practices of conscious agents, and may be countered by alternative, counter-hege-monic, practices; if hegemony is a structure of ideology, then it will determine the subjectivity of its subjects in ways which radically diminish the prospects for counter-hegemonic practice, except in the characterisically attenuated form of a plurality of post-structuralist resistant readings. Hegemony as culture is thus a matter of material production, reproduction and consumption; hegemony as structure a matter for textual decoding. Where Williams's interpretation of Gramsci's work remained resolutely 'post-culturalist', Hall progres-sively assimilated it to a developing structuralist - and post-struc-turalist - paradigm. Hence, Hall's eventual view of Gramsci as antici-pating 'many of the actual advances in theorizing' brought about by 'structuralism, discourse and linguistic theory or psychoanalysis' (Hall, 1988a, p. 56).

These theoretical differences increasingly devolved, moreover, on to a particular substantive issue, that of 'Thatcherism'. During the 1980s and early 1990s, Hall and many of his colleagues remained fas-cinated by the problem of how to analyse the particularities and pecu-liarities of Thatcherite Toryism. The issues at stake were claimed for Cultural Studies, rather than, say, political science, insofar as they per-tained to the social construction of consent: 'What is particularly sig-nificant for our purposes', wrote Hall, 'is Thatcherism's capacity to become popular, especially among those sectors of society whose interests it cannot possibly be said to represent in any conventional sense of the term' (ibid., p. 41). Hall's analysis had commenced from the assumption that Thatcherism was substantially different from ear-lier forms of Conservatism, and that this difference centred on the par-ticular ways in which hegemony was established and maintained. What was at issue, he argued, was the 'move toward "authoritarian populism" - an exceptional form of the capitalist state which ... has been able to construct around itself an active popular consent' (Hall, 1983, pp. 22-3). Hall's solution to this conundrum would run closely par llel to the work of Ernesto Laclau and Chantal Mouffe, which he would later describe as 'seminal' and 'extraordinarily rich' (Grossberg, 1996, p. 145). They argued that the relationship between social position and cultural identity could only ever be an effect of discourse itself. To the notion of 'objective interests', they counterposed a 'contradictory plurality'; to the 'unity and homogeneity of class subjects', a 'set of precariously integrated positions which ... cannot be referred to any necessary point of future unification' (Laclau and Mouffe, 1985, pp. 84-5). 'The logic of hegemony', they concluded, was thus 'a logic of articulation and contingency' (ibid., p. 85), thereby effectively precluding the possibility of any determinate connection between any social position and any discursive or ideological construct. This is precisely the import of Hall's own conclusion that popular consent to Thatcherism had been secured through its effective articulation with key elements in traditional working-class culture. According to Hall, Thatcherism operated directly 'on popular elements in the traditional philosophies and practical ideologies of the *dominated* classes'. This was possible, he explained, because such elements 'have no intrinsic, necessary or fixed class meaning', and can therefore be recomposed in new ways, so as 'to construct the people into a populist political subject: *with*, not against, the power bloc' (Hall, 1983, p. 30). In subsequent reformulations, the account would be modified and augmented by what was in effect a theory of postmodernism redefined, in peculiarly British terms, as 'New Times'. Here Hall sought to 'disarticulate' the politics of the Anglo-American New Right from economic and cultural postmodernity. Thatcherism, he insisted, 'represents ... an attempt ... to harness and bend to its political project circumstances ... which do not necessarily have a 'New Right' political agenda inscribed in them (Hall, 1989b, pp. 116-17). A post-structuralist understanding of discourse as necessarily 'polysemic' was thus combined with a distinctly postmodern sense of popular passivity, so as to 'construct' much of the British working class as positively Thatcherite.

Unsurprisingly, the substantive analysis had appeared to Williams even more wrongheaded than the theoretical. Thus, the scale of Conservative electoral victory seemed to him more readily explicable in terms of the peculiar, 'first-past-the-post', British electoral system, than of any successfully Thatcherite ideological mobilisation (Williams, 1989d, p. 163). In *Towards 2000*, moreover, Williams showed very clearly that pro-Labour loyalties persisted amongst union members, the unemployed, and manual workers (Williams, 1983, pp. 156-57); and that the fall in the Labour vote was as much a consequence of the recent split in the Party as of any direct transfer to the Conservatives (ibid., p. 155). But Williams's objections were fundamentally neither empirical nor empiricist. They were fuelled, rather, by his dual sense of the importance of creative human agency, and of himself as an 'organic' working-class intellectual (Jones, 1982, p. 113), bound to his class of origin by ties of community and kinship, solidarity and 'loyalties' (Williams, 1985). It was simply unthinkable for Williams that the working class should prove as susceptible to bourgeois hegemony as Hall appeared to believe possible. That Hall could so readily think the unthinkable was not necessarily, of course, a sign of strength, though he often seemed to imply as much (Hall, 1988b, p. 20). Certainly, their predictably different responses to the 1984-85

British coalminers' strike inspire something less than complete confidence in Hall's political judgement. At the height of the strike in September 1984 Hall seriously argued, in the columns of the Labour Party journal, *New Socialist*, that the Labour-run, and soon to be abolished Greater London Council had 'become the most important front in the struggle against Thatcherism' (Hall, 1984, p. 37). Williams's own reactions were very different: 'The point of growth for a reviving socialism', he wrote in an article originally published in the same journal, 'is now in all these crisis-ridden communities ... It is here ... that new popular forces are forming and looking for some effective political articulation ... the miners have, in seeking to protect their own interests, outlined a new form of the general interest' (Williams, 1989e, p. 127).

We might note that in *Towards 2000* Williams was dealing with precisely the kind of 'structural determinants' that culturalism was supposed to ignore. Indeed, it is Williams's explanation, rather than Hall's, that seems in retrospect the more readily compatible with mainstream empirical sociology. As the distinguished British sociologist, J.H. Goldthorpe, observed of Hall:

> Not only is no evidence provided of the supposed 'hegemony' at work, but the argument for it involves ignoring the ... quite substantial findings to indicate that Thatcherism *cannot* be linked with any very significant belief and value changes within British society, and that many Conservative policies are well out of line with prevailing opinion. (Goldthorpe, 1990, p. 431)

The political risks in any such 'block diagnosis of Thatcherism' were apparent to Williams: that it 'taught despair and political disarmament in a social situation which was always more diverse, more volatile and more temporary' (Williams, 1989a, p. 175). But now that the despair - and perhaps something at least of the political disarmament - has passed, the more straightforwardly academic problem remains to determine the theoretical and empirical adequacy of Hall's analysis. Whatever we make either of postmodernism in general or of 'New Times' in particular, the accumulating empirical data on the continuing resilience of the connections between class identity and politics casts increasing doubt on the plausibility of his intervention. Theoretically, we need to ask why it was that Williams was able to read Thatcherism more accurately than Hall. At one level, the answer might rest with the legitimacy accorded the proper claims of experience. When Williams identified with the striking miners, for example, he clearly invoked the lived experience of the class and place of his birth and upbringing. But experience alone had never been *the* authenticating test, either in his own work or in Thompson's. The older left culturalists had in fact persisted in a long-standing commitment, inherited from Leavisism ironically enough, not so much to experience *per se*, as to the analysis of the connections between being, consciousness and experience. By contrast, Hall and the younger post-Althusserians progressively abandoned all three, initially in favour of the notion of ideology as structure, later still the even more 'immaterial' notion of discursive formation. In truth, structuralism never had paid very much attention to the structural determinants of culture, except insofar as they occurred within ideology or within language. And insofar as these were made available for analysis, they were understood as present, neither in experience nor in empirical data of the kind produced by history and sociology, but in the deep structures of textuality. Even the Leavises had known that historical reality could never simply be deduced from a close reading of the literary text. But as Colin Sparks observes, contemporary Cultural Studies has increasingly regressed 'beyond Hoggart and Williams, beyond the Leavises and the British marxists, to an essentially textualist account of culture'. If this has been Hall's achievement, then it is surely, as Sparks concludes, a quite 'fundamentally regressive step' (1996, p. 98).[1]

Cultural Studies and Postmodernism

This textualism is crucial to the more general theoretical 'postmodernisation' of British Cultural Studies, over which Hall presided. If the most obviously negative aspect of this process had been his misreading of the class politics of Thatcherism, the most obviously positive is its attempt to theorise the cultural politics of ethnic and racial difference. The issue had been broached in the Centre's early work on youth subcultures (Hall and Jefferson, 1976) and foregrounded in *Policing the Crisis*, its highly acclaimed 'Cultural Studies' account of 'mugging', which had shown how media constructions of black criminality worked so as to confer popular legitimacy on the growing state authoritarianism that would become 'Thatcherism' (Hall et al., 1978a). But in the 1990s these and the relatedly 'diasporic' issues of postcolonialism, multiculturalism, hybridity and globalisation came to occupy pride of place in Hall's work. In these years, Hall finally emerged as a commanding figure in Cultural Studies, not only nationally, but also internationally (cf. Gilroy et al., 2000). There is no denying either the necessity for, nor the importance of this work of 'decentring', in which liberalism is exposed as 'the culture that won' rather than the 'culture ... beyond culture', Britishness as itself subject to a 'major internal crisis of national identity' (Hall, 2000a, pp. 228-9). But Hall's approach to these matters remains deeply problematic, especially as it relates to his reading of Williams. The 'interruption' of 'race' into the work of the CCCS, to borrow Hall's own terms (Hall, 1992, p. 282), had posed an immediate challenge to the emphasis on class and community inherited from Williams, Thompson and Hoggart. This challenge was registered more generally in Paul Gilroy's work: not simply in the complaint that they're ain't no black in the Union Jack, but more specifically in an objection to the 'forms of nationalism endorsed by a discipline which, in spite of itself, tends towards a morbid celebration of England and Englishness from which blacks are systematically excluded' (Gilroy, 1992, p. 12). At one point, Gilroy famously accused Williams of an 'apparent endorsement of the presuppositions of the new racism' (ibid., p. 50).

The accusation was directed at the discussion of 'race' and racism in *Towards 2000*, where Williams contrasted the 'alienated superficialities' of 'formal legal definitions' of citizenship with the more substantial reality of 'deeply grounded and active social identities' (Williams, 1983, p. 195). Gilroy read Williams as replicating the distinction between 'authentic and inauthentic types of national belonging' pedalled by the more racist of British conservatives (Gilroy, 1992, p. 49). This is a misreading, it seems to me, but a significant one nonetheless, if only for the status it acquired in Hall's later work. Gilroy's critique of Williams, first aired in 1987, figures in Hall's work from the early 1990s right through to the present. The characteristic form of the figure was established in the 1992 Raymond Williams Lecture, delivered by Hall in Cardiff and subsequently published in *Cultural Studies*. There, he described Gilroy as having 'quite correctly' fastened on the 'racially exclusive form of social identity' implicit in Williams's discussion; but proceeded to 'honour' the latter, nonetheless, for his stubborn insistence on the '"actual, lived relationships" of place, culture and community', especially among politically and culturally subordinate peoples; and finally concluded that the 'new diasporas' of the 'late-modern' experience 'will *never* be unified culturally' because they are 'inevitably the products of several interlocking histories and cultures' (Hall, 1993, pp. 360-3). Identity, he continued, is now 'irrevocably ... an open, complex, unfinished game - always under construction' (ibid., pp. 360-2). This pairing of Gilroy and Williams figured similarly in Hall's Taiwan interview with Kuan-Hsing Chen (Hall and Chen, 1996, p. 394) and in his plenary address to the Third International Crossroads in Cultural Studies Conference at the University of Birmingham (Hall, 2000b). All three aspects of the figure seem questionable: in the first place, it is not clear that Gilroy's assessment of Williams is actually 'correct'; second, this honouring of Williams seems mere pointless piety insofar as Hall no longer believes such community to be possible; and third, Hall's enthusiasm for the diaspora might itself be judged an alienated superficiality of his own.

The suggestion that Williams's sense of full social identity is implicitly racially exclusive is simply misconceived. For, as Jones rightly points out, both Gilroy and Hall misunderstand the intended addressee of Williams's criticism. It is important here to distinguish the four different subject positions present in Williams's text: that of the 'unfamiliar neighbours', who serve as referent for the reported conversation; the 'English working man' who protests their arrival; the author of the 'standard liberal' reply to his protests; and the author-narrator of the text itself, quite explicitly identified here as from the 'Welsh border' (Williams, 1983, pp. 195-6). The reference to the English working man is thus in no sense an act of identification, as Gilroy seems to suppose: whatever the case in the mid-1950s, Williams identifies as Welsh in *Towards 2000*. The liberal speaker, who reduces 'social identity to formal legal definitions', is clearly not black - since he refers to black people as 'they' - but almost certainly white and English, though nonetheless not a 'working man' (Williams, 1983, p. 195; Jones, 2000). In short, he is a middle-class liberal. In thus pointing to the limitations of liberal anti-racism, Williams nowhere denies that 'blacks can share a significant "social identity" with their white neighbours', as Gilroy suggests (1992, p. 50); nor that 'relationships between blacks and whites in many inner-city communities' can be 'actual' and 'sustained', as Hall suggests (1993, p. 360). His point, rather, is that the appeal to legality is in itself an inadequately counter-hegemonic response to hegemonic racism (Jones, 2000). The possibility and desirability of shared social identities between black and white neighbours are, in fact, precisely what motivate Williams's reference to the 'massive and diverse immigration' into the Welsh mining communities during the nineteenth century. 'These are the real grounds of hope', he concludes: 'It is by working and living together, with some real place and common interests to identify with, and as free as may be from external ideological definitions, whether divisive or universalist, that real social identities are formed' (Williams, 1983, p. 196). Where - really - is the evidence of racial exclusivity, implicit or otherwise, in any of this?

Hall's 'reverence' for Williams - this is the word he used at Birmingham in June 2000 - is no doubt genuine: 'Williams was a major influence on my intellectual and political formation', he wrote (Hall, 1993, p. 349); and 'Williams has his strengths, his important insights; he is a major figure' (Hall and Chen, 1996, p. 394). But what had seemed to Hall most 'striking' about Williams, that is, his capacity to judge 'Cambridge' by the quite different standards of another subordinate 'knowable community', is also what seems increasingly irrelevant to the '"new" situation' of late-modernity (Hall, 1993, pp. 350, 353). Hence, the judgement that Williams's conception of culture had reconstituted itself 'as a narrow, exclusive nationalism' (Hall and Chen, 1996, p. 394). I can find no evidence of such exclusivity in Williams. Nor is there much point to Hall's insistence - supposedly in opposition to Williams's 'serious misjudgement' - that formal, legal definitions of citizenship 'cannot be made conditional on cultural assimilation' (Hall, 1993, p. 360). For Williams had never argued that they could. He insisted, to the contrary, and on the very same page Gilroy and Hall misread,[2] that 'a merely legal definition of what it is to be 'British' ... is necessary and important, correctly asserting the need for equality and protection within the laws ... the most active legal (and communal) defence of dislocated and exposed groups and minorities is essential' (Williams, 1983, p. 195).

But there is something at issue, clearly, between Williams and Hall (and Gilroy): there must be more to it than a simple misreading or misunderstanding. The key sentences in these pages from *Towards 2000*, I would argue, to which neither Hall nor Gilroy directly refer, are those that follow immediately on the reference to the 'alienated superficialities' of 'the nation':

> That even some socialists should reply in such terms ... is another sign of the prepotence of market and exchange relations. One reason is that many ... socialists, and especially those who by the nature of their work or formation are themselves nationally and internationally mobile, have little experience of those rooted settlements from which ... most people derive their communal identities. (Williams, 1983, pp. 195-6)

This takes us to the heart of the difference between Williams and the later Hall, to their quite different, even opposed, valuations of 'rooted settlement' as against 'diasporic hybridity'. It is a difference which leads, in turn, to quite different evaluations of 'socialism' as against 'liberalism', since the hybrid subjects who *produce themselves anew and differently'* (Hall, 1993, p. 362) are only able to do so, in practice, by way of 'market and exchange relations'. For Gilroy certainly, for Hall to a substantial extent, rooted settlement and diasporic hybridity are coded racially as, respectively, white and black. Hence, the supposed racial exclusivity of Williams's sense of social identity. But I can find no evidence that Williams intended it thus. More seriously, I can see no good reason, apart from the immediate contingencies of everyday life in Britain under Thatcherism, to imagine it thus.

At this point, let me speak briefly to my own subject position as diasporic intellectual. Like Hall, I travelled thousands of miles from the place of my birth to the site of my career: I was born and brought up in the northern English county of Yorkshire, but have lived and worked for more than twenty years in the Australian city of Melbourne. Like Hall, I belong to one of the larger immigrant groups, many of whom are in fact working class in occupation. Like Hall, I am a university professor and, as such, enjoy an affluent, middle-class lifestyle: writing books, giving papers, travelling the world, going to international conferences. Like Hall, I take much pleasure from the cultural and intellectual cosmopolitanism of the city in which I live. Like Hall, I have been nationally and internationally mobile, by nature of my work, and thus have comparatively little direct experience of what Williams called rooted settlements. Whatever the delights of the diaspora - and these are real - they are far more obviously available to middle-class than to working-class migrants. Unlike Hall, I am white. But in Australia immigrants are disproportionately white or yellow. Here, black people are typically not immigrants at all, but rather the native first peoples, many of whom continue to live in settlements far more 'rooted' than anything Williams imagined. The point is an obvious one, but serves to question the racial coding of both the diasporic and the settled. To stretch the point further than perhaps one should, it is Williams's subject position, neither 'British' nor 'English' - which is how Gilroy misrepresents him - but rather Welsh, which most closely approximates to that of the aboriginal. The young Williams once quipped: 'I come from an old place; if a man tells me that his family came over with the Normans, I say "Yes, how interesting; and are you liking it here?"' (Williams, 1989b, p. 15). It is a nice joke, variants of which must surely be told by aboriginal peoples the world over.

Whatever the delights of the diaspora, full racial justice will sooner or later require recognition of the moral value of the most deeply settled of human cultures, like those of the indigenous Australians, the Inuit and the Amazon 'Indians'. This is no mere local eccentricity, but a pressing question both in Australia and throughout the Americas. Such recognition seems unlikely to be forthcoming from dominant cultures determined to transcend even their own limited histories of rooted settlement. Late capitalism invites us to produce ourselves anew and differently, on a daily basis, whenever it insists that we consume. And this is what Hall's work comes perilously close to celebrating: the alienated superficialities of the market. In this respect, it is fully representative of a more general tendency in post-Birmingham Cultural Studies to transform itself into 'commodity studies, or image studies' (Cevasco, 2000, p. 438). I borrow the latter phrase from a Brazilian writer, who describes herself as living and practising Cultural Studies 'under the dark shadow cast by the centre'. But we all live in this shadow, even those who live at its core. I will hazard the guess that it will be Williams, rather than the later Hall, whose work will eventually speak the more powerfully to the cultural contradictions of the twenty-first century, whether fought out in its peripheries or its centres.

Cultural Studies and Cultural Policy

In the early 1980s, the major theoretical differences between Williams and Hall, and between cultural materialism and Cultural Studies, had revolved around their respectively culturalist and structuralist appropriations of Gramsci. But, as the decade proceeded, post-structuralist thematics, particularly those deriving from Foucault, became more obviously present in Cultural Studies. Hall's later writings on Thatcherism clearly owe much to this Foucauldian influence (Hall, 1988a, pp. 51-3). An even more developed 'Foucauldianism' appears in the work of Tony Bennett, Hall's eventual successor to the Open University chair of sociology. Bennett had served as Chairman of the Open University U203 course, but moved to Australia in 1987 to become Director of the Institute for Cultural Policy Studies at Griffith University in Brisbane, where he remained until 1998. Like Hall, Bennett displayed a considerable flair for academic entrepreneurship. Like Hall, he would happily acknowledge a clear debt to Williams (Bennett, 1989, pp. 86-7). Indeed, he is careful to cite Williams's own role in the British Arts Council as prefiguring his own interest in cultural policy (Bennett, 1998, p. 36).[3] But like Hall, Bennett also moved away from Williams in response to post-structuralism and postmodernism, albeit in rather different directions. Where for Hall the central, pressing problem had become the linked questions of Thatcherism and the cultural politics of race, for Bennett it would be that of the relationship between Cultural Studies and cultural policy.

This shift toward 'cultural policy studies' was never simply pragmatic, but rather evolved from a very particular vision of the role of the intellectual, and a correspondingly particular version of cultural politics, both of which derived in part from Foucault. Foucault's genealogy had sought to relativise discourse, not by any radical reconstruction of the notion of signification, such as is attempted by Derrida, but by the attempt to substitute relations of power for relations of meaning. For Foucault, power in modern society had become essentially ubiquitous and, in its ubiquity, open and indeterminate, productive rather than simply oppressive: 'it induces pleasure, forms knowledge, produces discourse', he wrote: 'It needs to be considered as a productive network which runs through the whole social body' (Foucault, 1980, p. 119). There is, then, no single structure of power, but rather a play of powers; and no possibility of an objectively structuralist account of discourse, but only that of a strategic, or tactical, intervention into this play. The proper political function of the intellectual can, therefore, no longer be that of the Sartrean 'universal intellectual', who acts as 'the consciousness/conscience of us all', but must become that of the 'specific intellectual', who will work 'within specific sectors, at the precise points where their own conditions of life or work situate them' (ibid., p. 126). If Williams's role in cultural theory can perhaps be considered Sartrean (*The Times* described him as a British equivalent to Sartre), then Bennett's, by contrast, is determinedly 'specific'.

The underlying theoretical rationale behind Bennett's own commitment to cultural policy studies was first articulated in *Outside Literature*, the original title of which, interestingly enough, was planned to be *Against Literature* (Bennett, 1985, p. 49). In a reversal of Williams's intellectual journey towards Marxism, Bennett here set out to exorcise the ghosts of his own misspent Marxist youth (cf. Bennett, 1979). For Bennett, 'it no longer seems ... fruitful to regard Marxism as ... adequate to the theorisation of social phenomena' (1990, p. 7).

Marxism's central failure in the field of Cultural Studies, in Bennett's view, was its enduring loyalty to the 'idealist concerns of bourgeois aesthetics' (ibid., p. 33). To such idealism he sought to counterpose a thoroughgoing 'cultural materialism', though one which derived more obviously from Foucault than from Williams. Bennett's argument commenced from a general critique of the base/superstructure model, in which he proposed an alternatively 'sociological' understanding of literary relations as in themselves social relations. At first sight, this seems little more than a restatement of Williams's own position. But as we have seen there are at least two alternative routes by which to sidestep the dualism between base and superstructure, 'real' history and 'less real' literature: either, like Williams, one chooses to historicise literature; or, like Foucault and Derrida, one chooses to narrativise history. As we noted in Chapter 4, in the course of our discussion of the sociology of form and genre, Bennett decisively opted for the latter, choosing to see history as little more than a discursive regime for the maintenance and transformation of the past in the present (ibid., p. 50).

History thus disposed of, he proceeded to a critique of Marxist aesthetics as little more than a re-run of bourgeois 'philosophical aesthetics'. Here, the argument begins from premises very similar to Williams's own deconstruction of 'the aesthetic' in *Marxism and Literature*. Philosophical aesthetics misconstrue literary and artistic judgement as universal modes of cognition, Bennett argues, rather than as socially specific applications of the particular rules of value shared by particular valuing communities. They thereby 'fetishise the objects of value and deploy a discourse of disqualification in relation to those subjects who do not ... conform to their edicts' (ibid., p. 160). In aesthetic discourse, then, the relative intolerance characteristic of all discourses of value effectively 'becomes absolute' (ibid., p. 165). Hence, Bennett's rejection of all such notions of aesthetic value, whether Leavisite or Marxist. Thus far, the case against aesthetics seems theoretically unassailable. But in the book's fourth and concluding part, Bennett developed an essentially parallel critique of Marxist literary criticism, which radically called into question, not only more conventionally Marxist versions of critical practice, but also, if only by implication, Williams's own. Bennett's argument is that critics like Eagleton, Said and Jameson each in effect replicate an original Arnoldian, and later Leavisite, sense of the proper 'function of criticism'. In short, they have tended 'to re-align criticism with a totalising conception of social and cultural critique' (ibid., p. 194). They thus aspire to secure a political relevance for criticism 'by going back to being what it once was - a set of interpretive procedures oriented towards the transformation of the consciousness of individual subjects' (ibid., p. 195). This was, of course, the established function of Foucault's 'universal intellectual'. For Bennett himself, by contrast, the Foucauldian notion of the 'specific intellectual' demands 'more specific and localised assessments of the effects of practices of textual commentary conducted in the light of the institutionally circumscribed fields of their social deployment' (ibid., p. 10). Rather than denounce the world, he proposed to reform the university - and as much else of the culture industries as seemed practically reformable.

There is some limited overlap between Bennett's position here and that deployed in *Marxism and Literature*, and again in *Keywords*, where Williams indicts criticism as 'ideological', on the grounds that it 'actively prevents that understanding of response which does not assume the habit (or right or duty) of judgement' (Williams, 1976a, p. 76). Both Bennett and Williams envisage criticism's supersession by a kind of Cultural Studies that will be essentially sociological in character. Their different understandings of sociality nonetheless point towards very different kinds of cultural sociology. As Williams makes clear in the *Politics and Letters* interviews, his own objections to criticism are levelled, not so much at judgement *per se*, which seems to him 'inevitable', but at the peculiar 'pseudo-impersonality' of literary-critical judgement (Williams, 1979a, pp. 334-6). Indeed, his generally humanist reading of the importance of social agency and of social consciousness, as also his continuing sense of class loyalty, actually required non-specialist, value judgements of a more or less explicit kind. For if the long revolution is to be continued, then everyday arguments, about culture and society, politics and letters, must succeed in changing people's minds, that is, 'transforming' the 'consciousness of individual subjects'. There is quite simply no other way to proceed for a politics that will not only be democratic, but also inspired, as it were, 'from below'. For Bennett, by contrast, a 'specific intelligentsia' can effectively prosecute an essentially technocratic micropolitics 'from above'. Cultural policy studies will thus stand in relation to Cultural Studies much as Fabian social engineering had to sociology. Bennett aspires, in short, to examine 'the truth/power symbiosis which characterises particular regions of social management - with a view not only to undoing that symbiosis but also ... installing a new one in its place' (1990, p. 270).

If *Outside Literature* was essentially a work of negative critique, its positive corollary, the case for cultural policy studies as distinct from that against post-literary criticism, is outlined in *Culture: A Reformer's Science*. Here, Bennett argues that culture has become 'so deeply governmentalised' that it no longer makes sense to think of it 'as a ground situated outside the domain of government ... through which that domain might be resisted' (1998, p. 30). The New Left's understanding of higher and secondary education, as more or less freely available to the political project of groups of intellectuals, is simply politically naïve, he cautions: 'the institutions and spaces of public education are ... contexts which necessarily confer their own logic and social direction on the work that is conducted within them' (ibid., p. 49). It follows, then, that Cultural Studies must set aside cultural critique, so as to lay stake to some definite set of 'knowledge claims and method-ological procedures' convertible into practically utilisable 'clearly defined skills and trainings' (Bennett, 1998, p. 52). In practice, he con-cludes, these skills and trainings will need to be policy-oriented: 'intel-lectuals working in cultural studies needed to begin to "talk to the ISAs" - that is Althusser's famous Ideological State Apparatuses' (ibid., p. 33). This, then, is what Bennett means by 'disciplining' Cultural Studies: 'The destiny, if not the mission, of cultural studies may thus, in the long haul, prove to be that of allowing everyday life and cultural experience to be fashioned into instruments of govern-ment via their inscription in new forms of teaching and training' (ibid., p. 51). No doubt, Bennett is right to insist that the changing norms and practices of secondary school English teaching were more important than the New Left as a primary 'conditioning context' of British Cultural Studies (ibid., p. 49). But it was the New Left's intervention into this context, nonetheless, that provided Cultural Studies with its initial subject matter and with its founding texts. No doubt, Bennett is right to define the object of study in Cultural Studies as 'the relations of culture and power' (ibid., p. 53). But these relations can be cri-tiqued, as well as studied or serviced. No doubt, any institutionalised pedagogy must have something in particular to offer to its students. But the inference Bennett draws, that the relevant skills and training need necessarily be policy-oriented, seems unwarranted. In practice, these competencies are surely more likely to be of use in secondary school-teaching, where the linkage of literature (the novel, anyway) and the mass media (especially the press, film and television) has become increasingly commonplace. Bennett himself is determined that Cultural Studies should not become 'the heir of literary studies in its English formation', a prospect he finds positively 'depressing' (ibid., p. 52). No doubt, for Bennett, as for Hall, this hostility provides the basis for a perfectly adequate theorisation of their own personal career paths and biographical choices: both were trained in English Literature, both moved into Cultural Studies, both eventually became Professors of Sociology. Depressing or not, and turning Bennett's 'tough-mindedness' against itself, I will hazard the prediction that Cultural Studies is more likely to evolve in a post-literary than in a sub-sociological direction. And this is so for reasons that Bennett would readily accept: because 'Literature', constructed as the antithet-ical 'Other' of print and other 'fictions', is already a theoretically inde-fensible category; and because state education systems will nonethe-lesss still be required to educate, in one way or another, the subjectiv-ities of their populations.

In *The Politics of Modernism*, Williams had asked exasperatedly of cultural theory: 'Is there never to be an end to petit-bourgeois theorists making long-term adjustments to short-term situations?' (Williams, 1989a, p. 175). I doubt that he had Bennett in mind here, though the immediately preceding reference to Thatcherism could be read as pointing towards Hall. But clearly, both Bennett and Hall were deeply implicated in the theoretical moment of (post-) structuralism, which Williams's polemic takes as its target. Moreover, these more general theoretical objections are at one point quite specifically directed at Cultural Studies and at the Open University (ibid., p. 157). Whatever Williams's own intentions, it seems to me that Bennett and Hall have indeed made long-term theoretical adjustments to what were actually short-term political situations.[4] Bennett himself is clearly sensitive to this charge and has addressed it very directly. 'In the political and cultural situations which now exist in the societies where cultural studies has made some headway', he writes: 'the long-term vision that Williams proposes ... loses its coherence and purchase. For this particular petit-bourgeois theorist ... the issue is not one of making long-term adjustments to short-term situations, but of making long-term adjustments because the long-term situation itself now has to be thought in new ways' (Bennett, 1998, p. 37). The matter at issue thus hinges on how we read the long-term, rather than on how we read Williams. This in turn devolves into two analytically distinct questions: the relative cultural significance attaching to social class and the labour movement on the one hand, 'difference' and the new social movements on the other; and the role of the state in cultural management. Each of these provides Bennett with reason to think the new situation in his own new ways (Bennett, 1998, pp. 37, 30): in short, the business of Cultural Studies should be to negotiate and facilitate the relations between these various social interests and the state bureaucracies.

But Bennett seems to me mistaken on both counts. The new global 'anti-capitalist' movements serve to remind us that the aspiration to commonality and the effects of social class are of greater long-term political and cultural significance than 1990s notions of difference tended to suggest. And neither culture in general nor higher education in particular is anything like as 'governmentalised' as Bennett assumes. His notion of 'governmentality' refers to a far more explicitly 'statist' process than that identified in Foucault (Bennett, 1998, p. 144). But if governmentality is the work of the state in particular, rather than of power in general, then the most striking feature of postmodern late capitalism is surely its opposite: the commodification and consequent 'de-governmentalisation' of cultural texts, practices and institutions. I suspect that sober retrospective analysis will show that Thatcherite Toryism impinged much less on British popular consciousness than Hall sought to argue; but also that much less was achieved by way of cultural renovation under Australian Labor, even at the micropolitical level, than Bennett seemed to believe possible. A thoroughgoing cultural materialism such as Williams had established, which acknowledges the claims of agency *and* structure as neither structuralisms nor post-structuralisms were able to do, might well have spared Cultural Studies both sets of embarrassment.

Media, Culture and Society

Much closer to Williams's later work is the kind of cultural and media studies associated with Nicholas Garnham and his colleagues and former colleagues at the University of Westminster, the most influential probably being James Curran. Garnham himself is Professor of Media Studies and Founding Director of the Centre for Communication and Information Studies at Westminster, author of *Capitalism and Communication* and *Emancipation, the Media and Modernity* (Garnham, 1990; Garnham, 2000) and co-author of *The Economics of Television* (Collins et al., 1988). Curran, who moved from Westminster in 1985 to head the Department of Media and Communications at Goldsmiths' College in the University of London, is the co-author of *Power Without Responsibility* (Curran and Seaton, 1997), a highly acclaimed history of British press and broadcasting informed theoretically by a culturalist reading of Gramsci, and co-editor of such widely used media studies texts as *Cultural Studies and Communications* (Curran et al., 1996), *Mass Media and Society* (Curran and Gurevitch, 2000) and, more recently, *De-Westernizing Media Studies* (Curran and Park, 2000). Both were founding editors in 1979 of the Westminster house journal, *Media, Culture and Society*, which from its beginning included Williams, Hoggart and also Bourdieu in its editorial advisory board. The journal's opening manifesto, written by Curran, sought to place it in relation to an intellectual environment dominated, on the left, by the kind of theoreticist structural Marxism increasingly associated with Hall, Birmingham and the Open University, and on 'the right', by essentially empiricist studies of 'media effects'. The new journal, Curran promised, would favour neither orthodoxy, but would 'encourage research and debate within and between these two traditions' (Curran, 1979, p. 2). In retrospect, this appears more than a little disingenuous. As its editors would concede in 1986, *Media, Culture and Society* had then still published nothing from the 'media effects' tradition and nor did it intend to do so (Collins et al., 1986b, p. 2). Moreover, they continued, the journal 'was in large measure conceived as a counter-argument' to Althusserian and post-Althusserian structural Marxism (ibid., p. 4). Its distinctive contribution, they now acknowledged, was a stress, first, on the ways in which culture is produced, and second, on media and communication policy viewed, not from a technical or administrative vantage point, but from that of a 'critical intelligentsia', serving a 'democratic public interest' (ibid., pp. 4-5). Though there is no explicit reference to Williams here, this is nonetheless more or less exactly the project identified in his own later work.

The *Media, Culture and Society* approach has on occasion been represented as little more than a return to Marxist 'political economy'

(Turner, 1996, pp. 180-1). But this is, surely, a misrepresentation of a developing position which owes at least as much to cultural materialism as to historical materialism. Even Garnham's most aggressively political-economic critique of the Birmingham tradition, first published in the journal in 1979, actually takes as its theoretical starting point Williams's *Marxism and Literature* (Garnham, 1990, p. 20). Even Colin Sparks, perhaps the most orthodoxly Marxist of the *Media, Culture and Society* editors, viewed Williams's work as establishing 'valuable and progressive positions' (1980, p. 134). In the 1979 essay cited above, Garnham had, in fact, expressed some reservation about Williams's position: it 'suffers from a misleading reductionism by failing to distinguish between the material and the economic' (Garnham, 1990, p. 25). The criticism seems to me misdirected, for, as we have seen, Williams made exactly this distinction and, indeed, made use of it in ways which clearly anticipate Garnham's own interests. In any case, the following year Garnham and Williams were to work closely together on a special issue of *Media, Culture and Society*, intended as an introduction for English-speaking audiences to Bourdieu's sociology of culture (Garnham, 1980; Garnham and Williams, 1986). By 1983, moreover, Garnham was happy to assert a much closer identification between his work and Williams. Arguing against both media effects research and structural Marxism as sharing a common idealism, he insisted on the need for a 'major shift in perspective and emphasis', within media and Cultural Studies, towards 'what is coming to be called ... cultural materialism' (Garnham, 1983, p. 321). Garnham's emphases here on 'the irreducible material determinants of the social process of symbolic exchange', as also on the need for communication scholars 'both as citizens and scholars ... to decide ... which side they are on' (ibid., p. 329), are each deeply reminiscent of Williams.

It would be absurd to suggest that every single article in every single issue of *Media, Culture and Society* is somehow directly inspired by Williams. But it is not absurd to suggest that the journal's continuing project derives direct theoretical inspiration from that stress on cultural production which distinguished *Marxism and Literature* and *Culture*; nor that its substantive focus is still very much that defined in *Communications* and *Television: Technology and Cultural Form*. It is in such studies of the institutional production of culture, rather than in postmodern textualism or in technocratic cultural policy studies, that Williams's central theoretical legacy seems the more fully present. Moreover, this legacy continues to be invoked in various of the journal's position statements: a 1991 editorial described him as 'the single most important writer in the development of cultural theory in Britain' (Corner, 1991a, p. 134); the lead article by Garnham, introducing a 1995 special issue on intellectuals, deliberately cited Williams's commitment to the role of the 'critical intellectual' in opposition to the 'widespread defenestration of the intellectual' in postmodernism (Garnham, 1995a, pp. 371-3). Garnham's antipathy towards the increasingly postmodernist character of contemporary Cultural Studies clearly echoes Williams's own. This, too, has become characteristic of the journal's wider project. As three of Garnham's colleagues insisted in another position statement: 'This project ... is incompatible with the philosophical basis of postmodernism' (Scannell et al., 1992, p. 3). Here, however, the argument is couched in distinctly Habermasian terms, as a defence of Enlightenment reason against postmodern irrationalism and of the 'public sphere' against the globalisation of the cultural market (ibid., pp. 3, 13; cf. Habermas, 1985; Habermas, 1989). But an analogous case could have been derived from Williams, as a defence, respectively, of the long revolution and the common culture. We shall return to this comparison between Williams and Habermas in Chapter 7. For the moment, suffice it to note that Habermas's own initial theorisation of the social structures of the public sphere itself owed something to Williams's *Culture and Society* (Habermas, 1989, pp. 37, 258n).

In the mid-1980s, Garnham had explicitly described his work as 'cultural materialist'. During the 1990s, he would continue to invoke Williams's legacy against the postmodernisation of Cultural Studies (Garnham, 1995b, pp. 62-3; Garnham, 1997, p. 57). But both his own position and that of the journal more generally were defined increasingly in relation to Habermasian critical sociology, rather than cultural materialism. For both, the major implied difference with Williams seemed to be over the status of the 'literary'. Garnham clearly found the latter's interest in literature perplexing: witness his complaint that Williams's key insights should be 'hidden in a book of literary theory' (Garnham, 1990, p. 20).[5] The journal persistently ignored literary texts, as part of its more general aversion to textual analysis, and also the institutions of literary production, which might reasonably be considered to fall within the remit of its political economy.[6] In my view, it was at fault on both counts. If the textualism of post-Birmingham Cultural Studies is indeed open to objection, then this is best countered, surely, by a fully elaborated account of cultural process, which would necessarily include the textual moment, as well as analysis of the conditions of its institutional production, distribution and reception. The academic division of labour aside - and this is neither a good reason nor one actually advanced by Garnham - an exclusively institutional focus makes very little sense: institutions matter culturally only because they produce texts; and texts matter culturally because they mean something. As to the literary mode of production, this is as significant a part of the late-capitalist communications system as any other and one increasingly dominated by the same international conglomerates that control the other media. Again, it makes very little sense to pretend either that literature does not exist or that it occupies some altogether different, institutional and discursive space.

In addition to these quasi-empirical objections, we need to note how literature figured in Williams as a site for what Jones has termed '"emancipatory" ideology critique', that is, the immanent analysis of the 'emancipatory promise' inherent in the utopian claims of ideologies, a promise which can turn them into a 'court of critical appeal' rather than ideological legitimation (Jones, 1999, pp. 43-4). This procedure is as central to Williams's criticism, Jones observes, as it is to Adorno or to Marcuse. Garnham's own commitment to social critique is, of course, long-standing, but his work tends to underestimate the intimate connection in Williams between critique and criticism. There is a peculiar irony here, given Garnham's own recent interest in the role of the 'aesthetic' as a counterweight to postmodern relativism: *Emancipation, the Media and Modernity* makes impressive use of a variant of post-Kantian discourse ethics to ground a non-relativist aesthetic, at one point oddly reminiscent of Leavis (Garnham, 2000, p. 162). This is a necessary labour, I would argue, and one long overdue for *Media, Culture and Society*. Its conclusion, that we need to move the argument towards 'the development of a common culture and a respect for those cultural differences ... that have been tested in comparison with alternative interpretations and evaluations' might have been Williams's own. 'Within such a process', Garnham continues, 'the media ... are of crucial importance as the public sphere within which ... such a *sensus communis* can be created' (ibid., p. 164).

This is indeed what will be entailed in any effective resumption of the long revolution, but on the condition: first, that we understand the common culture as achievable only through a radical democratisation of the major economic, political and cultural institutions; and second, that we understand the arts themselves as media crucial to the making of any such culture. In principle, no doubt, Garnham would readily accede to both stipulations. So habitual are the assumptions of even very recent academic specialisation, however, that he barely registers the unnecessary slippage, the avoidable reduction, in the shift from a theoretical reaffirmation of William's 'deeply unfashionable' belief in the value of 'inherited artistic traditions' to a practical concern with 'evaluative judgements of media content' (Garnham, 2000, pp. 146-7), where the term 'media' is clearly intended as exclusive of the arts. There has been much of value in *Media, Culture and Society*, but much, too, that is merely the routinised product of routine academic 'research'. If the academy as culture industry warrants critique, both in itself and in its deep and growing complicity with the dominant culture industries, then a deconstruction of the category 'media' would be as good a place to begin as any.

Back to the Future - or Backs to the Wall?

Williams's theoretical legacy has been enormously influential and it remains powerfully present, even if at times unacknowledged, in each of the areas that concerned us in this chapter: first, the kind of self-declared 'Cultural Studies', cast in the postmodern, post-Birmingham mode, at once both textualist and populist, which tends increasingly to occupy the commanding heights of the new discipline, if only by virtue of its successful importation into the United States by Grossberg and others; second, the kind of sub-sociological 'cultural policy studies', apolitical in content and technocratic in form, reimported into Britain from Australia by Bennett; third, the kind of 'materialist' media sociology, or political economy of the media, championed by Garnham, Curran and others loosely associated with *Media, Culture and Society*. Although only the first of these enjoins an explicit cultural populism, all three tend in practice to ignore 'the arts' in the sense that Williams understood the term. For the development of a Cultural Studies approach to art and literature, we need to look elsewhere, to the body of work addressed in the chapter that follows. In the meantime, however, we should register how much Williams had argued against these specialisations and sub-specialisations, whether between politics and letters, between minority culture and mass civilisation, or between textual, institutional and policy analysis. It would be a mistake to dignify with the pathos of *Kulturpessimismus* what is, in large measure, merely an institutional effect of the sociology of the academy. But I am unavoidably reminded, nonetheless, of Adorno's insistence to Benjamin that avant-garde art and popular cinema were the 'torn halves of an integral freedom, to which however they do not add up' (Adorno, 1980, p. 123). Judged by Williams's own standards - by our capacity to name and make possible a common recognition of whether particular ways of thinking bear the seeds of life or of death - these specialisations, and their attendant institutionalisations, their conferences, journals and chairs, their pelf and place, represent at least as much an obstacle as a means to the creation of a common culture, at least as much a retreat as an advance from Williams's cultural materialism.

The proper response to this situation is surely to attempt to reverse these specialisations, in the hope of recovering for Cultural Studies something at least of its original intellectual purchase and political promise. This is certainly the import of much in Hoggart's later writings, as also in those of Williams's biographer, Fred Inglis. Hence, for example, Hoggart's insistence that 'no one who is not able to read *Persuasion* closely, to speak analytically and imaginatively about it, can be trusted to "read" television soap operas'; or that an 'achieved democracy must work for critical literacy, must believe that very many more in all parts of society can be encouraged towards that level; must bank on their own and others' potentialities' (1995, pp. 176, 336). Even more unfashionably, Inglis has defined Cultural Studies as 'the study of how to live well and do right in the narrative station to which chance has called each of us' (1993, p. 247). They are both right and in exactly the sense that Inglis intends by this word. But, in both, the force of the reaction against relativism threatens to drag us back to the (not so left) 'culturalism' of the 1950s. So, in what might be Hoggart's own contribution to 'the myth of Raymond Hoggart', the Williams respectfully cited as colleague and contemporary in *The Way We Live Now* turns out to have said 'much the same thing' as T.S. Eliot about culture and to have known in advance that cultural materialism could lead one 'astray' (Hoggart, 1995, pp. 108, 84). Moreover, this Williams is clearly preferable to that other Williams, who had thought there were no masses, but only manipulative ways of seeing people as masses (ibid., p. 243). My point is, not so much that Hoggart disagrees with Williams, but rather that he tends to represent the real substance of the latter's work as much closer to his own than it ever actually was.

This is yet more evident and even more of a problem in Inglis's *Raymond Williams*, a book intended as an act 'of homage' and 'practical judgement' (1995, p. 307). It is both, no doubt, but there is a very clear pattern, nonetheless, to the distribution of homage and critical judgement: Inglis is good on Pandy, Cambridge and the War, and warmly appreciative of Williams as a man, as left-Leavisite literary critic and as Old New Left activist; but he visibly recoils from his subject wherever Williams failed to live his life as if he were Raymond Hoggart. So the *May Day Manifesto* is 'richly impossible' and even 'plain comic'; *The Country and the City* abuses 'local knowledge and experience' to the advantage of 'grand theory' or 'mere propaganda'; cultural materialism is both a 'ringing oxymoron' and 'redundant'; and, as we have seen, *Marxism and Literature* is simply 'unreadable' (ibid., pp. 199, 239, 249). As Jim McGuigan observed in the *New Left Review*: 'it is ... perplexing how low an opinion Inglis finally has of Williams's most important books' (1996, p. 105). It becomes less perplexing, however, when one realises that what Inglis most admires in Williams is, by and large, what the latter most shared with Hoggart; and that there was much less of this than either Inglis or Hoggart or even Hall seemed to realise. I suspect that Inglis would have written - and probably should still write - a much better book about Hoggart than about Williams. The details of the differences between Williams and Hoggart have been well documented elsewhere (Jones, 1994, pp. 398-406). But the most fundamental of these, it seems to me, is that to which Hoggart himself pointed in a 1990 interview with *Media, Culture and Society*. Asked about the idea of a common culture, he replied that: 'Actually, that phrase was Raymond's ... much more than mine. I always had some difficulties with it ... My starting point ... was always the separation, the enormous separation between the educated and the rest in this society' (Corner, 1991a/b, p. 150). Hence, Hoggart's enduring commitment to Coleridge's notion of a 'clerisy', which Williams had rejected as early as *Culture and Society* (Hoggart, 1995, pp. 300-1; Williams, 1963, pp. 235, 248-50). But, for all Hoggart's pessimism and Inglis's supposed realism, this will not do, not at all. The immediate prospects might appear dim for a democratic common culture of the kind to which Williams aspired, but, as anyone who worked as a professional 'intellectual' in the last quarter of the twentieth century should surely realise, those for a Coleridgean clerisy, Arnoldian 'remnant' or Leavisite 'sensitive minority' have been altogether extinguished. The remorseless commitment to cultural commodification in both Thatcherism and New Labour - and their equivalents in my own country and elsewhere - have radically reduced the immediately practical prospects for the creation of a common culture. But insofar as there is still hope, then it must lie with the continuation of the long revolution, rather than in a recoil against the present such as is implied in Hoggart and Inglis. To borrow Benjamin's Brechtian maxim: 'Don't start from the good old things but the bad new ones' (Benjamin, 1973b, p. 121).

Notes

1 Sparks's criticism is directed from a more or less conventionally Marxist perspective. But Brennon Wood has made much the same point from within sociology, as distinct from Marxism: 'Struggles (or consensus) over meaning do not exhaustively constitute reality; rather, culture operates as part of the social totality. The interpretation of culture refers meaning not only to further meanings (i.e. to discourse) but also to other institutionalized social relations' (1998, p. 410).

2 The misreading is also taken over by Bennett (1998, p. 26).

3 But it is interesting to note that Bennett's most sustained encounter with cultural policy (Bennett et al., 1999) makes absolutely no reference to Williams.

4 Bennett acknowledges that cultural policy studies remains indebted to distinctly 'Australian traditions of government', which 'have historically tended to be more strongly directive and utilitarian - more Benthamite, even - than those associated with British forms of liberal government' (1998, p. 7). It seems to me that a more general predisposition toward utilitarianism was compounded in this instance by immediate political circumstances as specific and particular as those which provoked Hall to the diagnosis of 'authoritarian populism': during the 1980s, while the British Labour Party languished in opposition, the Australian Labor Party won four successive general elections.

5 The original 1979 version of the essay actually read 'hidden, gnomically, in a book of literary theory' (Garnham, 1986, p. 9).

6 In its first 22 years, *Media, Culture and Society* devoted only one issue to literary production (Lorimer and Scannell, 1993).

6

Rethinking Minority Culture

I was not ... oppressed by Cambridge. I was not cast down by old buildings, for I had come from a country with twenty centuries of history written visibly into the earth: I liked walking through a Tudor court, but it did not make me feel raw. I was not amazed by the existence of a place of learning; I had always known the cathedral, and the bookcases I now sit to work at in Oxford are of the same design as those in the chained library. Nor was learning, in my family, some strange eccentricity: I was not, on a scholarship in Cambridge, a new kind of animal up a brand-new ladder. Learning was ordinary; we learned where we could. Always, from those scattered white houses, it has made sense to go out and become a scholar or a poet or a teacher. Yet few of us could be spared from the immediate work; a price had been set on this kind of learning, and it was more, much more, than we could individually pay. Now, when we could pay in common, it was a good, ordinary life. (Williams, 'Culture is Ordinary')

The entire direction of Williams's effort pointed towards a radical decentring of 'Literature', and its eventual supersession into a more general 'cultural sociology'. As Jonathan Dollimore, a self-proclaimed cultural materialist, but also a professor of English Literature, has rightly commented, theory such as this makes possible 'a truly inter-disciplinary approach to - some might say exit from - the subject' (1994a, p. 2). That said, we need to note both that much of Williams's work was indeed conducted within what would conventionally be regarded as literary or drama studies; and that his intellectual influence in these areas has remained substantial. From the mid-1960s onwards, in literary studies as in Cultural Studies, the newly imported continental European 'Theory', whether Western Marxist, structuralist or post-structuralist, came into direct and immediate conflict with an already dominant culturalism. But, whereas Cultural Studies had been, in part, the effect of a rupture within culturalism, a rupture clearly marked by *The Uses of Literacy* and *The Long Revolution*, literary studies proper remained very much the domain of a more or less unreconstructed Leavisism. If culturalist resistances to Theory were greater in English than elsewhere, so too were the issues at stake, at least in England itself. As has been argued on more than one occasion, the discipline of English studies had been constructed as occupying a peculiarly central location within the English national culture (Anderson, 1992, pp. 96-7; Baldick, 1983, p. 95; Doyle, 1982, p. 17). The nationalism, which we noted in Chapter 2 as characteristic of Leavisism, was at once both constitutive of and constituted by this centrality. The incursion of Theory, sometimes radical and always foreign, into what had been widely understood as the very heart of the national culture, thus precipitated what Peter Widdowson rightly termed a 'crisis in English studies': 'a question, posed from within, as to what English *is*, where it has got to, whether it has a future, whether it *should* have a future as a discrete discipline, and if it does, in what ways it might be reconstituted' (Widdowson, 1982, p. 7). Williams's cultural materialism had been one of a number of theoretical positions, and the only one from within the discipline, which had decisively contributed to the formulation of precisely such questions as these.

Cultural Materialism and the Crises in English Studies

The crisis in English studies was acted out in a number of different institutional and discursive spaces: in the 'Sociology of Literature' conferences organised annually from 1976 to 1984 by Francis Barker and his colleagues from the Department of Literature at Essex University; in the journal, *Literature and History*, edited in its first incarnation from 1975 to 1988 by Widdowson and others in the School of Humanities at Thames Polytechnic; in the more specifically literary interventions of socialist or feminist journals such as the *New Left Review* or *Feminist Review*; and, at least as a source of theoretical provocation, in the film studies journal, *Screen*. At a slightly later date, a self-proclaimed 'third generation' of radical literary theorists would coalesce around Oxford English Limited and the journal, *News From Nowhere*. At much the same time, recognisable 'schools' of 'cultural materialist' or 'new historicist' criticism began to emerge in Britain and the United States respectively, becoming especially influential in Renaissance studies. If the crisis had begun with that rupture within culturalism, from which Cultural Studies had emerged, then it proceeded thereafter through four reasonably well defined stages. In the first, the radical critique was overwhelmingly Marxist in character, its own internal debates in effect a confrontation between culturalist and structuralist Marxisms, represented respectively by Williams and Althusser. This was the point at which both *Literature and History* and the Essex conferences were launched; the point at which Hall could affirm, in his opening contribution to the first such conference, that 'every one of these developments has, in some way or another, been generated by Marxism' (Hall, 1976, p. 5). Williams's own position, poised somewhere between an earlier left culturalism and a not quite fully realised cultural materialism, still remained actively in play with these other, more explicitly Althusserian Marxisms, best represented in literary studies by Eagleton. Williams himself presented to the second Essex conference a paper which deployed his own theoretical distinction between dominant, residual and emergent with some panache (Williams, 1977b). He was from the beginning an editorial adviser to *Literature and History*, though, unlike Eagleton, never actually a contributor. He wrote regularly for the *New Left Review*, though the journal's increasingly Althusserian tenor must then have seemed better suited to Eagleton's work. In the second stage, during the late 1970s and early 1980s, we witness an interesting reversal, by which Williams's own work had now become more declaredly Marxist, while at much the same time Althusserian structuralism had imploded in on itself, leaving behind a legacy of variously Derridean, Foucauldian and Lacanian post-structuralisms. This is the theoretical moment of *Screen* and the occasion for Williams's development of cultural materialism, from *Marxism and Literature* through to *Culture*. This is also the political moment of a kind of radical feminism, often determinedly post-structuralist in its theoretical predilections, to which Williams would respond with some difficulty.

The third stage is that from the late 1970s until shortly after Williams's death, in which his work seemed to attract an increasing audience both amongst erstwhile Althusserian recidivists, Eagleton included, and amongst the still younger generation of scholars represented by Oxford English Limited. As the latter group affirmed in 1989: 'The whole project of Oxford English Limited from its inception owed much to Williams ... with Williams dead, who is there now to send one's books to?' (Oxford English Limited, 1989, p. 10). This third stage entailed more than mere piety toward a 'grand old man of the left', though there was certainly some of that, for example, in press commentary on Williams's political role within the Socialist Society, from 1982 on. It represented, rather, a serious theoretical shift towards a recognisable cultural materialism, the formation of a distinct theoretical tendency such as the young Eagleton had eagerly anticipated, but which Williams had sought to avoid (Eagleton, 1985, pp. 131-2). In addition to Williams himself, Dollimore cites as instances of such work: Terry Lovell, Janet Wolff, Eagleton, and his own co-editor, Alan Sinfield (Dollimore, 1994a, p. 15n; Lovell, 1980; Wolff, 1993; Eagleton, 1996a; Sinfield, 1983). Both Lovell and Wolff continued to combine a broadly cultural materialist theoretical position with distinctly feminist politics (Lovell, 1987, p. 5; Wolff, 1990, p. 5). As for Eagleton, some-thing close to his final judgement would be that written for the 1989 *Critical Perspectives* volume: 'Williams ... refused to be distracted by the wilder flights of Althusserian or post-structuralist theory and was still there, ready and waiting for us, when some of us younger theorists, sadder and wiser, finally re-emerged from one or two cul-de-sacs to rejoin him where we had left off' (Eagleton, 1989c, p. 6). The fourth and final stage runs from shortly after Williams's death until the pres-ent and is characterised by a peculiar process of simultaneous remem-brance and forgetting. On the one hand, Williams's theoretical legacy has been both institutionalised and memorialised in the cultural mate-rialist literary criticism of Dollimore, Sinfield and Holderness in Britain and in the new historicist criticism of Greenblatt, Gallagher and others in the United States; on the other, this has been effected at the price of a certain dilution of what was sometimes most specific to Williams's own argument, most obviously by way of the repeated resort to Foucault.

Easthope distinguished two main currents in what he termed British 'post-structuralist' literary theory: first, the kind of textual 'deconstruction' pursued by Colin MacCabe and Catherine Belsey (Belsey, 1980), which sought to analyse the ways in which the text makes available to the reader certain definable subject positions; and second, the kind of 'institutional' analysis, pursued most notably by Eagleton, but also by Bennett, which sought to problematise the insti-tutional conditions of the production of textual meaning. The latter is what Easthope meant by 'left deconstruction' (1988, p. 153). These are what Felperin referred to as 'textualist' and 'contextualist' versions of post-structuralism, which he associated with the work of Derrida and Foucault respectively (1985, pp. 71-2). This formulation seems appro-priate both to the North American and the Australian intellectual con-texts, at least during the 1980s: textualist deconstruction, such as his own in Australia or that of the Yale school in the United States, was by and large Derridean; contextualist deconstruction, such as that of Frow in Australia (Frow, 1986) or Greenblatt in the United States, by and large Foucauldian. But, as Easthope rightly stressed, MacCabe and Belsey had worked with a style of deconstruction that derived at least as much from Althusser, by way of *Screen*, as from Derrida (Easthope, 1988, pp. 134-5). Where Easthope was mistaken, it seems to me, was to see 'left deconstruction' as essentially Foucauldian. For, in Britain, this kind of work had derived its inspiration at least as much from Williams as from Foucault, and was thus not so much post-structural-ist as 'post-culturalist'.

The text in which Eagleton, for example, most clearly retracted his earlier Althusserian structuralism (Eagleton, 1981, p. 97), is precisely where he also: dismisses the Anglophone reception of Foucault as pro-viding 'a glamorous rationale for erstwhile revolutionaries unnerved into pessimism' (ibid., p. 58); comments on Derridean deconstruction that 'only a powerless petty-bourgeois intelligentsia would raise it to the solemn dignity of a philosophy' (ibid., p. 142); but attributes to Williams 'bold efforts to shift attention from the analysis of an object named "literature" to the social relations of cultural practice' (ibid., p. 97). Bennett's *Formalism and Marxism* was similarly indebted to Williams, rather than to Foucault (Bennett, 1979, pp. 13-16); and, insofar as the much later *Outside Literature* and *Culture: A Reformer's Science*, are indeed Foucauldian, then this represents a very significant theoretical shift on Bennett's part. Even Easthope credited Williams's 'Base and Superstructure' essay, a text which betrays not the slightest evidence of interest in Foucault, as the original source for left deconstruction in Britain (1988, p. 14). No doubt there are, as Dollimore has stressed, certain very clear affinities between cultural materialism and the new historicism (1994a, p. 3). But it was simply perverse for Easthope, writing in an expressly British context, to reduce the former to the latter. He was right, nonetheless, to contrast the line running from Williams, with that from Althusser, through *Screen*. From 1971, when its editorial board had been reconstructed around Sam Rohdie, *Screen*, the journal of the Society for Education in Film and Television (SEFT), had become the effective intellectual centre, initially for 'cultural' Althusserianism, later for textualist post-structuralism. Its influence extended well beyond the specialist area of film studies and, through MacCabe, even into Cambridge English studies.

The Structuralist Controversy, Williams and MacCabe

During the late 1970s and early 1980s, the developing hostilities within Cambridge English, between traditional literary humanism and radical (post-) structuralism, finally erupted into a strangely public 'structuralist controversy', providing the British with a rehearsal for what would later become the American 'culture wars'. The immediate matter at issue had been the appointment in 1976 of MacCabe, then a young Althusserian-inclined film theorist, to an Assistant Lectureship in English, and the subsequent bitterly fought disputes over whether the position would be upgraded to a permanent Lectureship. The eventual outcome during 1980-81 included: the failure of MacCabe's application for promotion; a decision by the English Faculty to remove the two most distinguished members, Williams and Frank Kermode, from its appointments committee; and a two-day special meeting of the University Senate to discuss the state of the English Faculty. Rejected by Cambridge, MacCabe went on to work in Scottish and American universities and eventually to become Director of Research at the British Film Institute. He has continued to write on film and lingistics (MacCabe, 1999), though less prolifically than these high-profile beginnings might have led one to expect. MacCabe was in any case perhaps only an incidental target for Christopher Ricks and the

Cambridge 'humanists'. As Lisa Jardine later observed: 'The MacCabe affair was intellectually null ... Ricks wasn't interested in politics, just in literary criticism. He was hostile, therefore, to Williams and Kermode so he went for MacCabe, who wasn't cut out to be an intellectual' (Inglis, 1995, p. 285). Neither Kermode nor Williams were in any obvious sense 'structuralists'. Indeed, Williams's own response to literary structuralism had been highly sceptical, as he would himself later recall: 'When this tendency ... appeared as an import from France in the sixties, I even risked saying that it seemed strange only because it was a long-lost cousin who had emigrated from Cambridge in the late twenties and early thirties' (Williams, 1984b, p. 206). But they had both attempted to engage in some sort of productive encounter with contemporary French theory, thereby ensuring the animosity of much mainstream English 'thought' (cf. MacCabe, 1985, pp. 17-31).

There is no doubting the practical effort at solidarity made on MacCabe's behalf by Williams. We need to remind ourselves, nonetheless, of the very considerable differences between their respective theoretical positions. MacCabe's training had been in English Literature and, though now better known for his work in cinema studies, he had written a radically structuralist and, as it turned out, deeply controversial study of Joyce. Theoretically, MacCabe's work sought to explain how different kinds of text differently position their readers: the revolutionary implications of Joyce's writing were thus in the way it 'produces a change in the relations between reader and text' (MacCabe, 1978, p. 1). Substantively, this led to a sustained assault on literary and cinematic 'realism', which threatened no less than a dramatic reversal of the then conventional polarities of pre-existing cultural radicalisms. Both orthodoxly Communist Marxism and Lukácsian 'critical' Marxism had typically privileged literary realism as against 'bourgeois' modernism (Lukács, 1963). Moreover, quite apart from Communist dogma, many radical writers and film-makers had strongly believed in the potentially subversive effect of realistic technique: by virtue of its capacity to expose to public view previously hidden aspects of contemporary social reality, realism, it was believed, could quite literally 'raise the consciousness' of its audiences. French post-structuralism had developed a powerful critique of such literary realisms, however, deriving in the first place from Barthes's distinction between readerly and writerly texts, that is, respectively, those which position the reader as passive consumer and those which demand that the reader actively participate as co-author of the text (Barthes, 1974, p. 4). In somewhat analogous terms, MacCabe argued that 'the classic realist text' positions the reading subject in what he called a 'relation of dominant specularity', that is, in terms of a relationship between the subject and the real, in which the real 'is not articulated - it is'. The structure of the classic realist text, MacCabe concluded, is to be found both in the bourgeois novel and in film, and it is one which, ironically, 'cannot deal with the real in its contradiction because of the unques-

tioned status of the representation at the level of the dominant discourse' (1985, p. 39). Echoing Barthes and invoking Brecht (Brecht,
1980), in direct defiance of the Lukácsian tradition, MacCabe insisted
on the essential conservatism of such formal realisms. The texts of
mass culture and high culture alike thus reveal a single underlying
structure which functions so as to secure mass subservience to the
dominant ideological discourse. Though MacCabe himself acquired a
very public status during the Cambridge version of the 'structuralist
controversy', we should note that such anti-realist nostrums were, in
fact, widely current at the time in radical intellectual circles.

Williams's own position, by contrast, represented what John
Docker has rightly termed a 'challenge to screen studies'. Docker cites
Television: Technology and Cultural Form, referring to the ways in which
Williams demonstrates, in defiance of *Screen* Theory, the clearly non-
realist basis of much popular television (1989, pp. 132-3). This is certainly so, though it was by no means Williams's express intention to
argue thus against *Screen*. More to the point is Williams's much more
sympathetic and much more historically nuanced account of literary
and cultural realism itself. Though certainly no dogmatically
Lukácsian socialist realist, there was an important sense, nonetheless,
in which Williams's own literary sympathies, both practical and critical, were at least on occasion of a distinctly realist kind. If the term has
any literary-critical purchase at all, then the first two novels of
Williams's Welsh trilogy (Williams, 1960; Williams, 1964) are clearly
'realist' in character; in *The Long Revolution*, he had concluded his
chapter on the contemporary novel with an insistence that 'a new realism is necessary, if we are to remain creative' (Williams, 1965, p. 316);
and his work on the drama had, of course, been preoccupied throughout with the 'naturalistic revolution'. In a lecture first delivered to a
SEFT/*Screen* weekend school in 1976, and shortly thereafter published
in the journal itself, Williams had mounted a spirited defence of realism, and did so moreover in ways that deliberately endorsed self-consciously radical, realist television, in this instance Allen, Garnett and
Loach's *The Big Flame*. Though MacCabe was nowhere cited by name,
the argument is very pointedly directed against analyses such as his.
Realism, Williams argued, is much better understood in terms of intention, specifically the threefold intention to social extension, historical
contemporaneity and secular action, than in terms of any particular
formal method (Williams, 1989c, pp. 228-9). Furthermore, whenever
we move to the level of specific analysis, he continued, both methods
and intentions are highly variable. The point, then, is not to reduce
realism to a particular formal method, as MacCabe had done, but to
pursue the 'analysis of a developing dramatic form and its variations'
(ibid., p. 239).

Despite MacCabe's, and *Screen's*, repeated invocation of Brecht, it is
clear in retrospect that it was Williams, the drama scholar, who was
actually the more properly Brechtian. For Brecht's central charge

against Lukács had been that of the imposition of 'merely formal, literary criteria for realism' (Brecht, 1980, p. 82) and this is exactly what MacCabe proposed, albeit negatively rather than positively valorised. Against Lukács (and others), Brecht had argued that: 'They are ... enemies of production. Production makes them uncomfortable ... And they themselves don't want to produce' (Benjamin, 1973b, p. 118). Williams was surely right to detect an analogously formalist dogmatism at work in the emerging anti-realist orthodoxies. We live in a society, he wrote:

> which is ... rotten with criticism, in which the very frustrations of cultural production turn people from production to criticism ... It is precisely because these makers [ie. Allen, Garnett and Loach] are contemporaries engaged in active production, that we need not criticism but analysis ... the complex seeing of analysis rather than ... the abstractions of critical classification. (Williams, 1989c, p. 239)

This seems to me very close to what should have been the last word on post-structuralist anti-realism.

It should not, of course, be read as the converse, a principled anti-modernism, such as Lukács had engaged in, nor even a principled anti-postmodernism. Williams's later novels, we need note, are much more obviously 'experimental' in character than any simple notion of realism might lead one to expect. For Williams, there could be no general, formal characterisation either of 'modernism' or of 'realism', and the two cannot thereby be counterposed to each other as antithetical abstractions, in the manner envisaged by Lukács and, in effect, by MacCabe. Moreover, what mattered most for a radical art was, for Williams, the capacity to point beyond the real: hence, his sympathy for what he termed 'the alternative method of a hypothesis within ... recognition', in *The Big Flame*, 'a hypothesis played out ... within a politically imagined possibility' (Williams, 1989c, p. 234). As Tony Pinkney has rather interestingly suggested, Williams might well have been, not so much the 'British Lukács', as the British Ernst Bloch (Pinkney, 1989, pp. 28-31). This utopian impulse, most obviously present in *The Volunteers* (Williams, 1978b) and in *The Fight for Manod* (Williams, 1979c), connects, no doubt, to the stress on production, on what Williams was still willing to name 'creativity'. This is perhaps the most fundamental of differences between the various cultural materialisms deriving from Williams and the post-structuralisms deriving from *Screen*. The original, Althusserian, *Screen* position, which had lain stress on how the text positions the reader, was eventually superseded by a later, more properly deconstructionist sense of a multiplicity of possible readerly responses. Both Barker's *The Tremulous Private Body* (Barker, 1984) and Belsey's *The Subject of Tragedy* (Belsey, 1985), for example, would construct the literary-historical past as, to all intents and purposes, a narrative effect of the present. It was only in the cultural materialist line, from Williams, that such historiographical relativism was determinedly refused.

Williams and Eagleton

The most significant figure in this latter line is almost certainly Eagleton, for many years Professor of English at Oxford University, now Professor of Cultural Theory at the University of Manchester. Though he has clearly occupied a much less representative position in relation to literary studies than Hall in relation to cultural studies, the trajectory of his intellecual career nicely traces the varying impact of Williams's work on radical literary criticism in Britain. Eagleton's early work had been written very much in the shadow of *Culture and Society* (Eagleton, 1968), so much so, in fact, as to excite some irritation on Williams's own part (Williams, 1979a, p. 110). As late as 1975, Eagleton's study of the Brontës had managed to combine a continuing debt to Williams with an emergent proto-Althusserianism (Eagleton, 1975). Only a year later, however, came *Criticism and Ideology*, and with it, not only a fairly full-blown Althusserianism, but also a trenchant critique of Williams. The full-blown Althusserianism consisted, on the one hand, in a highly formalist elaboration of 'the major constituents of a Marxist theory of literature', centred around the twin concepts of 'mode of production' and 'ideology' (Eagleton, 1976, pp. 44-63); and on the other, in the proposal for a structuralist 'science of the text', which would take, as its theoretical object, the way literature 'produces' ideology, in the sense of performing it (Eagleton, 1976, pp. 64-101).

As noted in Chapter 2, Eagleton's critique of Williams found his work guilty of a combination of idealist epistemology, organicist aesthetics and corporatist sociology, each with its roots in 'Romantic populism'. The defining characteristic of that Romanticism, Eagleton argued, as of the very notion of 'culture' itself, was a radical 'over-subjectivising' of the social formation, in which structure is reduced to experience (ibid., p. 26). This was very much what Hall would later refer to as the 'experiential pull' in Williams and Thompson. But where Hall would, at least notionally, concede experience its due, Eagleton prosecuted a much more rigorously structuralist case. For the young Eagleton, meanings are not culture, but ideology; and it follows, then, that the new solidaristic values and meanings which, in Williams, are seen as the active creation of men and women in the historical present, can, in fact, only ever be '*enabled* by revolutionary rupture', at some point in the historical future (ibid., p. 27). Williams's 'generous reverence for human capacities' thus entails, in Eagleton's view, 'a drastic misconception of the structures of advanced capitalist formations' (ibid., p. 28). In short, Williams had failed to understand the way working-class subjectivity is determined by bourgeois ideology; 'structure of feeling' was thus an essentially inadequate conceptualisation of ideology, misreading structure as mere pattern (ibid., pp. 33-4); and even Williams's use of the Gramscian notion of hegemony had been wrongly predicated on its experiential primacy and was, therefore, necessarily 'structurally undifferentiated' (ibid., p. 42). We can concede something to the power of Eagleton's critique of Williams's earlier culturalism, while insisting nonetheless on its markedly retrospective quality: the later cultural materialism, already substantially formed by 1976, was to prove much less susceptible to such charges of empiricism. Moreover, insofar as real differences did indeed persist, it was surely Eagleton's position that was the more 'idealist and academicist' (ibid., p. 25). His quintessentially Althusserian insistence on the determining power of ideology over the human subject was, as Thompson might have said, *'exactly* what has commonly been designated, in the Marxist tradition, as idealism' (Thompson, 1978, p. 205). It led almost unavoidably to an enormous condescension toward popular activity, whether political or cultural. The equally Althusserian defence of the notion of aesthetic value, coupled as it was with a substantive acceptance of the content of the literary canon and a passing sneer at the 'abstract egalitarianism' of Cultural Studies (Eagleton, 1976, pp. 162-3), is similarly academicist. As Felperin would unkindly observe: 'you can take the boy out of Cambridge, but you cannot take Cambridge out of the boy' (1985, p. 57).

The intent of these remarks is not to take Eagleton to task for views he would in any case soon abandon, but to emphasise the extent to which structuralism and cultural materialism offered alternative, very different, and in some ways opposed, ways out of the theoretical deadlock between idealist humanism and determinist Marxism. These differences revolved around their respective concepts of structure, agency and subjectivity: for structuralism, structure was all-determining, agency an illusion and subjectivity the ideological effect of structure; for cultural materialism, structure sets limits and exerts pressures, agency takes place within those limits and pressures, and takes the characteristic form of an unavoidably material production, and subjectivity, though socially produced and shared, is nonetheless both real and active. The analytical logic of structuralism pointed towards a perennial search for the impress of ideology concealed within the deep structures of the text. Though the enabling rhetoric was both radical and contextual, the substantive focus remained the business as usual of literary-critical canonical exegesis. And though later post-structuralisms might dispute that focus, they certainly need not do so. Post-structuralism of the Derridean kind can very easily settle for little more than the substitution of a plurality of possible 'deconstructive' readings for the ideal of a singular, because scientific, 'structural' reading, while nonetheless preserving, and in a perverse way reinforcing, the canon of texts available for critical investigation. By contrast, the analytical logic of cultural materialism pointed towards a necessary decentring both of texts into the contexts of their production, reproduction and consumption, and of Literature into culture, literary studies into Cultural Studies. If Williams's politico-theoretical rhetoric was a great deal less 'revolutionary' than Althusser's, the substantive case at issue was surely very much more so.

Certainly, this was to prove Eagleton's own eventual assessment. His next two books, *Walter Benjamin* and *The Rape of Clarissa*, published in 1981 and 1982 respectively, represent that moment in his work when a repudiation of Althusserianism coincides with a horrified fascination for post-structuralism and a developing respect for cultural materialism. This combination of repudiation, fascination and respect is actually announced in *Walter Benjamin*, but there the major theoretical rationale remained a political defence of revolutionary intransigence in obviously non-revolutionary situations (Eagleton, 1985, p. 139). The combination was more properly constitutive of the argument in *The Rape of Clarissa*, where a kind of feminist deconstruction goes hand in hand with what Eagleton terms 'historical materialism', but is surely, in its stress on 'literary modes of production' (Eagleton, 1982, p. viii), actually a cultural materialism. Following Habermas (Habermas, 1989), Eagleton proposed to understand this particular, eighteenth century, mode of literary production as formed within the context of the new bourgeois 'public sphere' (Eagleton, 1982, pp. 6-7). *The Rape of Clarissa* thus inaugurated an 'institutional' analysis of the social functions of literature and criticism, which provided the central organising theme for Eagleton's most fully cultural-materialist books, *Literary Theory* and *The Function of Criticism*. The former is, of course, a bestselling textbook, first published in 1983, with a second edition in 1996. The apparent conventionality of its form is belied, however, by the subversive intent of its argument. Its critical and often hostile account of various contemporary schools of literary theory is predicated on an institutional history of the development of English studies as a discipline, and culminates in a polemical call for the kind of 'political criticism' that will go beyond the limits of the institution (Eagleton, 1996a, pp. 15-46; 169-89). This argument is resumed and once again coupled to the Habermasian notion of the bourgeois public sphere in *The Function of Criticism*, first published in 1984. In both books, the stress falls on the institutional production of criticism, as it had for Williams. In both, too, the category of 'Literature' is radically decentred (Eagleton, 1996a, pp. 14, 172; Eagleton, 1984, pp. 107-8), as it had been for Williams. In the later book, moreover, Eagleton specifically invoked Williams as 'the most important critic of post-war Britain', whose concept of 'structure of feeling' he now deemed 'vital' in 'examining the *articulations* between different sign-systems and practices' (Eagleton, 1984, pp. 108-10). Generous though this may be, the compliment is actually less telling than the more general cultural materialism of the argument within which it occurs.

Eagleton's writing of the 1990s can be seen as an attempt to redeploy and reapply a whole set of essentially Williamsite categories to distinctly un-English contexts. *The Ideology of the Aesthetic* is an attempt at a critical history of the concept of the aesthetic, as it evolved in modern, (mainly) German thought, from Baumgarten to Habermas. Much less concerned with institutional analysis, the book was criticised as tending both to 'over-value theory' and to ignore the social organisation of aesthetics (During, 1991, pp. 177, 180-1). Eagleton actually conceded the latter point, or very nearly so, in his 'Introduction', but stressed simply that one cannot write about everything (Eagleton, 1990a, p. 5). And, in truth, sometimes theory does have to be taken seriously as theory. For the central purpose of Eagleton's argument here, in contradistinction to the radically relativist sociologising of much contemporary Cultural Studies, was to recover both the negative and positive moments within the 'aesthetic' tradition. The obvious, but little remarked upon, point of comparison is with Williams's own account of the English 'culturalist' tradition in *Culture and Society*: as Eagleton notes, 'the Anglophone tradition is in fact derivative of German philosophy' (Eagleton, 1990a, p. 11). Just as, in the prosperously utilitarian 1950s, it had taken a Welshman to seek out the positively emancipatory content of the derivative English tradition itself, so in the darkly utilitarian 1980s, a Lancashire Irishman would discover something at least of the same in the German original. Indeed, the book might well have been entitled *Kultur und Gesellschaft 1750-1980*, though, alas, that is not the form of the actually existing German translation of *Culture and Society* (Williams, 1972).

Eagleton's Irishness is arguably a less substantial construct than Williams's Welshness, but it has been a powerfully informing influence, nonetheless, on his more recent writing, prompting one good play, a rather bad novel, a comic travel book and a substantial body of radical cultural criticism (Eagleton, 1987; Eagleton, 1989d; Eagleton, 1995; Eagleton, 1998; Eagleton, 1999a). Interestingly, he had broached the matter in direct conversation with Williams as early as 1987: 'We both hail originally from the Celtic fringes,' Eagleton ventured, 'and both of us, relatively late in life, began turning back to those roots ... it took us both a long time to look back to the margins because, as students of English, we'd had our heads well and truly fixed by an ideology of "Englishness"' (Williams and Eagleton, 1989, p. 181). The weight that attaches to 'originally' here depends very much on what is meant by 'origin', whether birth, upbringing or ancestry. Williams was presumably too kind to point to the obvious difference between Pandy and Salford, that the one is in Wales, the other clearly not in Ireland. But Eagleton is indeed of Irish descent, and, though he would later concede his own (presumably non-ideological) 'Englishness' with a certain good grace,[1] he has made productive use of this ancestry to interrogate the cultural politics of Anglo-British imperialism in

Ireland. Like *The Ideology of the Aesthetic, Heathcliff and the Great Hunger* can be read as a reworking of Williams's *Culture and Society*, here taking Irish literature rather than German philosophy as its primary object. There is a parallel foregrounding of what had been left oddly tangential in Williams himself. So Eagleton traces the differences between English and Irish writing, showing how Williams's own keyword, 'Culture', had been differently troped against 'Nature'; and, more specifically, how Irishness itself had been troped as Nature to English Culture. So too he re-places many of the thinkers from Williams's 'culture and society tradition' - Burke, Shaw and Wilde - in relation to the quite different Irish 'tradition' running from Swift to Joyce and Yeats.

Eagleton's studies in Irish culture build on the legacy of Williams's Welshness in at least two respects: firstly, in their understanding of how Englishness and Irishness (/Welshness) had been defined and constructed, in relation to and against each other, through the processes and projects of hegemony; and secondly, in their insistence that cultural representations can and should be measured against the historical referents to which they really do sometimes bear some relation. So in the opening chapter of *Heathcliff and the Great Hunger*, Eagleton moves between the text of *Wuthering Heights*, the historical reality of the Irish Famine, its representation and non-representation in subsequent historiographical and literary texts, the Brontë family's peculiar Yorkshire Irishness, and the more general troping of Nature and Culture in English and Irish writing (Eagleton, 1995, pp. 1-26). Even more clearly than in Williams, this stress on the connectedness of texts and contexts, signs and referents, is unencumbered by any commitment to aesthetic realism. So Eagleton's account of the material and cultural obstacles to the development of an Irish literary realism actually concludes by stressing the vital importance of the non-realist tradition in Ireland (Eagleton, 1995, pp. 145-54). The point should be obvious: all texts, whether realist or not, refer to their contexts; and all texts, whether realist or not, can be analysed in their relation to those contexts. Neither a post-colonial revisionist nor a Sinn Fein nationalist, Eagleton's Irishness also echoes something of Williams's sense of himself as 'a Welsh European'. So Eagleton borrows from one of Williams's novels the analogy between class and nationalism. 'To have it, and to feel it, is the only way to end it', Williams has a character say (Williams, 1964, p. 322). Glossing Williams and Marx, Eagleton insists on the irony that 'to undo this alienation you had to go ... all the way through it and out the other side. To wish class or nation away, to seek to live sheer irreducible difference *now* ... is to play straight into the hands of the oppressor' (Eagleton, 1990b, p. 23).

A second key theme in Eagleton's recent work has been the critique of postmodern culture and politics. Here too a debt to Williams is apparent. If Eagleton's *The Illusions of Postmodernism* gives rather more credence to postmodernism's supposedly radical credentials than had

Williams in *Against the New Conformists*, its conclusions remain remarkable similar: 'Postmodern end-of-history thinking does not envisage a future ... much different from the present,' Eagleton writes, 'a prospect it oddly views as a cause for celebration.' But, he continues, what if the future does turn out to be different? What if it witnessed a revival of fascism, for example? How would postmodern thought cope with such illiberalism? The answers are as damning as anything in Williams:

> its cultural relativism and moral conventionalism, its scepticism, pragmatism, and localism, its distaste for ideas of solidarity and disciplined organization, its lack of any adequate theory of political agency: all these would tell heavily against it ... the left, now more than ever, has need of strong ethical and anthropological foundations ... And on this score, postmodernism is ... part of the problem rather than of the solution. (Eagleton, 1996b, pp. 134-5)

Williams's notion of a common culture figures in *The Illusions of Postmodernism* as one possible source for these strong foundations (Eagleton, 1996b, pp. 84-5). But the idea is even more explicitly foregrounded in his more recent contribution to the 'Blackwell Manifestos' series, *The Idea of Culture*. Once again, Eagleton takes postmodernism as his target; once again, he argues for the theoretical superiority of Williams's idea of a common culture over contemporary theories of radical difference. Part of the problem, he insists, is that Williams's version is often confused with Eliot's: 'Whereas for Eliot the culture is common in content,' he writes, 'its commonness for Williams lies chiefly in its political form.' The power and the paradox of Williams's position, Eagleton continues, are in their recognition that cultural diversity actually requires for its achievement the kind of common belief and action necessary for the creation of common institutions. 'To establish genuine cultural pluralism', he argues, 'requires concerted socialist action. It is precisely this that contemporary pluralism fails to see. Williams's position would no doubt seem to it quaintly residual, not to say positively archaic; the problem in fact is that we have yet to catch up with it' (Eagleton, 2000, p. 122).

The point of all this has not been to celebrate Eagleton's recantation from an earlier Althusserian apostasy, still less a return to the fold of Anglo-culturalist empiricism. For, in truth, there can be no apostasy where there is no orthodoxy, and Williams's cultural materialism was not so much a doctrine as a research project. Nor, despite erstwhile Anglo-Althusserian charges to the contrary, was Williams really in any fold, of either English or empiricist extraction. The point, then, is simply to suggest the uses to which some of Williams's ideas can be put in hands as creative as Eagleton's. The latter's own judgement warrants repetition: 'the notion of cultural materialism is ... of considerable

value ... it extends and completes Marx's own struggle against idealism, carrying it forcefully into that realm ("culture") always most
 ideologically resistant to materialist redefinition' (Eagleton, 1989b,
p. 169). Eagleton himself is still more of a Marxist than Williams had
been, insisting on the base/superstructure formula and on the general
priority of historical over cultural materialism. As he observes of Irish
society: 'When material history bulks so blatantly large, ... who needs
to engage in elaborate theoretical defences of the model of base and
superstructure?' (Eagleton, 1995, p. 8). But Eagleton's Marxism
remains directly compatible with a 'cultural materialist concern for ...
social and material conditions'. Carried into the academic institutions,
he insists, cultural materialism 'would make the most profound difference to what actually got done there' (Eagleton, 1989b, p. 169). In
politically better times, no doubt, he would prefer a more full-blooded
Marxism. But, in the meantime at any rate, for a professor of English -
as Eagleton has been until very recently - carrying cultural materialism into the academy has been quite a lot to be going on with. It has
been sufficient to prompt Harold Bloom, the leading contemporary
custodian of the humanist literary canon, to an apoplexy worthy of
Leavis: 'The wretched Eagleton ... can't read or write, he is nothing but
a pompom. He is wretched, he is not even to be pitied, but to be held
in total contempt' (cf. Bloom, 1994; Bloom, 2000a; Bloom, 2000b).
Presumably, this is very much the response for which Eagleton would
have hoped.

Cultural Materialism and the New Historicism

While Eagleton has preferred to identify his work with Williams rather
than with cultural materialism per se, Dollimore and Sinfield,
Professors of English respectively at the Universities of York and
Sussex, have been enthusiastically 'card-carrying' cultural material-
ists, to borrow a phrase from Claire Colebrook (Colebrook, 1997,
p. 184). As we noted in Chapter 1, much recent commentary has tended to conflate cultural materialism with Greenblatt's 'new historicism'.
We also noted how the cultural materialism in question tended to be
that of Dollimore and Sinfield, rather than of Williams himself. Their
co-edited collection *Political Shakespeare*, subtitled *Essays in Cultural
Materialism* (Dollimore and Sinfield, 1994a), has proved sufficiently
influential as to prompt the very large claim that 'cultural materialism
in Britain and New Historicism in America' constitute a 'new academic order' in Renaissance studies (Wilson, 1995, p. viii). As we shall see,
American 'new historicism' is a little different from what Williams had
meant by cultural materialism. Their linkage by Wilson might, then, be
read as indicative of how little Dollimore and Sinfield actually owe to
Williams. The rival claims of these different cultural materialisms have
been much canvassed, with opinion ranging from Dollimore's own

claim that his work derives from 'the considerable output of Williams himself' (1994a, p.2) to Gorak's that writers like Dollimore 'have reduced Williams's program to little more than a slogan' (1988, p. 90). Though Dollimore and Sinfield clearly subscribe to a looser sense of the term than that in Williams, their insistence on their own indebtedness suggests something more than mere fidelity to a 'slogan'.

As we noted in Chapter 1, in *Political Shakespeare* Dollimore had come close to defining cultural materialism as a kind of 'cultural analysis' more or less coextensive with Cultural Studies (Dollimore, 1994a, pp. 2-3). Elsewhere in the same volume, however, Dollimore and Sinfield together define their 'cultural materialism', rather more precisely, as 'a combination of historical context, theoretical method, political commitment and textual analysis' (Dollimore and Sinfield, 1994b, p. vii). The sense of 'culture' in 'cultural materialism', they continue, is 'analytic' or social-scientific, rather than 'evaluative'; the sense of 'materialism' anti-idealistic, insofar as it insists that culture 'does not (cannot) transcend the material forces and relations of production'. From the first, it follows that high culture is merely 'one set of signifying practices among others'; from the second, that literary texts should be studied 'in history', that is, in their relation to the institutions of cultural production which produce and reproduce them. Finally, Dollimore and Sinfield insist that cultural materialism has a distinctive politics, that of a 'commitment to the transformation of a social order which exploits people on grounds of race, gender and class' (Dollimore and Sinfield, 1994b, p. viii). Williams's influence is readily apparent here, even if class and nation were of more importance to his own work than either race or gender. That said, there can be little doubt that Williams would have acceded to most of what Dollimore and Sinfield propose; indeed, he had actually affirmed his own solidarity with the 'body of work ... beginning to be formed' in *Political Shakespeare* (Williams, 1994, p. 286).

Both Dollimore and Sinfield have subsequently come to focus on substantive issues very different from those that concerned Williams, most especially (gay) sexuality. For Dollimore, cultural materialism remained an important initial influence on this work, but only as one 'perspective' among many. His major study of sexual dissidence is thus self-consciously written at the 'points' where cultural materialism and a whole range of other perspectives - 'biography, literary and cultural theory, theodicy, social history, psychoanalysis, philosophy, feminism, and ... lesbian and gay studies' - 'intersect with, but sometimes also contest each other' (Dollimore, 1991, p. 21). There is much that Dollimore had learned from Williams, not least the complexity of the relations between the dominant, the alternative and the oppositional (ibid., pp. 51-2, 83). But here there is no attempt to attach theoretical priority to cultural materialism, as there had been in *Political Shakespeare*. Dollimore's later, ambitious study of death and desire in western culture, from classical antiquity to the present, seems to have escaped Williams's influence almost entirely (Dollimore, 1999). So much of what might once have been written under the sign 'Williams' is now clearly written under that of 'Foucault'. There is some warrant, then, for Higgins's view of Dollimore as remembering Williams only 'to remind us just how safely we can forget him' (Higgins, 1999, p. 172). Neither 'historical context' nor 'theoretical method', in any specifically cultural-materialist sense, figure very prominently in Dollimore's later work. There is textual analysis, of course, but there has never been anything distinctively cultural materialist about that. There is political commitment too: *Death, Desire and Loss* is both occasioned and inspired by the cultural politics of the AIDS pandemic (Dollimore, 1999, pp. ix-xiii). But there had been rather more to cultural materialism, even in Dollimore's own earlier formulations, than simply political criticism.

By contrast, Sinfield's guiding theoretical approach has remained determinedly, if also 'dissidently', cultural materialist (Sinfield, 1992, pp. 8-10; Sinfield, 1998, pp. 147-50). Nor is this simply a matter of intellectual sloganising, in the sense suggested by Gorak. On the contrary, Sinfield's version of gay politics has been characterised precisely by a stress on the capacities for resistance to dominance, clearly reminiscent of Williams. Cultural materialism, Sinfield insists, is committed to the attempt to theorise 'dissident perceptions and action' (Sinfield, 1994a, p. 17). This commitment is distinctive to it, moreover, rather than characteristic of post-structuralist theories more generally. 'Much of the importance of Raymond Williams', he writes, 'derives from the fact that ... when Althusser and Foucault were being read ... as establishing ideology and/or power in a necessarily unbreakable continuum, Williams argued the co-occurrence of subordinate, residual, emergent, alternative, and oppositional cultural forces' (Sinfield, 1992, p. 9). This insight has led Sinfield to explore the possibilities for alternative forms of cultural production available to 'a more intelligent and purposeful' post-gay subculture (Sinfield, 1998, p. 150). Again, the stress on the materiality of culture is indebted to Williams. Elsewhere, and in what is still probably Sinfield's single most important work - a simultaneous attempt to update both *Culture and Society* and *The Long Revolution* - he has taken issue with the universalism of Williams's early 'left-culturalism' (Sinfield, 1997, pp. 242-3, 300). But he does so, nonetheless, precisely on the grounds of a whole set of cultural materialist categories: cultural production; the distinction between dominant, residual and emergent; 'middle class dissidence', and so on (ibid., pp. 26-7, 31, 35). Indeed, in the opening chapter especially written for the book's second edition, Sinfield offers as succinct a summary as any of what exactly cultural materialism 'does':

> Cultural materialists investigate the historical conditions in which
> textual representations are produced, circulated and received. They

engage with questions about the relations between dominant and subordinate cultures, ... the scope for subaltern resistance, and the modes through which the system tends to accommodate or repel diverse kinds of dissidence. In this approach, the terms 'art' and 'literature' ... are neither spontaneous nor innocent. They are ... strategies for conferring authority upon certain representations, and hence upon certain viewpoints. (Sinfield, 1997, p. xxiii)

The differences between Dollimore's and Sinfield's later work are interestingly prefigured in an earlier co-authored essay, written in defence of cultural materialism and against Belsey's earlier criticisms of *Political Shakespeare*. Belsey had objected to their version of cultural materialism, alleging that it retained a more than residual sympathy for the notion of a 'real struggle' 'elsewhere' than in 'texts'; and had argued for her own version of a more general 'cultural history', able to 'appropriate and develop' the strategies used in English Literature, but searching for 'contradictions and conflicts' rather than 'coherence', and across the whole 'range of texts' rather than the merely literary (Belsey, 1989, pp. 165-6). Dollimore and Sinfield produced a compound reply, each addressing different issues. In the first part, Dollimore had denied believing that 'that the real struggle is always elsewhere than in the text', but insisted nonetheless that 'many struggles are not textual'. He then proceeded to argue an interestingly nuanced case for the political efficacy of certain kinds of heavily qualified radical humanism, in relation to the quasi-essentialist character of subordinate political identities and truth claims (Dollimore and Sinfield, 1990, pp. 92, 94-6). In the second, Sinfield had accused Belsey of a 'lingering attachment to Englit' and argued accordingly for the theoretical superiority of cultural materialism over her cultural history. 'Cultural materialism embarrasses Englit., even elaborated as CB proposes,' he continues: 'by requiring knowledges and techniques that we scarcely possess, or even know how to discover. These are in part the province of history and other social sciences ... A cultural history must address not only texts, but the institutions and formations that organize, and are organized by, textualities' (Dollimore and Sinfield, 1990, pp. 98-9). Dollimore and Sinfield clearly shared - and still continue to share - much common ground. But the difference of emphasis remains characteristic: where Dollimore insisted on the importance of alternative modes of textual analysis, Sinfield argued for modes of analysis different from and supplementary to the textual. So where *Death, Desire and Loss* is overwhelmingly textual in character (theorised and politicised, certainly, but textual nonetheless), Sinfield's work repeatedly insists that at some point we pay express attention to the material mechanisms of cultural production.

As we have said, these are essentially differences of emphasis, rather than of substance or of principle (even if they do tend to point toward diverging lines of inquiry and intervention). So too were those between Dollimore and Sinfield, on the one hand, and Greenblatt, on the other, in their respective contributions to the first edition of *Political Shakespeare*. What Dollimore and Sinfield have been to cultural materialism, Greenblatt is to the new historicism (though there are other new historicist writers, notably Catherine Gallagher, Walter Benn Michaels and Louis Adrian Montrose). Now Professor of English at Harvard, but for many years at Berkeley, California, where new historicism germinated, Greenblatt has become the pre-eminent representative of this particular variety of theorising. The founding text of a distinctively 'new historicist' critical practice is generally held to be his *Renaissance Self-Fashioning* (Greenblatt, 1980); and the term itself was coined in his 1982 Introduction to *The Power of Forms in the English Renaissance* (Greenblatt, 1982, p. 5). New historicism's starting point is in something like Geertz's 'thick description' (Geertz, 1973; Gallagher and Greenblatt, 2000, pp. 20-2), that is, the close analysis of the social, cultural and historical milieux in which a text is produced and received. New historicist analyses typically bring literary and non-literary discourse into juxtaposition, showing how social power and historical conflict permeate textuality itself. So, for example, Greenblatt sets the 'eucharistic anxiety' in *Hamlet* against the rhetoric of Protestant opposition to the Catholic Mass (Gallagher and Greenblatt, 2000, pp. 151-62). As Greenblatt describes it, his work is preoccupied with 'the embeddedness of cultural objects in the contingencies of history' (Greenblatt, 1990, p. 164). For Gallagher and Greenblatt, then, as much as for Dollimore and Sinfield, individual authors and texts are in no sense autonomous. Rather, the work of art is a product of the 'negotiation between a creator or class of creators, equipped with a complex, communally shared repertoire of conventions, and the institutions and practices of society.' These negotiations take place, he continues, through the 'circulation of materials and discourses' in the 'hidden places of negotiation and exchange' (Greenblatt, 1990, pp. 158-9).

Writing in the Introduction to the first edition of *Political Shakespeare*, Dollimore had cheerfully pointed to 'the important and shared concerns of cultural materialism and the new historicism' (Dollimore, 1994a, p. 4). Greenblatt has on occasion displayed a similar sense of commonality: he had studied at Cambridge and would readily attest to Williams's 'critical subtlety and theoretical intelligence'. 'In Williams's lectures', he recalled, 'all that had been carefully excluded from the literary criticism in which I had been trained ... came pressing back in upon the act of interpretation' (Greenblatt, 1990, p. 2). New historicism shares much with cultural materialism, then, not least this apparent debt to Williams[2] and a shared conception of culture as historical and material practice. Little wonder, then, that the two positions are often regarded as theoretically resonant, if not cognate. So Ryan insists that they 'are united by their compulsion to relate literature to history, to treat texts as indivisible from contexts, and to do so from a politically charged perspective forged in the present' (1996, p. xi); and Felperin describes cultural materialism quite simply as new historicism's 'counterpart in Britain' (1990, p. 1). There is something vaguely surprising, then, perhaps even slightly shocking, in Sinfield's capacity to damn the new historicism with very faint praise: its success, he writes, 'derives from its vagueness; it covers most clever work that is not celebrating the unity of the-text-on-the-page' (Sinfield, 1994b, p. 21). Elsewhere he has argued, even more pointedly, that: 'Apart from better resourcing, the reason for the quality of new historicists' work is that they really believe in literary research ... the very excellence ... may effect a kind of blinkering; sophistication, cleverness, abstruseness, difficulty, and professionalism screen out the wider culture' (Sinfield, 1992, p. 8). Sinfield, it should be clear, really does not 'believe' in 'literary' research. Clearly, there is more at issue here, both theoretically and politically, than simple professional jealousy (though what British - or Australian - academic wouldn't be jealous of American institutional largesse?). New historicism can, in one sense, be considered cultural materialism in a postmodern register, preoccupied with historicising texts and with the workings of power through culture, but focused on issues of individual subjectivity construction, gender and the workings of patriarchy, rather than on class and nation. Where Williams's cultural materialism had been concerned with the connections between social class and a collectively emancipatory politics, new historicism has tended to exhibit the characteristic preoccupations of the officially-sanctioned forms of political radicalism within the North American academy: subjectivity formation, desire, race, gender, sexuality, and so on. These latter are also analysable in more strictly cultural materialist terms, however, as Dollimore and Sinfield's own work clearly attests (Dollimore, 1991; Sinfield, 1994a; Sinfield, 1994b).

The more fundamental differences between cultural materialism and the new historicism are threefold: first, the theoretical question as to the subversive potential of apparently subversive texts; second, the political question as to the competing claims of academic professionalism and subordinate subcultures; and third, the epistemological question as to the status of the 'referent' to which texts refer. As to the first, the issue hinges on how to read and apply Foucault, whether as a theorist of incorporation or of disruption, and on how to understand in/subordination, whether as always-already necessarily contained or as at least potentially resistive. The title of Greenblatt's 1982 essay is nicely suggestive of the general character of the new historicist enterprise, both in its obvious debt to Foucault, and in its sense of the literary text's imbrication in the workings of Renaissance social structures. As Greenblatt readily concedes, Foucault's extended visits to Berkeley had 'helped to shape' his own literary-critical practice (Greenblatt, 1990, pp. 146-7). Just as for Foucault the apparently autonomous self had been a socio-discursive effect of quite specific forms of social power, so for the Greenblatt of *Renaissance Self-Fashioning* the texts and performances of Renaissance literature and drama are actively pro-ductive of the new forms of self. In new historicism, as in Foucault, this simultaneous stress on the discursivity of power and on the power of discourse easily leads to an overly 'functional' understanding of the self as effectively subordinated to and integrated within the social for-mation. So in much of Greenblatt's work the apparently subversive moment in apparently subversive texts is read as ultimately affirma-tive of and complicit with the dominant discursive formation. The obvious instance here is the essay included in *Political Shakespeare*, and much reprinted elsewhere, which reads the subversive perceptions in Shakespeare's second tetralogy as ultimately supportive of the kingly authority they appear to question (Greenblatt, 1994).

For Sinfield, this new historicist insistence on the affirmative prop-erties of apparently subversive texts amounts to little more than a reworking of the Althusserian 'entrapment model' of ideology and power. Entrapment is indeed important, he concedes, as a way of the-orising the dominant ideology. But it is much more important to theo-rise the scope for effective dissidence, he continues: 'This, centrally, is what Raymond Williams was concerned with in his later work' (Sinfield, 1994b, p. 24). Hence, Sinfield's continuing interest in Williams's accounts of the alternative and the oppositional, the resid-ual and the emergent. We should note that Sinfield sees the new his-toricist version of the entrapment thesis as essentially a misreading of Foucault, who, he insists, was actually 'a committed and active leftist' (ibid., p. 26). So too was Althusser, comes the obvious objection. But this is beside the point for, however we read Foucault, the central issue remains that of the limits and possibilities of dissidence. For cultural materialism, Sinfield continues to argue that 'dissident potential derives ... from conflict and contradiction that the social order inevitably produces within itself, even as it attempts to sustain itself' (Sinfield, 1992, p. 41). For new historicism, Gallagher argues that left-ist readings of the literary text as disruptive actually replicate the literary-critical consensus as to the disturbing, destabilising and estranging functions of art. New historicism's break with the consen-sus 'is not an attempt to demoralize the left,' she concludes, but rather 'an attempt to de-moralize our relationship to literature, to interrupt the moral narrative of literature's benign disruptions' (Gallagher, 1996, p. 53). The lines of disagreement can be overdrawn: asking whether sites of resistance are ultimately cooptable, Greenblatt comments sim-ply that 'Some are, some aren't' (Greenblatt, 1990, p. 165); confronting much the same issue, Sinfield concludes that 'there is no simple way through, but every reason to go on trying' (Sinfield, 1994b, p. 27). They are agreed, in short, that entrapment and dissidence are each theoreti-cally possibile. The difference is one of relative probabilities, then, but also of intent and purpose and, hence, necessarily of politics.

New historicism has generally been much more reticent than cultural materialism as to its politics. So where Dollimore and Sinfield had insisted on cultural materialism's commitment to the 'transformation' of the entire 'social order', no less, Gallagher describes the new historicism as 'a criticism whose politics are ... difficult to specify' (Gallagher, 1996, p. 45). Greenblatt himself famously defined the 'function of the new historicism' as 'to renew the marvelous at the heart of the resonant', a nice turn of phrase, to be sure, but hardly a political manifesto (Greenblatt, 1990, p. 181). As Wilson has observed: 'In the many maps New Historicists drew of themselves ... "cultural materialism" was noticed and noted as a ... more outspoken, more political, ... in "scholarly" terms less sophisticated, version of the same thing' (Wilson, 1995, p. 55). He might well have added that Sinfield's maps tend to return the favour. So for Sinfield, the new historicist fascination with ideological entrapment is not so much a profound insight as evidence of a 'sense of its own political scope ... tellingly homologous with its own professional entrapment' in the higher reaches of the North American academy (Sinfield, 1992, p. 290). Citing Williams's unease at the communal cost of individual upward social mobility, Sinfield's 'preferred alternative' to academic professionalism has been to 'work intellectually ... in dissident subcultures' of 'class, ethnicity, gender and sexuality' (ibid,., p. 294). The 'best chance for literary and leftist intellectuals to make themselves useful', he writes, is to commit themselves to 'a subcultural constituency' (Sinfield, 1997, p. xxiv). Elsewhere, he has quite explicitly urged the vocation of Gramscian 'organic intellectual' on the radical academy (Sinfield, 1994b, p. 75; Sinfield, 1998, p. 151). In more recent formulations, however, the subcultures in question are those of 'race, ethnicity, gender and sexuality', but not of class. This shift registers a dawning recognition that intellectuals might themselves constitute 'a kind of class', with class interests of their own (ibid., p. 158). For Gramsci himself, part of the point of the distinction between traditional and organic intellectuals had been precisely to theorise the possibility of a working-class intelligentsia. As we have seen, Williams had imagined himself in something very like this capacity. The difference between Williams and Sinfield is striking, then, given the latter's more generally cultural materialist enthusiasms.

In part, this is an effect of the priority for Sinfield of a particular form of non-class identity: in his 'instance' the subculture happens to be 'lesbians and gay men' (Sinfield, 1997, p. xxiv). But this is not Sinfield's main point. Rather, he wishes to insist that, whenever intellectuals as intellectuals engage sympathetically with other classes, they will engage 'with concerns that are not immediately or entirely theirs', but that no such 'disjunction' arises when they engage as gay (black, female, etc.) intellectuals in the gay (black, female) subculture (Sinfield, 1998, p. 158). There is much (rather depressing) good sense in this recognition of the cultural and social limitations of the class position of the intelligentsia.[3] But Sinfield's escape clause surely comes too easily. No subculture, and no member of any subculture, can ever exist in a social space unaffected by class. So that, whenever intellectuals intervene in any subculture, they will necessarily speak from their class position as intellectuals, whatever their sexuality, ethnicity or gender. The important difference between Williams and Sinfield may well be one of periodisation, between the last years of the elite university system and the first of mass higher education. For, as Wilson rightly observes, the idea of academic intellectuals 'becoming organic' to other social groups presupposes a 'degree of academic or intellectual exteriority' no longer 'immediately obvious', if only because the bureaucratised, mass university is a social institution much like any other (Wilson, 1995, p. 256). Wilson is smart enough to recognise that what applies to the working class will almost certainly also apply to the gay community. This might appear to return us to the apolitical professionalism of the new historicism, though it surely need not. For it is one thing to suggest that intellectuals will tend to act politically as intellectuals, pursuing their own collective interests, but nonetheless often by way of alliances with other classes and groups; quite another to argue that individualised professional expertise provides an effective substitute for a politics. Resonance and wonder are fine, but both labour and gay organisations typically require something different from their intellectuals; and those intellectuals are normally theirs only ever provisionally, hardly ever organically.

The third of our differences between cultural materialism and the new historicism is that over the epistemological status of the referent. As Ryan observes, new historicism consciously defined itself in opposition to older historicisms, which claimed to 'ground their accounts of literature in a factual historical reality that can be recovered and related to the poems, plays and novels that reflect it' (Ryan, 1996, p. xiii). So Greenblatt insists that: 'methodological self-consciousness is one of the distinguishing marks of the new historicism in cultural studies as opposed to a historicism based upon faith in the transparency of signs and interpretive procedures' (1990, p. 158). Neither Dollimore nor Sinfield - nor Williams nor Eagleton - ever believed in the transparency of either signs or interpretative procedures. Nor did they believe anything so foolish as that literature either does or should 'reflect' reality. But all four agree that signs do sometimes have referents, that there is a sense in which texts can be used both to represent and misrepresent other extra-textual 'realities', and that, as Dollimore had it, 'many struggles are not textual'. The kind of analysis conducted by Williams in *The Country and the City*, or by Eagleton at points in *Heathcliff and the Great Hunger* where literary text and historical context are productively compared, in part so as to test the extent to which texts misrepresent their contexts, tends to be precluded by the remorseless 'textualism' of new historicist criticism. This is not so much a matter of judging the truth or falsity of the textual representation - although this is by no

means entirely irrelevant - as of understanding how textuality per-
forms ideology. So, for example, Dollimore and Sinfield read the representation of the conquest and union with France in *Henry V* as a
dramatic 're-presentation' of the 'real' attempt by the Elizabethan state
to conquer and absorb Ireland. The play is 'fascinating', they conclude,
to the extent that it discloses *both* 'the struggles of its own historical
moment' *and* their 'ideological representation' (Dollimore and
Sinfield, 1985, p. 225). Such strategies are much less readily available
to a theoretical position as determinedly post-structuralist as the new
historicism. For, as Ryan observes, 'new historicism turns history into
a text and treats all texts as literary texts susceptible to the same interpretive techniques ... The poststructuralist price of the return to history is the evaporation of the world that produced all these words'
(Ryan, 1996, p. xiv).

Said and Williams

In this chapter, we have been concerned to trace the continuing influence of Williams's work in contemporary 'literary' studies. Given his
own disciplinary and geographical locations, we have necessarily been
preoccupied with English Literature, primarily as it has been practised
in England, only secondarily in the United States. It would be wrong,
however, to conclude without any comparison of Williams's work
with that of Edward Said, Professor of Comparative Literature at
Columbia University in New York. American rather than English,
Palestinian rather than American, Comparatist rather than Anglicist,
Said nonetheless remembers Williams as 'a good friend and a great
critic' (Said, 1993, p. xxxi). This is so, moreover, despite his obvious -
that is, obviously right, even if overstated - objection that in Williams
'the imperial experience is quite irrelevant' (ibid., p. 47).[4] Said is, of
course, a major critic in his own right, his *Orientalism*, first published
in 1978, the founding text of what has since become known as 'postcolonial theory'. The combination of 'Third Worldist' cultural politics
and post-structuralism, which the latter term denotes, has become an
important, perhaps even characteristic, feature of the contemporary
radical academy. And, insofar as it has been constituted by any particular body of work, it is above all that associated with Said on the one
hand, Gayatri Chakravorty Spivak on the other. Their two careers are
very easily run together as paradigmatically, but also caricaturally,
'postcolonial': both have been preoccupied with the cultural legacies
of imperialism, both are from what was once known as the 'Third
World', both teach in 'the West', both make theoretical use of post-
structuralism. It has become conventional at this stage to distinguish
Said's debt to Foucault from Spivak's to Derrida. And there is a certain
point to the convention: Spivak is both the translator into English of
Derrida's *Of Grammatology* and a famously 'obscure' deconstructionist

critic (Derrida, 1974; Eagleton, 1999c; Spivak, 1999, pp. 423-31); Said's understanding of 'Orientalism' had been as a 'discourse' in the specifically Foucauldian sense of 'an enormously systematic discipline by which European culture was able to manage - and even produce - the Orient ... during the post-Enlightenment period' (Said, 1995, p. 3). That said, we should add that Said's work has never been simply (or even complexly) post-structuralist. On the contrary, there is a great deal of healthy eclecticism in his writing and many other influences at work, most obviously perhaps that of Gramsci (ibid., p. 7).

These influences also include Williams: while *Marxism and Literature* is not among the theoretical resources for *Orientalism*, both *Culture and Society* and *The Long Revolution* certainly were (ibid., pp. 14, 28). One of Said's former students has even claimed that *The Country and the City* 'provided the initial motivation and, in part, the model for *Orientalism*' (Brennan, 1992, p. 77).[5] I remain unconvinced that this is so, but there is no doubting Said's own judgement that this was 'Williams's richest book' (Said, 1993, p. 98). When Said admits that his work 'depended very much on Raymond's' or when he claims to have 'learned so much from Raymond' (Williams and Said, 1989, pp. 181, 192), it is tempting to dismiss the first as overstatement, the second as mere politeness. After all, Said's attempt to chide Williams for his over-identification with the dominant forms of Anglo-Britishness provides one of the key lines of argument in this very discussion. Said returned to the argument, moreover, in the first Raymond Williams Lecture, where he insisted that Williams's 'intellectual and moral presence' had been inextricably connected to, both enabled and limited by, its 'Anglocentrism' (Said, 1990, pp. 81, 83). The criticism has been restated and reformulated more forthrightly by other, younger, postcolonial critics: Parry contrasts Said's 'exemplary graciousness' with Williams's 'visceral ... attachment' to 'identitarian thought'; Radhakrishan points to the 'asymmetry and unevenness' between their respective 'subject positions' (Parry, 1992, p. 22; Radhakrishnan, 1993, pp. 288-9). All this is fair comment, no doubt. But, for all the obvious and important differences, there is more in 'common' between Williams and Said than the latter's acolytes are sometimes inclined to concede. If not in *Orientalism*, then certainly in *The World, the Text and the Critic*, Said had acknowledged the 'great lesson' of *The Country and the City* that 'for every poem or novel in the canon there is a social fact being requisitioned for the page' (Said, 1984, p. 23). At one point, he had even used the term 'cultural materialism' to describe his own preferred 'methodological attitude' (ibid., p. 177). In the Memorial Lecture, moreover, Said is quite explicit that Williams's primary legacy is essentially methodological:

> Just as Williams ... enables us to move directly beyond ... the ideological capture of the *text* and into the life of communities, so too

does his work posthumously and over time enable us to perceive the generous perspectives on other literatures and societies afforded and made possible by his approach to English literature and society. (Said, 1990, p. 82)

In short, the method is fine, even if the substantive focus, which gave it its strength, appears unnecessarily circumscribed in theoretical retrospect. So, when Said asks of Williams, 'What ... is there in it for us ...?', the answer is to use the latter's 'work in and about England', so as to address 'related aesthetic, political and cultural problematics', as they appear in other, un-English, un-European, un-Western, locales and texts (Said, 1990, p. 84). In this particular instance, Said uses Williams's reading of Orwell as a way into his own of Camus.

This is more than simply a matter of methodology, in any positivist sense of the term: it is also a matter of the most basic assumptions about the nature of art, society and what it means to be human. The deeper commonality between Williams and Said is at its most apparent in the latter's magnum opus, *Culture and Imperialism*, which takes as its central theme the 'general relationship between culture and empire' and sets out to show how literature itself created 'structures of feeling' that supported, elaborated and consolidated European imperialism (Said, 1993, pp. xi, 14). Note the methodological and terminological borrowing from Williams; but note too the expansion of analytical focus beyond the narrow confines of England and Englishness. More importantly, note also what is not being done. In general, postcolonial criticism has tended to rely on post-structuralist theories of 'difference' to decentre and deconstruct liberal humanist notions of an 'essential' (read 'white' and 'European') 'truth' and 'humanity'. The manoeuvre works well enough as a relativisation of the dominant 'metropolitan' cultures, but only at the price of a threatened relativisation of subaltern identities and truth claims. For, if both Europeanness and otherness are constituted within and through discourse, then there can be no extradiscursively 'real' postcolonial identity, to which a postcolonial cultural politics might appeal. One way out of this dilemma is suggested by Spivak's notion of 'strategic essentialism': '*strategically* adhering to the essentialist notion of consciousness', while simultaneously drawing on the 'strengths' of 'antihumanist critique' (Spivak, 1987, pp. 206-7). But Said himself opts neither for relativism nor even for strategic essentialism. There 'seems no reason except fear and prejudice to keep insisting on ... separation and distinctiveness', he writes:

It is more rewarding - and more difficult - to think concretely and sympathetically, contrapuntally, about others than only about 'us'. But this also means not trying to rule over others, not trying to classify them or put them in hierarchies, above all, not constantly reiterating how 'our' culture or country is number one (or *not* number one, for that matter). (Said, 1993, p. 408)

For Said, then, as for Dollimore, and for Williams before him, the solution turns out to be, not so much a strategic essentialism as a radically nuanced version of essentialist humanism itself. Here more than anywhere, in this insistence on the continuing political and intellectual relevance of a radicalised humanism, Williams and Said come to occupy very much the same 'post-culturalist' theoretical space.

Notes

1 Thus Eagleton: 'perhaps the most I can hope to qualify for is William Carleton's beautifully guarded compliment to William Thackeray: "He writes very well about Ireland, for an Englishman"' (1995, p. ix).

2 Gallagher is less obviously impressed, but nonetheless also pays her dues to Williams's legacy (cf. Gallagher and Greenblatt, 2000, pp. 60-6).

3 On this subject, cf. Frow (1995, pp. 121-30); Milner (1999, pp. 148-64); Milner (2000).

4 The statement is more or less true of *Culture and Society* and *The Long Revolution*. But imperialism can hardly have been irrelevant to their author, who had been deprived of his commission precisely for his refusal to serve in an imperialist war. Recalled to the British Army for service during the Korean War, Williams had told his commanding officer: 'I would be no damn use to you, I'd be on the other side' (Williams, 1979a, p. 88).

5 This observation appears to be based on personal experience: 'Some of the statements I attribute to Said ... were made in seminars, lectures, or in conversation' (Brennan, 1992, pp. 92-3n).

7

Towards 2050

> Men fight and lose the battle, and the thing that they fought for comes about in spite of their defeat, and when it comes turns out not to be what they meant, and other men have to fight for what they meant under another name... (Morris, A Dream of John Ball)

> Late ... capitalism ... constitutes ... the purest form of capital yet to have emerged, a prodigious expansion of capital into hitherto uncommodified areas. This purer capitalism of our own time thus eliminates the enclaves of precapitalist organization it had hitherto tolerated and exploited in a tributary way. (Jameson, Postmodernism, or, the Cultural Logic of Late Capitalism)

Thus far we have discussed Williams's work, and cultural materialism more generally, mainly in relation to the specifics of British intellectual life, to some limited extent in relation to my own Australian situation. But neither the history of British cultural studies nor that of the wider post-war Anglophone intellectual culture can be written in such circumscribed terms: insofar as the intelligentsia is concerned, perhaps the single most important development over the last thirty years has been the relatively rapid rate of translation of key theoretical texts between the major western European languages, in particular English, French and German. The impress of German critical theory and French structuralism remains continuously present in the British, American and Australian debates themselves. More importantly, perhaps, we need to note the presence of roughly commensurate sets of theoretical dilemmas in other intellectual cultures powerfully subject to the simultaneous influence of literary humanism and Communist Marxism. The obviously relevant instances here are Germany and France, the two European countries that provided a home to Western Marxism and, to date, the only western countries to witness the creation and subsequent destruction of mass Communist Parties.[1] In this chapter, then, we proceed to a brief comparison between British cultural materialism and certain roughly equivalent developments in recent German and French thought: Habermas's theory of communicative action, Foucault's 'genealogy' and Bourdieu's cultural sociology.

Cultural Materialism as Post-Culturalism

Habermas's work can be represented as, in a significant sense, cultural materialist. More explicitly sympathetic to Marx than either Foucault or Bourdieu, he interprets the base/superstructure model, very similarly to Williams, as a historical rather than ontological proposition, 'the mark of a seal that must be broken' (Habermas, 1990, p. 16). His early theorisation of the bourgeois 'public sphere' (Habermas, 1989), as also the later borrowing from Weber of the notion of increasingly autonomous and professionalised cultural spheres as constitutive of a distinctive cultural modernity (Habermas, 1985, p. 9), both suggest the possibilities for an institutional analysis of culture. Habermas's theoretical affiliations have been to Western Marxism rather than to any kind of structuralism: he readily admits his indebtedness to 'Lukács, Korsch, Gramsci and the Frankfurt School' (Habermas, 1979b, p. 83), that is, to the more expressly humanist and culturalist elements within the Marxian legacy. This is a Marxism which learnt much from Weber and from German sociology, most importantly, that modern capitalism remains subject to a developmental logic of rationalisation. Weber's rationalisation thesis, as also his elaboration of the different types of rational action, are central to Habermas. Indeed, the latter's defence of Enlightenment reason, against both French post-structuralism and the darkly pessimistic 'dialectic of Enlightenment' of his own former mentors, Adorno and Horkheimer (Habermas, 1987a), can be seen as resuming the earlier meliorist expectations not only of Marx, but of Weber.

There are obvious parallelisms between Williams and Habermas, which have on occasion been remarked upon (Eagleton, 1990a, pp. 404, 409). Both subscribed to a kind of radical-democratic anti-capitalism which takes its inspiration partly from Marxism, partly from post-Romantic idealism, in Habermas's case that of Weber, in Williams's that of Leavis. Both were as enthusiastically sympathetic to the postmodern 'new social movements' (Habermas, 1981) as they were suspicious of postmodern theoretical relativism. For Habermas, as for Williams, the long revolution continues, but it does so in the peculiar guise of a reason immanent within sociality itself. For Habermas, as for Williams, the theoretical model of an emancipated culture, deriving from the allegedly constitutive properties of actually existing culture, provides the criteria by which both to critique existing social reality and to elaborate the utopian possibilities for real social change. For Williams, the model was that of a truly common culture, for Habermas that of unimpeded communication: through the structure of language, he wrote, 'autonomy and responsibility are posited for us. Our first sentence expresses unequivocally the intention of universal and unconstrained consensus' (Habermas, 1971, p. 314). The end result is the theory of communicative action itself (Habermas, 1984; Habermas, 1987b).

Habermas's departures from Communist Marxism are at least as radical as those of Williams, and in one respect very much more so: for Habermas, the old class struggle between capital and labour has been rendered archaic by the emergence of the post-war welfare state, on the one hand, the struggles of the new social movements on the other (Habermas, 1981, p. 33). As empirical propositions about the nature of contemporary social reality, these seem to me highly implausible, even when applied to the unusually affluent working class and unusually influential Green movement of the Federal German Republic. Williams's sense of the continuing importance of social class seems to me much more persuasive. Quite apart from this fundamental political difference, there are differences also of intellectual approach, which are partly disciplinary and partly national-cultural in origin. For Williams, the concretely experiential remains stubbornly relevant, not so much as the antithesis but as the complement to abstract reason. As Eagleton rightly observed: 'Williams's subtle sense of the complex mediations between such necessarily universal formations as social class, and the lived particularities of place, region, Nature, the body, contrasts tellingly with Habermas's universalist rationalism' (Eagleton, 1990a, p. 409). It is my guess that, for Williams, class was as much a matter of lived particularity as of universal formation, and that it was at this level, as much as at any other, that he chose to refuse the false opposition between old and new social movements. Be that as it may, it seems difficult to avoid the conclusion that for Habermas the disciplinary claims of sociology appear to pose a recurrent threat to the claims of particularity. In itself this should serve to remind us that both Cultural Studies in general and Williams's cultural materialism in particular emerged from a distinctively British intellectual environment barely touched by sociology. This may not be quite the burden it once seemed.

We have had previous cause to compare cultural materialism with various forms of structuralism and post-structuralism. It might be imagined, then, that there is little more to be said about Foucault certainly, perhaps even about Bourdieu. But it could also be argued that, in the strictest sense of the term, neither Foucault nor Bourdieu can be considered properly 'post-structuralist'; that the title belongs more appropriately to Derridean deconstruction and its anticipation in the later Barthes. Unlike Barthes, Foucault himself deliberately refused the self-description, 'structuralist' (Foucault, 1980, p. 114); and moreover, as structuralism gave way to post-structuralism, he was to prove publicly dismissive of Derrida's work (Foucault, 1972b, p. 602). Somewhat analogously, Bourdieu sought to distance himself from the 'objectivism' of structuralist anthropology (Bourdieu, 1977a, pp. 1-30); and he too was to prove similarly dismissive of Derrida (Bourdieu, 1984, p. 495). Yet there is a sense, nonetheless, in which both inhabit a more generally post-structuralist intellectual universe. As we noted in Chapter 5, from Durkheim and Saussure through to Barthes and Lévi-Strauss structuralism had displayed a recurrent aspiration to scientificity, its central project to discover the truth beneath the text hidden within the text's own deep structures. By contrast, post-structuralism betrayed that aspiration by an equally recurrent insistence that there could be no such single truth within the text, that signs always signify again. And this scepticism *vis-à-vis* discourse, a scepticism which seeks to identify the possibilities within discourse which discourse itself seeks to repress, is, in fact, as characteristic of Foucault and Bourdieu as of Derrida and Barthes.

More importantly for our purposes, both Foucault and Bourdieu take much more seriously than does its author Derrida's insistence that deconstruction, as distinct from critique, should interfere 'with solid structures, "material" institutions, and not only with discourses or signifying representations' (Derrida, 1987, p. 19). For Foucault, institutional and discursive practices, powers and knowledges, are inextricably interconnected, and in ways that are necessarily internal to each other. Thus, when he rejected the Marxist base/superstructure model, Foucault did so in terms oddly reminiscent of Williams, which stressed, not simply the autonomy of the 'superstructures', but more importantly their materiality (Foucault, 1980, p. 118). For Bourdieu, too, the 'symbolic power' of ideology is not some secondary effect of an economy located elsewhere, but is itself fully material. Thus, when Bourdieu rejected the 'crude reductionism' of much Marxism, he did so, again in terms oddly reminiscent of Williams, by emphasising that ideologies 'owe their structure and their most specific functions to the social conditions of their production and circulation - that is to say, to the functions which they fulfil ... for the specialists competing for the monopoly of the established competence in question' (Bourdieu, 1977b, p. 116). If cultural materialism reduced to essentials holds simply, in Bennett's phrase, 'that cultural practices should be regarded as forms of material production' (Bennett, 1990, p. 13), then clearly, there is much, both in Foucault and perhaps even more so in Bourdieu, that is in this generic sense 'cultural materialist'.

There are, nonetheless, very significant differences between Williams's cultural materialism and that of both Foucault and Bourdieu. The contrast with Foucault is particularly striking. Where Williams persisted in seeing a history and an evolution, a long revolution that was in some quite fundamental senses progressive, Foucault detected only difference and rupture. *Discipline and Punish* (Foucault, 1977b), as also the earlier, more structuralist *Madness and Civilisation* and *The Birth of the Clinic* (Foucault, 1965; Foucault, 1973a), were each built around binary oppositions between the classical *episteme* of the eighteenth century and our own modern *episteme*. These discursive regimes were contrasted with each other as equally systemic, equally valid, equally regulative. There is, then, no progress, only difference and, at times, Foucault's remorseless demystification of the pretensions to scientificity of modern psychiatry, medicine and penology appeared almost to suggest a preference for the eighteenth century. Where Williams persisted in seeing the possibilities for a macropolitics that would continue the long revolution, and for a kind of intellectual engagement that would be at worst 'organic' to the working class, at best 'universal', Foucault aspired only to a 'specific' micropolitics. Where Williams persisted in seeing human society and culture as the products of human agency, albeit an agency often alienated from itself, Foucault's position remained resolutely anti-humanist. The strength of the new sciences of psychoanalysis and structural anthropology, he wrote in 1966, was in their ability 'to do without the concept of man ... they dissolve man' (Foucault, 1973b, p. 379). This anti-humanism clearly persisted from the earlier archaeology into the middle period genealogy: 'genealogy', he insisted, requires 'a form of history which can account for the constitution of knowledges ... without having to make reference to a subject' (Foucault, 1980, p. 117).

Foucault's historical relativism and his modestly libertarian micropolitics remain connected to this anti-humanism by way, not so much of a presence, as of an absence: that of an ethics. Where in William humanist historiography and epistemology both sustain and are sustained by a humanist ethic, there is no such equivalent in Foucault. This is not to suggest that a practical ethics is necessarily logically incompatible with a theoretical anti-humanism, only that Foucault himself was unable to construct one until the later volumes of *The History of Sexuality*, and that, when it did appear, it was a poor, pathetic thing, an aestheticist mythologisation of the phallocratic sexual mores of Greek slaveowners (Foucault, 1985). Williams's humanism was, of course, not the 'liberal humanism' so often derided, and rightly so, by post-Althusserian postmodernists, deconstructionists and post-structuralist feminists for its false universalism. It was, rather, a specifically 'materialist' humanism, which acknowledged the differences in our present condition, precisely so as to distinguish eradicable inequity from desirable plurality, and thereby to proceed, not to the abstractly universal, but to a concrete commonality. In a world which becomes progressively more totalised, by the pressure of global environmental crisis as much as by the drive toward globalisation, Foucault's refusal of a humanist ethics, as also that in postmodern post-structuralism more generally, seems closer to an ethic of irresponsibility than to one of self-mastery.

No such verdict could be pronounced on Bourdieu, whose life and work are much nearer to Williams in tone and purpose, and whose earlier writings excited the latter's positive admiration. In the late 1990s, Bourdieu became by far the most prominent academic intellectual to join in active solidarity with the new 'anti-globalisation' movements. The latter phrase is a misnomer, of course, since in its campaigns for the internationalisation of human, democratic and trade union rights, this 'movement of many movements' (Klein, 2001, p. 81) is at least as 'global' in scope as its corporate opponents. Its real target has been globalisation on corporate terms, what Naomi Klein calls 'the privatization of every aspect of life, and the transformation of every activity and value into a commodity'; its real aim 'a radical reclaiming of the commons' (ibid., p. 82). The movement tends to date its origins from 1994-95, the years of the Zapatista rising in Mexico and the public-sector strikes in France. But Bourdieu's *La Misère du monde*, first published in hardback in 1993, and in paperback in 1998, had clearly foreshadowed many of its political preoccupations. The book's combination of ethnographic interviews and sociological commentary had mounted a stunning indictment of 'economic liberalism' - what in Britain was known as 'Thatcherism'; in the United States, 'Reaganism'; in Australia, bizarrely enough, 'economic rationalism' - as setting up precisely the preconditions for 'an unprecedented development of all kinds of ordinary suffering' (Bourdieu et al., 1999, pp. 4, 181-8). A bestseller in France, it became a major source of political inspiration to the new movement, both in the original and in its 1999 English translation, *The Weight of the World*.

Bourdieu was also directly involved in militant 'anti-globalisation' activism: he spoke in solidarity with mass meetings of striking railway workers in 1995 and of unemployed workers in 1998 (Bourdieu, 1998a, pp. 24n, 88n); he launched the 1996 petition for an 'Estates General of the Social Movement' and its May Day 2000 successor, the appeal for a pan-European Estates General; he co-founded the radical 'Raisons d'agir' group and its associated publishing house; he had publicly called 'for a left Left' (Bourdieu, 1998b); he was a regular contributor to the radical monthly, *Le Monde diplomatique*, which was published in French and in English translation. For an Anglophone observer of my generation and intellectual formation, it was difficult not to be reminded of Williams's performance in this self-same role as activist-intellectual. If Williams was a British Sartre, then Bourdieu is close to becoming a French Williams. Certainly, there is a great deal more point to this comparison than to any with Anthony Giddens, Bourdieu's counterpart in recent British Sociology, whose work has amounted to little more than a sustained apologia for the post-Thatcherism of Blair's 'New Labour' Party (Giddens, 1994; Giddens, 1998). In his 1988 obituary, Garnham made something of a virtue out of the necessity that Williams 'was a man who worked, largely alone with the assistance of his wife, outside the institutional bases of communication studies ... He never received foundation or research council funding for communications research' (Garnham, 1988, p. 124). That this might have been, at best, a cruel virtue is suggested by the results of the relatively well-funded, collaborative research undertaken by Bourdieu. The obvious instance, at least insofar as Cultural Studies is concerned, is *Distinction*, which was based on a detailed sociological survey, conducted by interview and by ethnographic observation, of the cultural preferences of over 1200 people from three different urban areas (Bourdieu, 1984, p. 503). But resources of a similar magnitude are also brought to bear in *The State Nobility* (Bourdieu, 1996a) and in *The Weight of the World* itself.

The points of similarity between Bourdieu and Williams are at once both intellectual and political: a shared sense of the continuing importance of social class to the social structures of advanced capitalism; a shared suspicion of the pretensions to exclusive legitimacy of bourgeois 'high culture'; a shared sympathy for popular cultural aspirations; and a shared assessment of the centrality of culture to the social organisation of contemporary capitalism. Bourdieu's pointed contrast between 'the aesthetic disposition' of legitimate taste, on the one hand, which 'presupposes the distance from the world ... which is the basis of bourgeois experience' (Bourdieu, 1984, p. 54), and 'the popular aesthetic', on the other, 'based on the affirmation of continuity between art and life' and 'a deep-rooted demand for participation' (ibid., p. 32), both echoes and confirms much of what Williams had argued about modernism, postmodernism and popular culture. At a further, perhaps deeper level, there is an interesting parallelism between Williams's theory of determination and Bourdieu's theory of practice. Both attempted to theorise human sociality in terms of the strategic action of individuals within a constraining, but nonetheless not determining, context of values, a 'structure of feeling' in Williams, the 'habitus' in Bourdieu (Bourdieu, 1977a, pp. 72-95). These are understood, in each case, as simultaneously structured and structuring, as materially produced (ibid., p. 72) and, interestingly, as very often generation-specific (ibid., p. 78).

But there are also important differences. Where Williams insisted on the concretely experiential quality of such structures, the equivalent in Bourdieu is much more abstract, a system of durable dispositions rather than a pattern of felt experience. Where Williams worked with a model of theory as explicitly critical, Bourdieu's work tended to affect a quasi-positivistic objectivism. Though *Distinction* was certainly 'a social critique of the judgement of taste', it was less obviously a critique of the aesthetic disposition itself: here, the moment of critique remained well concealed behind a carefully cultivated mask of scientific 'objectivity'. Even in *The Weight of the World*, clearly the most explicitly engaged of his scholarly works, Bourdieu still insisted that sociological 'science' could itself uncover 'the possibilities for action' political programmes will need to take advantage of (Bourdieu et al., 1999, p. 629). Where Williams conceived of the intellectual function as primarily critical, and of intellectuals as significantly productive of emergent sensibility, Bourdieu detected mainly the dominated fraction of the dominant class, the self-interested traders in cultural capital. There is, thus, a certain cynical quality to Bourdieu's insistence that 'all practices, including those purporting to be disinterested or gratuitous' can be treated as 'economic practices directed towards the maximizing of material or symbolic profit' (Bourdieu, 1977a, p. 183). Such cynicism can easily lead to a radical overestimation of the reproductive powers of the social *status quo*. Hence, what Garnham and Williams termed the 'functionalist/determinist residue' (Garnham and Williams, 1986, p. 129) in Bourdieu's concept of reproduction, a residue that, in theoretical terms at least, remains more than residual.

Bourdieu struggled to find ways of thinking the role of the intellectual which would allow for his own developing aspiration to activism. Hence, the interest in what he termed the 'corporatism of the universal', that is, the idea that intellectuals have a kind of collective self-interest in the defence of the culture sphere, which somehow translates into something close to a traditional humanist politics (Bourdieu, 1989; Bourdieu, 1996b, pp. 339-48). The problem should be obvious, however: this approach both contradicts his own earlier scepticism about the intelligentsia's pretensions to distinction and also radically understates the more general moral significance of his own political intervention. It matters, then - and perhaps more than Garnham and Williams were willing to acknowledge - that Bourdieu's activist politics, increasingly admirable though they undoubtedly were, still seemed extrinsic to his massively 'reproductive' sociology. As a British socialist recently observed: 'Bourdieu's political stance ... is ... less a reflection than an antidote to aspects of his theoretical vision' (Wolfreys, 2000, p. 99). Though Garnham and Williams resisted this description, Bourdieu's work is still best understood in its, admittedly fraught, relation to Durkheimian structural anthropology: the positivistic rendering of the empirical as the externally measurable and observable, the sense of the efficacy of collective representations, even the conception of 'sociology' as embracing what the English speakers still distinguished as 'anthropology', all this is characteristically Durkheimian.[2] Indeed, one might venture the suggestion that Bourdieu's relation to French anthropology - dissenting, plebeian, but belonging, nonetheless - was akin to that between the young Williams and English Literature.

Although Williams and Habermas, Foucault and Bourdieu, do indeed share in a certain 'cultural materialism', there are significant divergences, nonetheless, between their respective positions. These seem to be explicable, at least in part, as a consequence of 'inherited' differences between British culturalism, German critical theory and French structuralism. In short, Williams stands in an essentially analogous relation to the culturalist tradition as do Habermas to the (Western) Marxist, Foucault and Bourdieu to the structuralist. Williams's cultural materialism is thus best understood, neither as a culturalism nor even a left-culturalism, but rather as what we have termed 'post-culturalism'. We have noted how the theoretical literature in Cultural Studies tended to contrast Williams's 'culturalism' with the long tradition of French structuralism. What we now know as post-structuralism developed by way of a reaction against precisely this structuralist intellectual tradition. But there is an equivalently long culturalist tradition behind Williams, reaching back from Eliot and Leavis to Arnold and beyond. And Williams's relation to this tradition is essentially 'post-culturalist'. This is so in more than the simply chronological sense. As we have seen, the post-structuralist discovery that all knowledge is social and all meaning plural led to an emergent preoccupation with the role of the reader and related concepts. We also noted how, before Williams, the culturalist tradition had itself typically subscribed, not to a scientism, but nonetheless to a kind of 'objective idealism' by which truth was seen to inhere in the cultural tradition itself. We observed how Williams's deconstruction of this notion, through the idea of the selective tradition, effected a relativising turn similar to that of post-structuralism in relation to structuralism. It did so by virtue of an appeal to the role of the collective reader. It gestured in the direction of a recognition of the intrication of power within discourse such as that acknowledged by both Foucault and Bourdieu; and a recognition of the materiality, historicity and social arbitrariness of the linguistic sign similar to that in Foucault and Derrida. All of this remained coupled to a sense of genuinely free communicative action - a truly common culture - as normative, of which even Habermas might have approved. Little wonder, then, that Eagleton should have described Williams's work as prefiguring and pre-empting 'the development of parallel left positions by, so to speak, apparently standing still' (1984, p. 109).

Cultural Materialism and Cultural Studies

Theoretically, the central point at issue between Williams's cultural materialism and the various post-structuralisms concerned neither the autonomy nor the effectivity, nor even the materiality, of culture, but rather the ontological status of the human subject, that is, the question of theoretical humanism versus theoretical anti-humanism. As Higgins observes, in an argument directed at Dollimore and Sinfield as much as at Yale deconstruction or the new historicism: 'For Williams, the self or subject is never simply an effect of language ... Language does not simply determine self-consciousness; it also enables it' (Higgins, 1999, p. 174). I am myself reasonably convinced that Williams, and Marx, though not most Marxists, were right in this matter: that there is, in fact, a human nature, and that this nature is best grasped by Marx's understanding of the human 'species being' as constituted by our capacity for conscious, collective and creative production (Marx,

1975b, pp. 327-30). We are, then, quite centrally the makers of our own history and the producers of our own culture. It is because Williams held to this view that his cultural materialism became, at its core, a theory of cultural *production*. And it is in this sense that it was indeed, as he insisted, 'a Marxist theory'. Such propositions are necessarily pregnant with intellectual and political consequence. For these respective humanisms and anti-humanisms bear very differently, both on literary and Cultural Studies, considered as specialist academic disciplines, and also on the wider prospects for an emancipatory politics.

To take the disciplinary question first, it must now be obvious that those of us who still choose to think of ourselves as 'Marxists' - as distinct from culturalists, structuralists, post-structuralists - are increasingly confronted with the problem of how to relate to a Cultural Studies that is quite clearly not Marxist. There is a precedent for this situation, not in Cultural Studies itself, but in history, which seems to have been the preferred discipline for Communist academics, both in Britain and Australia (I cannot speak for the United States) in the years immediately following the Second World War. It occurs to me that we might profitably learn from this previous experience of those Marxist historians, at least as it was to be eventually theorised by E.P. Thompson. In most of the stories of Cultural Studies, including my own, Thompson normally rates only a bit-part as one of the early 'founding fathers', but then tends to leave the stage much earlier than either Williams or Hoggart. As indeed he really did: for *The Poverty of Theory* was intended as a wholesale attack on much that Cultural Studies then most admired: on Althusser in particular, but also on 'Theory' and 'structuralism' more generally. It was also - and quite deliberately - a performative act of identification with the discipline of history, as distinct from Cultural Studies, sociology, or English (like Hall, Thompson had been trained in the latter). Here Thompson directly addressed the relationship between history as a discipline and historical materialism as a particular argument in relation to it. He was insistent on two points: that historical evidence has a determinate objectivity, an independent existence quite apart from any significance the historian may accord it (Thompson, 1978, pp. 231-5); and that there is a common 'historical logic', defined in terms of both theoretical and evidential procedures, to which both Marxist and non-Marxist history must submit. If Marxist concepts are 'found to be more "true", or adequate to explanation, than others', he explained:

> this will be because they stand up better to the test of historical logic, and not because they are "derived from" a true Theory outside this discipline ... I refuse ... to escape from criticism by leaping from the court of appeal. For historical knowledge, this court lies within the discipline of history and nowhere else ... Appeal may take two

forms ... evidential ... and ... theoretical ... But both forms of appeal may be conducted only within the vocabulary of historical logic. The court has been sitting in judgement upon historical materialism for one hundred years, and it is continually being adjourned. (ibid., pp. 236-7)

Note the interesting homology between how Thompson conceived of his own interventions into the discipline of history and how Popular Front Communism, of which he had once been part, had conceived of its into the labour movement and the peace movement. In both cases, the intervention is judged by how well it stands up to the demands of the discipline/movement.

Whatever his sources, however, Thompson was surely right and Althusserian theoreticism surely equally mistaken. The proper business of historical materialism in relation to history, and of cultural materialism in relation to Cultural Studies, must be to make use of its own capacity for distinctive conceptualisation, so as to produce empirically powerful propositions, amenable to testing according to the particular logics of the discipline itself. Which poses the interesting question as to why this Thompsonian option was not available to Williams, in many respects the more politically 'moderate' figure. The answer is obvious: Cultural Studies was not yet a discipline. The only equivalent to Thompson's history would thus have been 'English Literature', an essentially hostile formation, which could only ever have been a kangaroo court. As Williams himself explained: 'The reason my attack was ... so radical was that I had decided, from within the tradition of literary criticism itself, that its categories of literature and of criticism were so deeply compromised that they had to be challenged *in toto*' (Williams, 1979a, p. 326). But that was then and this is now; and in the interim Cultural Studies has begun to emerge as something roughly approximating a conventional academic discipline. Now that we have finally erected the tribunal of Cultural Studies before which to plead, now clearly is the time to begin pleading: for cultural materialism certainly and perhaps even for Marxism too. In short, it is time to recognise Williams's work as a significant resource of hope in its own right, not least for the positive value it attaches to the idea of a common culture.

There is probably no idea in Williams so thoroughly discredited as this now is. But, as we noted in Chapter 3, much of that discredit attaches to a quite unwarranted conflation of Williams's argument with that in Eliot and Leavis. We should be grateful, then, for Eagleton's recent attempt to recover the original intention. 'The paradox of Williams's position', he writes, is that the conditions for a truly common culture: 'can be laid only by politically securing ... , in effect, socialist institutions. And this ... involves common belief, commitment and practice. Only through a fully participatory democracy, including one which regulated material production, could the channels of access be fully opened to give vent to ... cultural diversity' (Eagleton, 2000, p. 122). This is exactly so. We might add, however, that this is only one of three senses in which Williams uses the concept of a common culture (or some close synonym). At times, it does indeed function exactly as Eagleton says, that is, as a normative political ideal, an equivalent to the idea of democratic socialism itself, in the sense of a 'participatory democracy, regulating material production'. At others, however, it functions much more theoretically, as an equivalent to the concept of totality in Lukács, totalisation in Sartre, or cognitive mapping in Jameson, that is, as an injunction to see the whole, to find the connections (Lukács, 1971, pp. 27-8; Sartre, 1976, p 46: Jameson, 1991, p. 54). At yet others, it functions practically, as an equivalent to the notion of solidarity in labour and socialist practice. All three usages seem to me indispensable and none to lead to the cultural authoritarianism one finds in Leavis and Eliot. We live in dangerously interesting times, where a rampantly hegemonic corporate capitalism threatens to empty the 'social' of virtually all content and meaning. In such times, I fail to see how we can even begin to cope, let alone hope, without resort to some notion such as this, in all of its three senses.

Cultural Materialism and Socialist Politics: Towards 2050

As noted in the previous chapter, Dollimore and Sinfield described cultural materialism as combining 'historical context, theoretical method, political commitment and textual analysis'. The political commitment was to be of a necessarily radical kind, moreover: 'socialist and feminist commitment', they continued, 'confronts the conservative categories in which most criticism has ... been conducted' (Dollimore and Sinfield, 1994b, p. vii). There can be no doubt that Williams's own work was indeed so politically motivated, nor that his was a deliberately radical politics, explicitly directed toward the 'politics of culture', in Eagleton's phrase, as distinct from 'cultural politics'. The possibility remains, however, that this is a matter of mere contingency: the nexus between political and cultural theory certainly seems so in the (post-) structuralist tradition. But in Williams's cultural materialism, a simultaneous stress on the human capacity for conscious creativity on the one hand, on the material determination of the possibilities and limits of such creativity on the other, seems much more amenable to alignment with an emancipatory than an exploitative or oppressive politics. For Williams this had meant a continuing commitment to the radical libertarian and socialist currents within the labour movement and, later, a developing sympathy for Welsh nationalism. In both cases, the more obviously communitarian and solidaristic aspects of the politics sat fairly comfortably with equivalently communitarian and solidaristic elements in the cultural theory. As he told a 1977 Summer School of the Welsh nationalist party, Plaid Cymru, a 'truly prospective', as distinct from 'merely retrospective', radical nationalist politics could produce 'the kind of complex liberation which genuine community ... could be' (Williams, 1989f, pp. 117-18).

Williams knew, of course, that Labour governments have been as much a part of the problem as of the solution; he knew too that the building of nation states had been 'intrinsically a ruling-class operation' (Williams, 1983, p. 181); he even knew that in the 1930s Welsh nationalism had been 'on the cultural Right ... Wales was offered ... as the last noble fragment of a classical and catholic world' (Williams, 1989g, p. 59). His own socialism, as also his own Welshness, were of a very different kind. But the objection remains that even such labourisms and such radical nationalisms as his, whatever their original emancipatory intent, articulate a by now demonstrably residual, rather than emergent, structure of feeling, in a world that is increasingly globalised, increasingly post-industrial, increasingly individualised, in short, increasingly 'postmodern'. Hence, for example, O'Connor and Redhead's damning comment that 'we are not going to hear', from Williams, 'anything that may shock the sensibilities of the "Labour Movement"' (O'Connor and Redhead, 1991, p. 125). Such charges are particularly telling, moreover, if made from the vantage point of a postmodern feminism, since the old working-class or old Welsh community, as much as Habermas's 'life world', was sustained, both in reality and very often also as a normative ideal, by an obviously patriarchal sexual division. It is not that feminists have ignored Williams (cf. Mitchell, 1984; Rowbotham, 1985; Lovell, 1989). Nor even that Williams had entirely ignored feminism: when challenged in 1979, he had readily conceded that it was not only a political weakness, but 'an intellectual failing not to confront the problem' (Williams, 1979a, p. 150). Both in the *Politics and Letters* interviews and in the later *Towards 2000*, there is evidence of a real attempt at solidarity with the women's movement, for example in his support for 'the transitional demand of payment for housework' (Williams, 1979a, p. 149). But it is clear that Williams himself was never able adequately either to theorise or even to articulate emotionally such questions of sexual politics. There is no equivalent anywhere in his work to Bourdieu's attempts to theorise masculine domination in general and the social position of gays and lesbians in particular (Bourdieu, 2001).

The year after his death, Jane Miller had asked exasperatedly of Williams how a thinker so willing to 'rethink absolutely' even the most central tenets of Marxism could be so unwilling to 'countenance even the questions which feminists have addressed' (Miller, 1990, p. 48). Six years later, in a review of Inglis's biography, Jim McGuigan would provide one possible answer: 'Were he still alive Williams would be seventy five this year. I do not personally happen to know any really feminist seventy-five-year-old men, which is no excuse for them or for Williams but merely a sociological observation' (McGuigan, 1996,

p. 107). This is an excuse, of course, and one followed by an excuse for an excuse. But thinking of my own father - still living I'm pleased to say, but very much of Williams's generation - and his friends, I am tempted to concede the point. McGuigan fails, nonetheless, to register the reasons why feminists like Miller felt entitled to be disappointed with Williams. As Cora Kaplan puts it:

> Williams's ... perspectives and those of feminist critics and historians often run parallel and occasionally dovetail, both in their critique of an older Marxist analysis of culture and in their interest in and reservations about structuralist and post-structuralist theory. This convergence may ... partly explain ... his own reticence and reservations about feminism, for it often seems as if these analyses ... are in a kind of unacknowledged competition for the same ground. (1995, p. 213)

Kaplan's own reading of the 1840s, and of Williams's readings of the 1840s, persuasively analyses a peculiarly salient instance of precisely such 'unacknowledged competition'. More generally, however, her observation also seems to explain the double response to Williams's work from within feminism, described thus by Morag Shiach: 'some respond to what they feel ought to be its implications, others ... with frustration and anger to what it does not say' (1995, p. 57). So, for example, Carol Watts, writing in the avowedly Williamsite journal *News from Nowhere*, argued that, whatever the limitations of Williams's own particular effort, cultural materialism could 'contribute to a feminist historical materialism' and 'connect(s) with a field of feminist study which is thriving - women's culture and literature, theories of representation' (Watts, 1989, p. 106). Tracing a middle course somewhere between Watts and Miller, Shiach herself insists that: 'Feminists can find much of use to them in the work of Raymond Williams; they cannot, however, find many women' (Shiach, 1995, p. 51). Her own conclusion seems salutory: 'Williams's work will not simply deliver a feminist politics but it may help in the difficult political and theoretical task of developing a feminist analysis of the role of gender in the construction and maintenance of the contemporary social formation' (ibid., p. 57).

Despite Williams's obvious weaknesses as a feminist, O'Connor and Redhead's more general comments seem to me both manifestly false and manifestly unfair. On the contrary, Williams's later work engaged very directly with the postmodern politics of the late twentieth century. As Francis Mulhern would observe, only two years short of the millennium itself: '*Towards 2000* will soon be literally out of date, but it will remain actual and exemplary for its refusal to trim its reasoning to the measure of capitalist possibility, for its commitment to the renewal of rational historical imagination' (1998, p. 115). The book had been characterised by a sustained attempt at theoretical innovation and exploration. It was here that Williams's work most clearly registered the paradigm shift from the 'New New Left' of the 1960s and 1970s to the 'postmodern left' of the 1980s and 1990s. Its most explicitly 'postmodern' moment, entailing a radical reversal of sensibilities on Williams's part, was in its strong sense of the internationalisation of the contemporary world order. This, in turn, provided the materials for a critique of 'official' nationalism and of Labour's complicity therewith. To the 'official community' of nation states such as 'the Yookay', Williams now sought to counterpose an internationalism that would nonetheless be compatible with the 'lived and formed identities' of the 'minority peoples', not only the Welsh, but the Scots, Irish and West Indian, and even the English 'regions' (Williams, 1983, p. 197). If this concern with localised, 'knowable' communities was not in itself novel, the radical antipathy to the British nation state and to its culture most certainly was: the particularities of the Welsh and the complexities of a 'paranational' world system both became more pressing here than the peculiarities of a Britain understood as English, an England understood as 'the South', a South understood as its ruling and intermediate classes.

Here, too, Williams coined the term 'Plan X' to describe the 'new politics of strategic advantage' characteristic of the postmodern political-economy. This is what we have since learned to name as 'globalisation', the politics, not only of Thatcherism and Reaganism, but of the World Trade Organisation and the International Monetary Fund, the World Bank and the World Economic Forum, of Clinton and Bush, and also, as Bourdieu reminded us, of Blair, Jospin and Schröder (Bourdieu, 1998b).[3] Williams's own description of 'X Planning' remains startlingly prescient:

> [W]hat is new ... is that it has genuinely incorporated a reading of the future, and one which is quite as deeply pessimistic ... as the most extreme readings of those ... campaigning against ... the extending damage of ecological crisis ... The difference of "Plan X" people is that they do not believe that any of these dangers can be halted or turned back. Even when there are technical ways they do not believe that there are possible political ways. Thus ... their real politics and planning are not centred on these, but on an acceptance of the indefinite continuation of extreme crisis and extreme danger. (Williams, 1983, p. 244)

Note how the argument is stated with uncharacteristic force, with few of the careful qualifications so common elsewhere in Williams's work. The urgency of tone clearly attested to a powerful sense of growing alarm, which in retrospect seems entirely appropriate.

Here, too, Williams quite deliberately identified the new social

movements - the peace movement, the ecology movement, the feminist movement, and the movement of 'oppositional culture' - as major
'resources for a journey of hope' beyond capitalism (Williams, 1983,
pp. 249-50). One clear measure of the distance travelled by Williams
since the 1970s is provided by his ability here to recognise and
applaud the achievements both of feminist scholarship and of the
women's movement itself. Despite O'Connor and Redhead, the labour
parties did not, in fact, figure as such a resource in *Towards 2000*, but
rather as a problem to be negotiated. Their central function, Williams
wrote, 'is to reproduce the existing definitions of issues and interests.
When they extend to new issues and interests, they usually lead them
back into a system which will isolate, dilute and eventually compro-
mise them' (ibid., p. 250). This is surely a proposition able to offend the
sensibilities of much of the labour movement, both in Britain and elsewhere. One Australian writer even (mis) read Williams's argument as
tantamount to the suggestion that the new movements had challenged
the very basis of the traditional institutions of the labour movement
(Johnson, 1987, p. 175). At one level, this is so, for Williams was indeed
arguing against the labour parties as they had traditionally functioned. But Johnson nonetheless underestimated the strength of
Williams's commitment to class politics as such: the new reality 'is
often *mis*interpreted', he insisted, as 'getting beyond class politics'
(Williams, 1983, p. 172 - my emphasis).

These 'new' issues, followed through, in Williams's view, 'lead us
into the central systems of the industrial-capitalist mode of production
and ... into its system of classes' (Williams, 1983, pp. 172-3). For the
Williams of *Towards 2000*, it is true, the labour movement could 'go
either way'. But this was an alternative in which only one option is
truly bearable: for if organised labour becomes finally incorporated,
then socialism would be 'left stranded as a theory and a sect' (ibid.,
p. 173). What is true is that Williams, unlike Thompson, had by now
clearly understood the labour parties, if not the labour movement, and
certainly not the working class, as obstacles to social change.
O'Connor and Redhead seem to have required of a radical politics that
it positively disengage, not only from Labourism as both political ideology and party, but from the very notion of class itself. They thus
asked much more than that Williams should shock the sensibilities of
the labour movement: they asked, in short, that he abandon the central
insights, not only of Marxism, but of much mainstream academic sociology, into the operation of structured social inequality in late-capitalist societies. It hardly seems a price worth paying. In my view, it was
precisely in the strength of Williams's endorsement of the new social
movements, and of his deliberately nuanced appraisal of the labour
movement, that he succeeded in recuperating the positive, but not the
negative and fashionably *déclassé*, moment within postmodern leftism.
Again, he was surely prescient: for one of the disinctive features of the
anti-globalisation movement has been this developing alliance

between environmentalists and other new social movement activists, on the one hand, and those sections of the labour movement least hegemonised by the Old Left parties, Labourist or Communist, on the other. This was as true of Seattle in November 1999 as of Paris in December 1995. 'The real struggle has broadened so much', Williams wrote in *Towards 2000*, 'the decisive issues have so radically changed, that only a new kind of socialist movement, fully contemporary in its ideas and methods, bringing a wide range of needs and interests together in a new definition of the general interest, has any real future' (ibid., p. 174). This still seems about as right as we are likely to get it, even as we begin to move on beyond 2000 and towards 2050.

I have singled out environmentalism as one of the key aspects of the anti-globalisation movement with deliberate intent, for the new movement has been, above all, an alliance of disaffected trade unionists, small farmers and peasants, radical 'Greens' and ecologists. Here again, Williams's work was prescient, for, like Adorno's, his Marxism had clearly anticipated contemporary ecopolitics and ecocriticism and, indeed, it has on occasion been recognised as such (Head, 1998, p. 37). If Williams had seemed unable to theorise questions of sexual politics with real adequacy, his environmentalist credentials were much more substantial: in the early 1980s, at a time when such commitments were still unfashionable on the Left, he had served as Vice-President of the Socialist Environment and Resources Association. His sympathy for 'Third World' peasant revolution were noted in Chapter 4. Here we should also note how closely this had been combined, in *The Country and the City*, with a deeply ecological sense of the connectedness of people and land. As Said would observe, the book gained 'much of its force from its direct and unflinching look at the land itself' (Said, 1990, p. 82). Unlike most post-Romantic treatments of country life, Williams's was neither sentimentalising nor reactionary, but rather, in Hartman's phrase, 'a careful, engaged, and at the same time politically conscious description of country life and its fatal alteration' (Hartman, 1997, p. 92n). There are direct continuities between themes aired in *The Country and the City*, the ecological arguments advanced in *Towards 2000*, and the combination of environmentalist and peasant politics within today's anti-globalisation movement. A countryman himself,[4] Williams 'had the luck ... to repair and rebuild old drystone walls; to hedge and ditch ... and to see from skilled men how the jobs should be done' (Williams, 1973a, pp. 301-2). He surely spoke the language of José Bové, of the Confédération Paysanne, albeit in Welsh rather than French vernacular, when he insisted that: 'Neither will the city save the country nor the country the city. Rather the long struggle within both will become a general struggle, as in a sense it has always been' (Williams, 1973b, p. 301).

Reviewing the successes and failures of the twentieth-century Left, in a 1997 version of what the Communist Left would have termed 'Results and Prospects', Sinfield puzzles over why the post-1968 New

New Left should have been thrown into such disarray by the collapse of a Soviet Union it had always reviled. His short answer is that it was not and that the crisis of the Western Left is more plausibly explained by the more or less contemporaneous collapse of post-war welfare-capitalism. Despite all the Left's 'revolutionary rhetoric', he writes:

> we hadn't really worked out a system to supersede welfare-capital-ism ... we envisaged capitalism continuing, though with vastly more of the 1945 promises realized ... *That is the failure that has perplexed us*, not the failure of Soviet-style, centralized direction. Capitalism ... can't be made compatible with a significant element of socialism. And this is so stunning that we cannot afford to recognize it. (Sinfield, 1997, pp. xx-xxii)

There is much truth in this; indeed, it is another way of saying, as Eagleton does, that the Left had been far too concerned with cultural politics, far too little with the politics of culture, and with the politics of politics that must necessarily accompany them. This was much less true of Williams, however, than of most of the rest of us. He may not quite have worked out a 'system', but the institutional moment persistently commanded his attention, compelling him repeatedly to sketch in, as best he could, the details of what might once have been possible under capitalism, what might still be possible beyond it. In this, his work was both exemplary and exceptional. Mulhern has recently argued very persuasively that contemporary 'Cultural Studies' reproduces the selfsame 'metacultural' discursive form as that found in traditional 'Kulturkritik' (Mulhern, 2000, p. 156).[5] 'Metacultural discourse', he writes:

> is a form of resistance through ritual, offering ... a 'magical solu-tion' to the poverty of politics in bourgeois society ... metaculture ..., in either mode, invents an authoritative subject, 'good' culture, be it minority or popular, whose function is to mediate a symbolic metapolitical resolution of the contradictions of capitalist moder-nity. (ibid., pp. 168-9)

As Mulhern appears to recognise, Williams's work provides an important exception to this observation, insofar as it set out to establish 'an integrally socialist politics of culture' (ibid., p. 72) in opposition both to elitist 'Kulturkritik' and to populist Cultural Studies. The key question for Williams, as it still must be for us, was thus essentially politico-institutional: that of the radical incompatibility of large-scale capital-ism with democracy; and of how, then, in the face of a capitalism as hubristic as any in the long history of modernity, to create and strength-en the institutions of political, economic and cultural democracy. As

Williams spells it out in *Towards 2000*:

> What is really astonishing is that ... the ... active promoters, the ide-
> ologists and the agents, of this continuing world-wide process ...
> speak to the rest of us, at least from one side of their mouths, about
> the traditional values of settlement, community and loyalty. These
> great disrupters, not only of other people's settlements but of many
> of those of their own nominal people, have annexed and appropri-
> ated ... many of the basic human feelings about a necessary and
> desirable society. They retain this appropriation even while their
> hands are endlessly busy with old and new schemes in which the pri-
> orities are wholly different: schemes through which actual people
> and communities are depressed or disappear, under the calculations
> of cost-benefit, profit and advantageous production. (Williams,
> 1983, pp. 186-7)

For Williams, the proper alternative to all this would be a 'variable
socialism - the making of many socialisms' (ibid., p. 198). We have
been told repeatedly since his death by capitalism's growing army of
intellectual apologists - some only recent converts to their cause - that
now 'the history of socialism as the avant-garde of political theory
comes to a close' (Giddens, 1994, pp. 68-9); that 'today quite plainly *is*
different ... The difference is the failure of socialism' (Giddens, 1995, p.
xiii). It comes as welcome relief, then, to encounter Sinfield's 'hunch'
that 'socialism will be rediscovered, spontaneously by a new generation, in 2020 or so', as a direct response to capitalism's 'own contradictions' (Sinfield, 1997, p. xx). For myself, I am both more and less
optimistic than this. Optimistically, I doubt we will need to wait quite
so long as Sinfield fears: from Paris to Seattle, and even here in
Melbourne, a new generation is already learning the language of
resistance. Pessimistically - or perhaps realistically - I am less sure that
this will turn out to be the language of 'socialism' ('communism',
'Marxism', etc.): other people may well have to fight for what we
meant under another name. The one currently on offer is 'anti-globalisation': it will do for now.

Notes

1 Italy comes close to a third such instance. But the parallels are less
straightforward: the PCI was never as fully Bolshevised as its French or
German counterparts; and it continues to enjoy a significant afterlife among
the undead of the PDS.

2 No doubt, Weber is also an important source of inspiration. Bourdieu
describes Weber as opening the way to a 'radical materialism', capable of
seeking out 'the economic determinants', even 'in areas where the ideology
of "disinterestedness" prevails' (Bourdieu, 1993, p. 12). This is, of course,

very close to thumbnail sketch of Bourdieu's own long-range project. But if Bourdieu takes his cynicism from Weber, the general model of society remains much closer to Durkheim.

3 The equivalents in Australia are Hawke and Keating.

4 As Eagleton observed: 'He looked and spoke more like a countryman than a don' (1989c, p. 1).

5 Mulhern uses the term 'Kulturkritik' to refer to the English tradition of Arnold, Eliot and Leavis as well as to the original German (2000, pp. xv-xvi).

Bibliography

Adorno, T. (1976) 'Sociology and empirical research'. (Translated by G. Bartram). In P. Connerton (ed.) *Critical Sociology*. Harmondsworth: Penguin.

Adorno, T. (1980) 'Letters to Walter Benjamin'. (Translated by J. Zohn). In E. Bloch et al. *Aesthetics and Politics*. London: Verso.

Adorno, T. and Horkheimer, M. (1972) *Dialectic of Enlightenment*. (Translated by J. Cumming.) New York: Herder and Herder.

Adorno, T. and Horkheimer, M. (1979) *Dialectic of Enlightenment*. (Translated by J. Cumming.) London: Verso.

Adorno, T. and Marcuse, H. (1999) 'Correspondence on the German student movement'. (Translated by E. Leslie). *New Left Review*, (I) 233.

Ahmad, A. (1992) *In Theory: Classes, Nations, Literatures*. London: Verso.

Althusser, L. (1969) *For Marx*. (Translated by B. Brewster.) London: Allen Lane.

Althusser, L. (1971) *Lenin and Philosophy and Other Essays*. (Translated by B. Brewster.) London: New Left Books.

Althusser, L. and Balibar, É. (1970) *Reading Capital*. (Translated by B. Brewster.) London: New Left Books.

Altick, R. (1978) 'The sociology of authorship', in P. Davison, R. Myersohn and E. Shils (eds), *Literary Taste, Culture and Mass Communication. Vol.10: Authorship*. Cambridge: Chadwyck-Healey.

Anderson, P. (1976) *Considerations on Western Marxism*. London: New Left Books.

Anderson, P. (1980) *Arguments Within English Marxism*. London: New Left Books.

Anderson, P. (1992) *English Questions*. London: Verso.

Anderson, P. (1998) *The Origins of Postmodernity*. London: Verso.

Anderson, P. (2000) 'Renewals', *New Left Review*, (II) 1.

Baldick, C. (1983)*The Social Mission of English Criticism 1848-1932*. Oxford: Oxford University Press.

Barker, F. (1984) *The Tremulous Private Body: Essays on Subjection*. London: Methuen.

Barthes, R. (1968) *Elements of Semiology*. (Translated by A. Levers and C. Smith.) New York: Hill and Wang.

Barthes, R. (1973) *Mythologies*. (Translated by A. Lavers.) St. Albans: Paladin.

Barthes, R. (1974) *S/Z*. (Translated by R. Miller.) New York: Hill and Wang.

Barthes, R. (1975) *The Pleasure of the Text*. (Translated by R. Miller). New York: Hill and Wang.

Barthes, R. (1976) *Sade, Fourier, Loyola*. (Translated by R. Miller.) New York: Hill and Wang.

Barthes, R. (1977) *Image-Music-Text*. (Translated by S. Heath). New York: Hill and Wang.

Belsey, C. (1980) *Critical Practice*. London: Methuen.

Belsey, C. (1985) *The Subject of Tragedy: Identity and Difference in Renaissance Drama*. London: Methuen.

Belsey, C. (1989) 'Towards cultural history - in theory and practice', *Textual Practice*, 3, 2.

Benda, J. (1927) *La trahison des clercs*. Paris: Grasset.

Benjamin, W. (1973a) 'The work of art in the age of mechanical reproduction', in *Illuminations*. (Translated by H. Zohn). Glasgow: Collins.

Benjamin, W. (1973b) *Understanding Brecht*. (Translated by A. Bostock.) London: New Left Books.

Bennett, T. (1979) *Formalism and Marxism*. London: Methuen.

Bennett, T. (1985) 'Really useless "knowledge": a political critique of aesthetics', *Thesis Eleven*, 12.

Bennett, T. (1986) 'Introduction: popular culture and "the turn to Gramsci"', in T. Bennett et al. (eds), *Popular Culture and Social Relations*. Milton Keynes: Open University Press.

Bennett, T. (1989) 'Holding spaces', *Southern Review*, 22, 2.

Bennett, T. (1990) *Outside Literature*. London: Routledge.

Bennett, T. (1998) *Culture: A Reformer's Science*. London: Sage.

Bennett, T., Emmison, M. and Frow, J. (1999) *Accounting for Tastes: Australian Everyday Cultures*. Cambridge: Cambridge University Press.

Bennett, T. et al. (eds) (1981) *Culture, Ideology and Social Process: A Reader*. London: Batsford Academic/Open University Press.

Bennett, T. et al. (eds) (1986) *Popular Culture and Social Relations*. Milton Keynes: Open University Press

Bentham, J. (1962) 'The rationale of reward', in *The Works of Jeremy Bentham*. Vol. II. New York: Russell and Russell.

Blackburn, R. (1988) 'Raymond Williams and the politics of a new left', *New Left Review*, (I) 168.

Bloom, H. (1994) *The Western Canon: The Books and School of the Ages*. New York: Harcourt Brace and Co.

Bloom, H. (2000a) 'There are no great English novelists: interview with Joanna Coles', *The Times*, 28 November.

Bloom, H. (2000b) *How to Read and Why*. London: Fourth Estate.

Bloom, H. et al. (1979) *Deconstruction and Criticism*. New York: Seabury Press.

Bourdieu, P. (1977a) *Outline of a Theory of Practice*. (Translated by R. Nice.) Cambridge: Cambridge University Press.

Bourdieu, P. (1977b) 'Symbolic power'. (Translated by C. Wringe.) In D. Gleeson (ed.), *Identity and Structure: Issues in the Sociology of Education*. Driffield: Nafferton Books.

Bourdieu, P. (1984) *Distinction: A Social Critique of the Judgement of Taste*. (Translated by R. Nice.) London: Routledge and Kegan Paul.

Bourdieu, P. (1989) 'The corporatism of the universal: the role of intellectuals in the modern world'. (Translated by C. Betensky.) *Telos*, 81.

Bourdieu, P. (1993) *Sociology in Question*. (Translated by R. Nice.) London: Sage.

Bourdieu, P. (1996a) *The State Nobility: Elite Schools in the Field of Power*. (Translated by L.C. Clough.) Cambridge: Polity Press.

Bourdieu, P. (1996b) *The Rules of Art: Genesis and Structure of the Literary Field*.

(Translated by S. Emanuel.) Cambridge: Polity Press.

Bourdieu, P. (1998a) *Acts of Resistance: Against the New Myths of Our Time.* (Translated by R. Nice.) Cambridge: Polity Press.

Bourdieu, P. (1998b) 'Pour une gauche de gauche', *Le Monde*, 8 April.

Bourdieu, P. (2001) *Masculine Domination.* (Translated by R. Nice.) Cambridge: Polity Press.

Bourdieu, P. et al. (1999) *The Weight of the World: Social Suffering in Contemporary Society.* (Translated by P.P. Ferguson et al.) Cambridge: Polity Press.

Brailsford, H.N. (1961) *The Levellers and the English Revolution.* London: Cresset Press.

Bradley, C.H.J. (1998) *Mrs Thatcher's Cultural Policies: 1979-1990.* Boulder: Social Science Monographs.

Brecht, B. (1980) 'Against Georg Lukács'. (Translated by S. Hood.) In E. Bloch et al. *Aesthetics and Politics.* London: Verso.

Brenkman, J. (1995) 'Raymond Williams and marxism', in C. Prendergast (ed.), *Cultural Materialism: On Raymond Williams.* Minneapolis: University of Minnesota Press.

Brennan, T. (1992) 'Places of mind, occupied lands: Edward Said and philology', in M. Sprinker (ed.), *Edward Said: A Critical Reader.* Oxford: Blackwell.

Bukharin, N. (1977) 'Poetry, poetics and the problems of poetry in the USSR', in M. Gorky et al., *Soviet Writers' Congress 1934: The Debate on Socialist Realism and Modernism.* London: Lawrence and Wishart.

Caudwell, C. (1946) *Illusion and Reality.* London: Lawrence and Wishart.

Centre for Contemporary Cultural Studies (1978) *On Ideology.* London: Hutchinson/Centre for Contemporary Cultural Studies.

Cevasco, M.E. (2000) 'Whatever happened to cultural studies: Notes from the periphery', *Textual Practice*, 14, 3.

Clarke, J. et al. (1976) 'Subcultures, cultures and class: a theoretical overview', in S. Hall and T. Jefferson (eds), *Resistance Through Rituals: Youth Sub-cultures in Post-war Britain.* London: Hutchinson/Centre for Contemporary Cultural Studies.

Clarke, J. et al. (eds) (1979) *Working-Class Culture: Studies in History and Theory.* London: Hutchinson/Centre for Contemporary Cultural Studies.

Colebrook, C. (1997) *New Literary Histories: New Historicism and Contemporary Criticism.* Manchester: Manchester University Press.

Coleridge, S.T. (1972) *On the Constitution of the Church and State.* London: J.M. Dent.

Collins, R. et al. (eds) (1986a) *Media, Culture and Society: A Critical Reader.* London: Sage.

Collins, R. et al. (1986b) 'Introduction', in R. Collins et al. (eds), *Media, Culture and Society: A Critical Reader.* London: Sage.

Collins, R. et al. (1988) *The Economics of Television: The UK Case.* London: Sage.

Corner, J. (1991a) 'Editorial', *Media, Culture and Society*, 13, 2.

Corner, J. (1991b) 'Studying culture: reflections and assessments: an interview with Richard Hoggart', *Media, Culture and Society*, 13, 2.

Crawford, R. (ed.) (1998) *The Scottish Invention of English Literature.* Cambridge: Cambridge University Press.

Cross, N. (1985) *The Common Writer: Life in Nineteenth-Century Grub Street.* Cambridge: Cambridge University Press.

Curran, J. (1979) 'The media and politics', *Media, Culture and Society*, 1, 1.

Curran, J. and Gurevitch, M. (eds) (2000) *Mass Media and Society.* London: Arnold.

Curran, J., Morley, D. and Walkerdine, V. (eds) (1996) *Cultural Studies and Communications*. London: Arnold.

Curran, J. and Park, M.-J. (eds) (2000) *De-Westernizing Media Studies*. London: Routledge.

Curran, J. and Seaton, J. (1997) *Power Without Responsibility: The Press and Broadcasting in Britain*. London: Routledge.

Derrida, J. (1973) *Speech and Phenomena and Other Essays on Husserl's Theory of Signs*. (Translated by D.B. Allison.) Evanston: Northwestern University Press.

Derrida, J. (1974) *Of Grammatology*. (Translated by G.C. Spivak.) Baltimore: Johns Hopkins University Press.

Derrida, J. (1978) *Writing and Difference*. (Translated by A. Bass.) Chicago: University of Chicago Press.

Derrida, J. (1982) *Margins of Philosophy*. (Translated by A. Bass.) Chicago: University of Chicago Press.

Derrida, J. (1987) *The Truth in Painting*. (Translated by G. Bennington and I. McLeod.) Chicago: University of Chicago Press.

Derrida, J. (1994) *Specters of Marx: The State of the Debt, the Work of Mourning, and the New International*. (Translated by P. Kamuf.) London: Routledge.

Docker, J. (1989) 'Williams' challenge to screen studies', *Southern Review*, 22, 2.

Dollimore, J. (1991) *Sexual Dissidence: Augustine to Wilde, Freud to Foucault*. Oxford: Oxford University Press.

Dollimore, J. (1994a) 'Introduction: Shakespeare, cultural materialism and the new historicism', in J. Dollimore and A. Sinfield (eds), *Political Shakespeare: Essays in Cultural Materialism*. Manchester: Manchester University Press.

Dollimore, J. (1994b) 'Shakespeare understudies: the sodomite, the prostitute and their critics', in J. Dollimore and A. Sinfield (eds), *Political Shakespeare: Essays in Cultural Materialism*. Manchester: Manchester University Press.

Dollimore, J. (1999) *Death, Desire and Loss in Western Culture*. Harmondsworth: Penguin.

Dollimore, J. and Sinfield, A. (1985) 'History and ideology: the instance of *Henry V*', in J. Drakakis (ed.), *Alternative Shakespeares*. London: Methuen.

Dollimore, J. and Sinfield, A. (1990) 'Culture and textuality: debating cultural materialism', *Textual Practice*, 4, 1.

Dollimore, J. and Sinfield, A. (eds) (1994a) *Political Shakespeare: Essays in Cultural Materialism*. Manchester: Manchester University Press.

Dollimore, J. and Sinfield, A. (1994b) 'Foreword to the first edition: cultural materialism', in J. Dollimore and A. Sinfield (eds), *Political Shakespeare: Essays in Cultural Materialism*. Manchester: Manchester University Press.

Doyle, B. (1982) 'The hidden history of English studies', in P. Widdowson (ed.), *Re-Reading English*. London: Methuen.

During, S. (1991) 'The ideology of the aesthetic', *Arena*, first series, 94.

During, S. (ed.) (1999) *The Cultural Studies Reader*. Second edition. London: Routledge.

Durkheim, E. (1964) *The Division of Labor in Society*. (Translated by G. Simpson.) New York: Free Press.

Durkheim, E. (1976) *The Elementary Forms of the Religious Life*. (Translated by J.W. Swain.) London: George Allen and Unwin.

Dworkin, D.L. (1993) 'Cultural studies and the crisis in British radical thought', in D.L. Dworkin and L.G. Roman (eds), *Views Beyond the Border Country: Raymond Williams and Cultural Politics*. London and New York: Routledge.

Eagleton, T. (1968) 'The idea of a common culture', in T. Eagleton and B. Wicker (eds), *From Culture to Revolution: The Slant Symposium 1967*. London: Sheed and Ward.

Eagleton, T. (1975) *Myths of Power: A Marxist Study of the Brontës*. London: Macmillan.

Eagleton, T. (1976) *Criticism and Ideology*. London: New Left Books.

Eagleton, T. (1981) *Walter Benjamin or Towards a Revolutionary Criticism*. London: Verso.

Eagleton, T. (1982) *The Rape of Clarissa: Writing, Sexuality and Class Struggle in Samuel Richardson*. Oxford: Basil Blackwell.

Eagleton, T. (1984) *The Function of Criticism: From 'The Spectator' to Post-Structuralism*. London: Verso.

Eagleton, T. (1985) 'Criticism and ideology: an interview', *Thesis Eleven*, 12.

Eagleton, T. (1986) *Against the Grain: Essays 1975-1985*. London: Verso.

Eagleton, T. (1987) *Saints and Scholars*. London: Verso.

Eagleton, T. (ed.) (1989a) *Raymond Williams: Critical Perspectives*. Cambridge: Polity Press.

Eagleton, T. (1989b) 'Base and superstructure in Raymond Williams', in T. Eagleton (ed.), *Raymond Williams: Critical Perspectives*. Cambridge: Polity Press.

Eagleton, T. (1989c) 'Introduction', in T. Eagleton (ed.), *Raymond Williams: Critical Perspectives*. Cambridge: Polity Press.

Eagleton, T. (1989d) *Saint Oscar*. Lawrence Hill, Derry: Field Day.

Eagleton, T. (1990a) *The Ideology of the Aesthetic*. Oxford: Basil Blackwell.

Eagleton, T. (1990b) 'Nationalism: irony and commitment', in T. Eagleton, F. Jameson and E.W. Said (eds), *Nationalism, Colonialism and Literature*. Minneapolis: University of Minnesota Press.

Eagleton, T. (1995) *Heathcliff and the Great Hunger*. London: Verso.

Eagleton, T. (1996a) *Literary Theory: An Introduction*. (First published in 1983.) Oxford: Blackwell.

Eagleton, T. (1996b) *The Illusions of Postmodernism*. Oxford: Blackwell.

Eagleton, T. (1998) *Crazy John and the Bishop and Other Essays on Irish Culture*. Notre Dame, IN: University of Notre Dame Press.

Eagleton, T. (1999a) *The Truth About the Irish*. Dublin: New Island Books.

Eagleton, T. (1999b) *Scholars and Rebels in Nineteenth-Century Ireland*. Oxford: Blackwell.

Eagleton, T. (1999c) 'In the gaudy supermarket', *London Review of Books*, 21, 10.

Eagleton, T. (2000) *The Idea of Culture*. Oxford: Blackwell.

Easthope, A. (1988) *British Post-Structuralism Since 1968*. London: Routledge.

Easthope, A. (1991) *Literary Into Cultural Studies*. London: Routledge.

Eliot, T.S. (1962) *Notes Towards the Definition of Culture*. London: Faber.

Eliot, T.S. (1963a) 'Tradition and the individual talent', in *Selected Essays*. London: Faber.

Eliot, T.S. (1963b) 'The metaphysical poets', in *Selected Essays*. London: Faber.

Eliot, T.S. (1968) *Milton: Two Studies*. London: Faber.

Eliot, T.S. (1982) *The Idea of a Christian Society and Other Writings*. London: Faber.

Felperin, H. (1985) *Beyond Deconstruction: The Uses and Abuses of Literary Theory*. Oxford: Oxford University Press.

Felperin, H. (1990) *The Uses of the Canon: Elizabethan Literature and Contemporary Theory*. Oxford: Oxford University Press.

Fiori, G. (1970) *Antonio Gramsci: Life of a Revolutionary*. (Translated by T. Nairn.) London: New Left Books.

Foucault, M. (1965) *Madness and Civilisation: A History of Insanity in the Age of Reason*. (Translated by R. Howard.) New York: Vintage Books.

Foucault, M. (1972a) *The Archaeology of Knowledge*. (Translated by A.M. Sheridan.) London: Tavistock.

Foucault, M. (1972b) *Histoire de la folie á l'âge classique*. Paris: Gallimard.

Foucault, M. (1973a) *The Birth of the Clinic*. (Translated by A.M. Sheridan.) London: Tavistock.

Foucault, M. (1973b) *The Order of Things: An Archaeology of the Human Sciences*. New York: Vintage Books.

Foucault, M. (1977a) *Language, Counter-Memory, Practice*. (Translated by D.F. Bouchard and S. Simon.) Ithaca: Cornell University Press.

Foucault, M. (1977b) *Discipline and Punish: The Birth of the Prison*. (Translated by A.M. Sheridan.) Harmondsworth: Allen Lane.

Foucault, M. (1978) *The History of Sexuality*. (Translated by R. Hurley.) New York: Random House.

Foucault, M. (1980) *Power/Knowledge: Selected Interviews and Other Writings, 1972-1977*. (Edited by C. Gordon.) Brighton: Harvester Press.

Foucault, M. (1985) *The Use of Pleasure*. (Translated by R. Hurley.) New York: Pantheon Books.

Fox, R. (1979) *The Novel and the People*. London: Lawrence and Wishart.

Freadman, A. (1988) 'Untitled: (on genre)', *Cultural Studies*, 2, 1.

Frow, J. (1986) *Marxism and Literary History*. Oxford: Basil Blackwell.

Frow, J. (1995) *Cultural Studies and Cultural Value*. Oxford: Oxford University Press.

Gallagher, C. (1996) 'Marxism and the new historicism', in K. Ryan (ed.), *New Historicism and Cultural Materialism: A Reader*. London: Arnold.

Gallagher, C. and Greenblatt, S. (2000) *Practicing New Historicism*. Chicago: University of Chicago Press.

Garnham, N. (ed.) (1980) 'Class and culture, the work of Pierre Bourdieu', *Media, Culture and Society*, 2, 3.

Garnham, N. (1983) 'Towards a theory of cultural materialism', *Journal of Communication*, 33, 3.

Garnham, N. (1986) 'Contribution to a political economy of mass-communication', in R. Collins et al. (eds), *Media, Culture and Society: A Critical Reader*. London: Sage.

Garnham, N. (1988) 'Raymond Williams, 1921-1988: a cultural analyst, a distinctive tradition', *Journal of Communication*, 38, 4.

Garnham, N. (1990) *Capitalism and Communication: Global Culture and the Economics of Information*. London: Sage.

Garnham, N. (1995a) 'The media and narratives of the intellectual', *Media, Culture and Society*, 17, 3.

Garnham, N. (1995b) 'Political economy and cultural studies: reconciliation or divorce?', *Critical Studies in Mass Communication*, 12, 1.

Garnham, N. (1997) 'Political economy and the practice of cultural studies', in M. Ferguson and P. Golding (eds), *Cultural Studies in Question*. London: Sage.

Garnham, N. (2000) *Emancipation, the Media and Modernity: Arguments about the Media and Social Theory*. Oxford: Oxford University Press.

Garnham, N. and Williams, R. (1986) 'Pierre Bourdieu and the sociology of culture', in R. Collins et al. (eds), *Media, Culture and Society: A Critical Reader*. London: Sage.

Geertz, C. (1973) 'Thick description', in *The Interpretation of Cultures*. New York:

Basic Books.

Giddens, A. (1994) *Beyond Left and Right: The Future of Radical Politics*. Cambridge: Polity Press.

Giddens, A. (1995) *A Contemporary Critique of Historical Materialism*. Second edition. London: Macmillan.

Giddens, A. (1998) *The Third Way: The Renewal of Social Democracy*. Cambridge: Polity Press.

Gilroy, P. (1992) *There Ain't No Black in the Union Jack: The Cultural Politics of Race and Nation*. London: Routledge.

Gilroy, P., Grossberg, L. and McRobbie, A. (eds) (2000) *Without Guarantees: In Honour of Stuart Hall*. London: Verso.

Goldmann, L. (1964) *The Hidden God*. (Translated by P. Thody.) London: Routledge and Kegan Paul.

Goldmann, L. (1969) *The Human Sciences and Philosophy*. (Translated by H.V. White and R. Anchor.) London: Jonathan Cape.

Goldmann, L. (1971) *Immanuel Kant*. (Translated by R. Black.) London: New Left Books.

Goldmann, L. (1975) *Towards a Sociology of the Novel*. (Translated by A. Sheridan.) London: Tavistock.

Goldthorpe, J.H. (1990) 'A response', in J. Clark, C. Modgil and S. Modgil (eds), *John H. Goldthorpe: Consensus and Controversy*. London: Falmer Press.

Gorak, J. (1988) *The Alien Mind of Raymond Williams*. Columbia: University of Missouri Press.

Gramsci, A. (1957) *The Modern Prince and other Essays*. (Translated by L. Marks.) London: Lawrence and Wishart.

Gramsci, A. (1971) *Selections from the Prison Notebooks*. (Translated by Q. Hoare and G. Nowell Smith.) London: Lawrence and Wishart.

Green, M. (1978) 'Raymond Williams and cultural studies', In P. Davison et al. (eds), *The Cultural Debate Part I*. Cambridge: Chadwyck-Healey.

Greenblatt, S. (1980) *Renaissance Self-Fashioning: From More to Shakespeare*. Chicago: University of Chicago Press.

Greenblatt, S. (1982) 'Introduction', in S. Greenblatt (ed.), *The Power of Forms in the English Renaissance*. Norman: Pilgrim Books.

Greenblatt, S. (1990) *Learning to Curse: Essays in Early Modern Culture*. London: Routledge.

Greenblatt, S. (1994) 'Invisible bullets: Renaissance authority and its subversion, *Henry IV* and *Henry V*', in J. Dollimore and A. Sinfield (eds), *Political Shakespeare: Essays in Cultural Materialism*. Manchester: Manchester University Press.

Greenfield, C. and Williams, P. (1989) 'Raymond Williams: the political and analytical legacies', *Southern Review*, 22, 2.

Grossberg, L. (1996) 'On postmodernism and articulation: an interview with Stuart Hall', in D. Morley and K.-H. Chen (eds), *Stuart Hall: Critical Dialogues in Cultural Studies*. London: Routledge.

Grossberg, L. et al. (1988) *It's a Sin: Essays on Postmodernism, Politics and Culture*. Sydney: Power Publications.

Grosz, E. (1989) *Sexual Subversions: Three French Feminists*. Sydney: Allen and Unwin.

Habermas, J. (1971) *Knowledge and Human Interest*. (Translated by J.J. Shapiro.) Boston: Beacon Press.

Habermas, J. (1979a) 'Interview with Jürgen Habermas'. (Translated by. R.

Smith.) *New German Critique* 18.

Habermas, J. (1979b) 'Conservatism and capitalist crisis', *New Left Review*, (I) 115.

Habermas, J. (1981) 'New social movements', *Telos*, 49.

Habermas, J. (1984) *The Theory of Communicative Action vol. I, Reason and the Rationalisation of Society*. (Translated by T. McCarthy.) Boston: Beacon Press.

Habermas, J. (1985). 'Modernity - an incomplete project'. (Translated by S. Ben-Habib.) In H. Foster (ed.), *Postmodern Culture*. London: Pluto Press.

Habermas, J. (1987a) *The Philosophical Discourse of Modernity*. (Translated by F. Lawrence.) Cambridge: Polity Press.

Habermas, J. (1987b) *The Theory of Communicative Action vol. II Lifeworld and System: A Critique of Functionalist Reason*. (Translated by T. McCarthy.) Cambridge: Polity Press.

Habermas, J. (1989) *The Structural Transformation of the Public Sphere*. (Translated by T. Burger.) Cambridge: Polity Press.

Habermas, J. (1990) 'What does socialism mean today? The rectifying revolution and the need for new thinking on the left'. (Translated by B. Morgan.) *New Left Review*, (I) 183.

Hall, S. (1976) 'A critical survey of the theoretical and practical achievements of the last ten years', in F. Barker et al. (eds), *Literature, Society and the Sociology of Literature*. Colchester: Department of Literature, University of Essex.

Hall, S. (1978) 'The hinterland of science: ideology and the sociology of knowledge', in Centre for Contemporary Cultural Studies, *On Ideology*. London: Hutchinson/Centre for Contemporary Cultural Studies.

Hall, S. (1980a) 'Cultural studies: two paradigms', *Media, Culture and Society*, 2, 1.

Hall, S. (1980b) 'Cultural studies and the centre: some problematics and problems', in S. Hall et al. (eds), *Culture, Media, Language*. London: Hutchinson/Centre for Contemporary Cultural Studies.

Hall, S. (1980c) 'Encoding/decoding', in S. Hall et al. (eds), *Culture, Media, Language*. London: Hutchinson/Centre for Contemporary Cultural Studies.

Hall, S. (1980d) 'The Williams interviews', *Screen Education*, 34.

Hall, S. (1981) 'Cultural studies: two paradigms', in T. Bennett et al. (eds), *Culture, Ideology and Social Process: A Reader*. London: Batsford Academic/Open University Press.

Hall, S. (1983) 'The great moving right show', in S. Hall and M. Jacques (eds), *The Politics of Thatcherism*. London: Lawrence and Wishart.

Hall, S. (1984) 'Face the future', *New Socialist*, September.

Hall, S. (1986) 'Popular culture and the state', in T. Bennett et al. (eds), *Popular Culture and Social Relations*. Milton Keynes: Open University Press.

Hall, S. (1988a) 'The toad in the garden: Thatcherism among the theorists', in C. Nelson and L. Grossberg (eds), *Marxism and the Interpretation of Culture*. London: Macmillan.

Hall, S. (1988b) . 'Thatcher's lessons', *Marxism Today*, March.

Hall, S. (1989a) 'Politics and letters', in T. Eagleton (ed.), *Raymond Williams: Critical Perspectives*. Cambridge: Polity Press.

Hall, S. (1989b) 'The meaning of new times', in S. Hall and M. Jacques (eds), *New Times: The Changing Face of Politics in the 1990s*. London: Lawrence and Wishart.

Hall, S. (1991) 'Introduction', in R. Simon, *Gramsci's Political Thought*. Second edition. London: Lawrence and Wishart.

Hall, S. (1992) 'Cultural studies and its theoretical legacies', in L. Grossberg, C. Nelson and P. Treichler (eds), *Cultural Studies*. New York: Routledge.

Hall, S. (1993) 'Culture, community, nation', *Cultural Studies*, 7, 3.

Hall, S. (2000a) 'Conclusion: the multi-cultural question', in B. Hesse (ed.), *Un/Settled Multiculturalisms: Diasporas, Entanglements, Transruptions*. London: Zed Books.

Hall, S. (2000b) 'Questioning multiculturalism'. Plenary address. *Third International Crossroads in Cultural Studies Conference*. Birmingham: University of Birmingham.

Hall, S. and Chen, K.-H. (1996) 'Cultural studies and the politics of internationalization: an interview with Stuart Hall', in D. Morley and K.-H. Chen (eds), *Stuart Hall: Critical Dialogues in Cultural Studies*. London: Routledge.

Hall, S. and Jefferson, T. (eds) (1976) *Resistance Through Rituals: Youth Sub-cultures in Post-war Britain*. London: Hutchinson/Centre for Contemporary Cultural Studies,

Hall, S., Williams, R. and Thompson, E.P. (eds) (1967) *New Left May Day Manifesto*. London: May Day Manifesto Committee.

Hall, S. et al. (1978a) *Policing the Crisis: Mugging, the State, and Law and Order*. London: Macmillan.

Hall, S. et al. (1978b) 'Politics and ideology: Gramsci', in Centre for Contemporary Cultural Studies *On Ideology*. London: Hutchinson/Centre for Contemporary Cultural Studies.

Hall, S. et al. (eds) (1980) *Culture, Media Language*. London: Hutchinson/Centre for Contemporary Cultural Studies.

Hampton, C. (1990) *The Ideology of the Text*. Milton Keynes: Open University Press.

Harris, M. (1968) *The Rise of Anthropological Theory: A History of Theories of Culture*. New York: Thomas Y. Cromwell.

Hartley, J. (1998) 'Editorial (with goanna)', *International Journal of Cultural Studies*, 1, 1.

Hartman, G. (1997) *The Fateful Question of Culture*. New York: Columbia University Press.

Head, D. (1998) 'The (im)possibility of ecocriticism', in R. Kerridge and N. Sammells (eds), *Writing the Environment: Ecocriticism and Literature*. London: Zed Books.

Higgins, J. (1999) *Raymond Williams: Literature, Marxism and Cultural Materialism*. London and New York: Routledge.

Hill, C. (1985) 'Censorship and English literature', in *The Collected Essays of Christopher Hill*, Vol. I: *Writing and Revolution in 17th Century England*. Brighton: Harvester.

Hobbes, T. (1960) *Leviathan*. Oxford: Blackwell.

Hoggart, R. (1958) *The Uses of Literacy*. Harmondsworth: Penguin.

Hoggart, R. (1970) *Speaking To Each Other*. Vol. II. *About Literature*. London: Chatto and Windus.

Hoggart, R. (1995) *The Way We Live Now*. London: Chatto and Windus.

Hoggart, R. and Williams, R. (1960) 'Working class attitudes', *New Left Review*, (I) 1.

Horkheimer, M. (1972) 'Traditional and critical theory', in *Critical Theory: Selected Essays*. (Translated by M.J.O. O'Connell.) New York: Seabury Press.

Inglis, F. (1993) *Cultural Studies*. Oxford: Blackwell.

Inglis, F. (1995) *Raymond Williams*. London: Routledge.

Irigaray, L. (1985a) *Speculum of the Other Woman*. (Translated by G.C. Gill.) Ithaca, New York: Cornell University Press.

Irigaray, L. (1985b) *This Sex Which is Not One*. (Translated by C. Porter with C. Burke.) Ithaca, New York: Cornell University Press.

Jameson, F. (1981) *The Political Unconscious: Narrative as a Socially Symbolic Act*. London: Methuen.

Jameson, F. (1990) *Late Marxism: Adorno, or, the Persistence of the Dialectic*. London: Verso.

Jameson, F. (1991) *Postmodernism, or, the Cultural Logic of Late Capitalism*. London: Verso.

Jameson, F. (1998a) *The Cultural Turn: Selected Writings on the Postmodern, 1983-1998*. London: Verso.

Jameson, F. (1998b) *Brecht and Method*. London: Verso.

Jardine, L. and Swindells, J. (1989) 'Homage to Orwell: the dream of a common culture and other minefields', in T. Eagleton (ed.), *Raymond Williams: Critical Perspectives*. Cambridge: Polity Press.

Johnson, L. (1987) 'Raymond Williams: a marxist view of culture', in D. Austin-Broos (ed.), *Creating Culture: Profiles in the Study of Culture*. Sydney: Allen and Unwin.

Johnson, R. (1979) 'Histories of culture/theories of ideology: notes on an impasse', in M. Barrett et al. (eds), *Ideology and Cultural Production*. London: Croom Helm.

Jones, P. (1982) `"Organic"intellectuals and the generation of English cultural studies: an introduction-to-cum-historical-survey-of the field', *Thesis Eleven*, 5/6.

Jones, P. (1994) 'The myth of "Raymond Hoggart": on "founding fathers" and cultural policy', *Cultural Studies*, 8, 3.

Jones, P. (1999) '"The problem is always one of method ..."': cultural materialism, political economy and cultural studies', *Key Words*, 2.

Jones, P. (2000) 'Williams's critical sociology of culture', *Raymond Williams: After 2000 Conference*. Melbourne: Overland.

Kaplan, C. (1995) '"What we have again to say": Williams, feminism, and the 1840s', in C. Prendergast (ed.), *Cultural Materialism: On Raymond Williams*. Minneapolis: University of Minnesota Press.

Klein, N. (2001) 'Reclaiming the commons', *New Left Review*, (II) 9.

Kristeva, J. (1984) *Revolution in Poetic Language*. (Translated by M. Waller.) New York: Columbia University Press.

Lacan, J. (1977) *Écrits: A Selection*. (Translated by A. Sheridan.) London: Tavistock.

Laclau, E. and Mouffe, C. (1985) *Hegemony and Socialist Strategy: Towards a Radical Democratic Politics*. (Translated by W. Moore and P. Cammack.) London: Verso.

Laing, S. (1991) 'Raymond Williams and the cultural analysis of television', *Media, Culture and Society*, 13, 2.

Leavis, F.R. (1932) 'Under which king, Bezonian?', *Scrutiny*, 1, 3.

Leavis, F.R. (1933) 'Restatements for critics', *Scrutiny*, 1, 4.

Leavis, F.R. (1938) *New Bearings in English Poetry*. London: Chatto and Windus.

Leavis, F.R. (1948) *Education and the University: A Sketch for an 'English School'*. London: Chatto and Windus.

Leavis, F.R. (1962a) *The Common Pursuit*. Harmondsworth: Penguin.

Leavis, F.R. (1962b) *The Great Tradition*. Harmondsworth: Penguin.

Leavis, F.R. (1962c) *Two Cultures?* London: Chatto and Windus.

Leavis, F.R. (1963) '*Scrutiny* a retrospect', *Scrutiny*, 20.

Leavis, F.R. (1972a) *Nor Shall My Sword*. London: Chatto and Windus.

Leavis, F.R. (1972b) *Revaluation*. Harmondsworth: Penguin.

Leavis, F.R. and Thompson, D. (1960) *Culture and Environment*. London: Chatto and Windus.

Leavis, Q.D. (1979) *Fiction and the Reading Public*. Harmondsworth: Penguin.

Lenin, V.I. (1970) *What Is to Be Done?* (Translated by S.V. Utechin and P. Utechin.) London: Panther.

Lentricchia, F. (1980) *After the New Criticism*. Chicago: University of Chicago Press.

Leslie, E. (1999) 'Introduction to Adorno/Marcuse correspondence on the German student movement', *New Left Review*, (I) 118.

Lévi-Strauss, C. (1972) *Structural Anthropology*. (Translated by C. Jacobson and B. Grundfest Schoepf.) Harmondsworth: Penguin.

Levy, B. and Otto, P. (eds) (1989) 'Special issue: Raymond Williams', *Southern Review*, 22, 2.

Lloyd, D. and Thomas, P. (1995) '*Culture and Society* or culture and the state', in C. Prendergast (ed.), *Cultural Materialism: On Raymond Williams*. Minneapolis. University of Minnesota Press.

Lorimer, R. and Scannell, P. (eds) (1993) 'The publishing industry', *Media, Culture and Society*, 15, 2.

Lovell, T. (1980) *Pictures of Reality: Aesthetics, Politics, Pleasure*. London: British Film Institute.

Lovell, T. (1987) *Consuming Fiction*. London: Verso.

Lovell, T. (1989) 'Knowable pasts, imaginable futures', *History Workshop*, 27.

Lukács, G. (1962) *The Historical Novel*. (Translated by H. and S. Mitchell.) London: Merlin Press.

Lukács, G. (1963) *The Meaning of Contemporary Realism*. (Translated by J. and N. Mander.) London: Merlin Press.

Lukács, G. (1971a) *History and Class Consciousness*. (Translated by R. Livingstone.) London: Merlin Press.

Lukács, G. (1971b) *The Theory of the Novel*. (Translated by A. Bostock.) London: Merlin Press.

MacCabe, C. (1978) *James Joyce and the Revolution of the Word*. London: Macmillan.

MacCabe, C. (1985) *Theoretical Essays: Film, Linguistics, Literature*. Manchester: Manchester University Press.

MacCabe, C. (1999) *The Eloquence of the Vulgar: Language, Cinema and the Politics of Culture*. London: British Film Institute.

Macherey, P. (1978) *A Theory of Literary Production*. (Translated by G. Wall.) London: Routledge and Kegan Paul.

Mandel, E. (1975) *Late Capitalism*. (Translated by J. de Bres.) London: New Left Books.

Marcuse, H. (1964) *One-Dimensional Man: Studies in the Ideology of Advanced Industrial Society*. Boston: Beacon Press.

Marx, K. (1970) *Capital*. Vol. I. (Translated by S. Moore and E. Aveling.) London: Lawrence and Wishart.

Marx, K. (1975a) 'A contribution to the critique of Hegel's philosophy of right: introduction'. (Translated by G. Benton.) In *Early Writings*. Harmondsworth: Penguin.

Marx, K. (1975b) 'Economic and philosophical manuscripts'. (Translated by G. Benton.) In *Early Writings*. Harmondsworth: Penguin.

Marx, K. (1975c) Preface (to *A Contribution to the Critique of Political Economy)'*, in *Early Writings*. Harmondsworth: Penguin.

Marx, K. and Engels, F. (1947) *Literature and Art*. New York: International Publishers.

Marx, K. and Engels, F. (1967) *The Communist Manifesto*. (Translated by S. Moore.) Harmondsworth: Penguin.

McGuigan, J. (1996) 'Reviewing a life: Fred Inglis's biography of Raymond Williams', *New Left Review*, (I) 215.

McIlroy, J. and Westwood, S. (eds) (1993) *Border Country: Raymond Williams in Adult Education*. Leicester: National Institute of Continuing Education.

Merleau-Ponty, M. (1974) *Adventures of the Dialectic*. (Translated by J. Bien.) London: Heinemann.

Merrington, J. (1968) 'Theory and practice in Gramsci's marxism', in R. Miliband and J. Saville (eds), *The Socialist Register 1968*. London: Merlin Press.

Mill, J.S. (1970) *The Subjection of Women*. Cambridge, Mass: MIT Press.

Mill, J.S. and Taylor Mill, H. (1970) *Essays on Sex Equality*. Chicago: University of Chicago Press.

Miller, J. (1990) *Seductions: Studies in Reading and Culture*. London: Virago.

Milner, A. (1994) 'Cultural materialism, culturalism and post-culturalism: the legacy of Raymond Williams', *Theory, Culture and Society*, 11, 1.

Milner, A. (1999) *Class*. London: Sage Publications.

Milner, A. (2000) 'Class and cultural production: the intelligentsia as a social class', *Arena* new series, 15.

Mitchell, J. (1984) *Women: The Longest Revolution*. London: Virago.

Morris, W. (1977) 'A dream of John Ball', in *Three Works by W. Morris*. London: Lawrence and Wishart.

Mulhern, F. (1981) *The Moment of `Scrutiny'*. London: Verso.

Mulhern, F. (1998) *The Present Lasts a Long Time: Essays in Cultural Politics*. Cork: Cork University Press.

Mulhern, F. (2000) *Culture/Metaculture*. London: Routledge.

O'Connor, A. (1989) *Raymond Williams: Writing, Culture, Politics*. Oxford: Blackwell.

O'Connor, J. and Redhead, S. (1991) 'Book review', *Theory, Culture and Society*, 8, 4.

Orwell, G. (1961) 'Why I write', in *Collected Essays*. London: Mercury Books.

Oxford English Limited (1989) 'Editorial: third generation', *News From Nowhere*, 6.

Parry, B. (1992) 'Overlapping territories and intertwined histories: Edward Said's postcolonial cosmopolitanism', in M. Sprinker (ed.), *Edward Said: A Critical Reader*. Oxford: Blackwell.

Parsons, T. (1949) *The Structure of Social Action*. New York: Free Press.

Phillips, D. (1976) 'Chronology', in D. Widgery (ed.), *The Left in Britain 1956-1968*. Harmondsworth: Penguin.

Pinkney, T. (1989) 'Raymond Williams and the "two faces of modernism"', in T. Eagleton (ed.), *Raymond Williams: Critical Perspectives*. Cambridge: Polity Press.

Plekhanov, G. (1956) *The Development of the Monist View of History*. (Translated by A. Rothstein.) Moscow: Foreign Languages Publishing House.

Plekhanov, G. (1978) 'Art and social life'. (Translated by E. Hartley et al.) In P. Davison et al. (eds), *Art and Social Life*. Cambridge: Chadwyck-Healey.

Prendergast, C. (1995) 'Introduction: groundings and emergings', in C. Prendergast (ed.), *Cultural Materialism: On Raymond Williams*. Minneapolis. University of Minnesota Press.

Radek, K. (1977) 'Contemporary world literature and the tasks of proletarian art', in M. Gorky et al., *Soviet Writers' Congress 1934: The Debate on Socialist Realism and Modernism*. London: Lawrence and Wishart.

Radhakrishnan, R. (1993) 'Cultural theory and the politics of location', in D.L. Dworkin and L.G. Roman (eds), *Views Beyond the Border Country: Raymond Williams and Cultural Politics*. London and New York: Routledge.

Robey, D. (ed.) (1973) *Structuralism: An Introduction*. Oxford: Oxford University Press,

Rowbotham, S. (1985) 'Picking up the pieces', *New Socialist*, October.

Ryan, K. (1996) 'Introduction', in *New Historicism and Cultural Materialism: A Reader*. London: Arnold.

Said, E.W. (1984) *The World, the Text, and the Critic*. London: Faber.

Said, E.W. (1990) 'Narrative, geography and interpretation', *New Left Review*, (I) 180.

Said, E.W. (1993) *Culture and Imperialism*. London: Chatto and Windus.

Said, E.W. (1995) *Orientalism: Western Conceptions of the Orient*. Harmondsworth: Penguin.

Sartre, J.-P. (1950) *What is Literature?* (Translated by B. Frechtman.) London: Methuen.

Sartre, J.-P. (1976) *Critique of Dialectical Reason*. (Translated by A. Sheridan-Smith.) London: New Left Books.

Sartre, J.-P. (1976/1977) 'Socialism in one country', *New Left Review*, (I) 100.

Saussure, F. de (1974) *Course in General Linguistics*. (Translated by W. Baskin.) Glasgow: Collins.

Scannell, P., Schlesinger, P. and Sparks, C. (1992) 'Introduction', in P. Scannell, P. Schlesinger and C. Sparks (eds), *Culture and Power: A Media, Culture and Society Reader*. London: Sage.

Sedgwick, P. (1976) 'The two new lefts', in D. Widgery (ed.), *The Left in Britain 1956-1968*. Harmondsworth: Penguin.

Shelley, P.B. (1931) *A Defence of Poetry* (with P. Sidney, *An Apology for Poetry*). (Edited by H.A. Needham.). London: Ginn and Co.

Shiach, M. (1995) 'A gendered history of cultural categories', in C. Prendergast (ed.), *Cultural Materialism: On Raymond Williams*. Minneapolis. University of Minnesota Press.

Sinfield, A. (1983) 'Literary theory and the "crisis" in English studies', *Critical Quarterly*, 25, 3.

Sinfield, A. (1992) *Faultlines: Cultural Materialism and the Politics of Dissident Reading*. Berkeley: University of California Press.

Sinfield, A. (1994a) *The Wilde Century: Effeminacy, Oscar Wilde and the Queer Moment*. London: Cassell.

Sinfield, A. (1994b) *Cultural Politics, Queer Reading*. London: Routledge.

Sinfield, A. (1997) *Literature, Politics and Culture in Postwar Britain*. Second edition. London: Athlone Press.

Sinfield, A. (1998) *Gay and After*. London: Serpent's Tail.

Sparks, C. (1980) 'Raymond Williams, culture and Marxism', *International Socialism*, second series, 9.

Sparks, C. (1988) 'Editorial', *Media, Culture and Society*, 10, 2.

Sparks, C. (1996) 'Stuart Hall, cultural studies and Marxism', in D. Morley and K.-H. Chen (eds), *Stuart Hall: Critical Dialogues in Cultural Studies*. London: Routledge.

Spivak, G.C. (1987) *In Other Worlds: Essays in Cultural Politics*. London: Methuen.

Spivak, G.C. (1999) *A Critique of Postcolonial Reason: Toward A History of the Vanishing Present*. Cambridge, Mass: Harvard University Press.

Thompson, E.P. (1955) *William Morris: Romantic to Revolutionary*. London: Lawrence and Wishart.

Thompson, E.P. (1957) 'Socialist humanism: an epistle to the philistines', *New Reasoner*, 1.

Thompson, E.P. (1963) *The Making of the English Working Class*. London: Victor Gollancz.

Thompson, E.P. (1976) 'Through the smoke of Budapest', in D. Widgery (ed.), *The Left in Britain 1956-1968*. Harmondsworth: Penguin.

Thompson, E.P. (1977) 'Postscript 1976', *William Morris: Romantic to Revolutionary*. Second edition. London: Merlin Press.

Thompson, E.P. (1978) *The Poverty of Theory and Other Essays*. London: Merlin Press.

Tönnies, F. (1955) *Community and Association*. (Translated by C.P. Loomis.) London: Routledge and Kegan Paul.

Trotsky, L. (1960) *Literature and Revolution*. (Translated by R. Strunsky.) Ann Arbor: University of Michigan Press.

Trotsky, L. (1970) *On Literature and Art*. (Edited by P.N. Siegel.) New York: Pathfinder Press.

Turner, G. (1996) *British Cultural Studies: An Introduction*. Sydney: Allen and Unwin.

Vološinov, V.N. (1973) *Marxism and the Philosophy of Language*. (Translated by L. Matejka and I.R. Titunik.) New York: Seminar Press.

Waites, B. et al. (eds) (1982) *Popular Culture: Past and Present*. London: Croom Helm/Open University Press.

Watts, C. (1989) 'Reclaiming the border country: feminism and Raymond Williams', *News From Nowhere*, 6.

Weber, M. (1948) *From Max Weber: Essays in Sociology*. (Edited by H.H. Gerth and C.W. Mills.) London: Routledge and Kegan Paul.

Weber, M. (1964) *The Theory of Social and Economic Organization*. (Translated by A.M. Henderson and T. Parsons.) New York: Free Press.

Webster, F. (2000) 'Sociology, cultural studies and disciplinary boundaries' Inaugural lecture. Birmingham: Department of Cultural Studies and Sociology, University of Birmingham.

Wellek, R. (1937) 'Literary criticism and philosophy', *Scrutiny*, 5, 4.

Wellek, R. and Warren, A. (1976) *Theory of Literature*. Harmondsworth: Penguin.

West, A. (1975) *Crisis and Criticism*. London: Lawrence and Wishart.

West, C. (1995) 'In memoriam: the legacy of Raymond Williams', in C. Prendergast (ed.), *Cultural Materialism: On Raymond Williams*. Minneapolis: University of Minnesota Press.

Widdowson, P. (1982) 'The crisis in English studies', in P. Widdowson (ed.), *Re-Reading English*. London: Methuen.

Widgery, D. (1976) 'Introduction: farewell Grosvenor Square', in D. Widgery (ed.), *The Left in Britain 1956-1968*. Harmondsworth: Penguin.

Williams, R. (1950) *Reading and Criticism*. London: Frederick Muller.

Williams, R. (1952) *Drama from Ibsen to Eliot*. London: Chatto and Windus.

Williams, R. (1953) 'The idea of culture', *Essays in Criticism*, 1.

Williams, R. (1954) *Drama in Performance*. London: Frederick Muller.

Williams, R. (1960) *Border Country*. London: Chatto and Windus.

Williams, R. (1962) *Communications*. Harmondsworth: Penguin.

Williams, R. (1963) *Culture and Society 1780-1950*. (First published 1958.) Harmondsworth: Penguin.

Williams, R. (1964) *Second Generation*. London: Chatto and Windus.

Williams, R. (1965) *The Long Revolution*. (First published 1961.) Harmondsworth: Penguin.

Williams, R. (1966) *Modern Tragedy*. London: Chatto and Windus.

Williams R. (ed.) (1968a) *May Day Manifesto*. Second edition. Harmondsworth: Penguin.

Williams, R. (1968b) *Drama in Performance*. Second edition. London: C.A. Watts.

Williams, R. (1970) 'Practical critic', The *Guardian*, 26 February.

Williams, R. (1971a) *George Orwell*. New York: Viking Press.

Williams, R. (1971b) 'Literature and sociology: in memory of Lucien Goldmann', *New Left Review*, (I) 67.

Williams, R. (1972) *Gesellschaftstheorie als Begriffsgeschichte: Studien z. histor. Semantik von Kultur*. (Translated by Dt. von Heinz Blumensath.) Munich: Rogner and Bernhard.

Williams, R. (1973a) *Drama from Ibsen to Brecht*. (First published 1968.) Harmondsworth: Penguin.

Williams, R. (1973b) *The Country and the City*. New York: Oxford University Press.

Williams, R. (1973c) 'Base and superstructure in Marxist cultural theory', *New Left Review*, (I) 82.

Williams, R. (1974a) *The English Novel: From Dickens to Lawrence*. (First published 1970.) St Albans: Paladin.

Williams, R. (1974b) *Television: Technology and Cultural Form*. Glasgow: Collins.

Williams, R. (1976a) *Keywords: A Vocabulary of Culture and Society*. Glasgow: Collins.

Williams, R. (1976b) *Communications*. Third edition. Harmondsworth: Penguin.

Williams, R. (1977a) *Marxism and Literature*. Oxford: Oxford University Press.

Williams, R. (1977b) 'Forms of English fiction in 1848', in F. Barker et al. (eds), *1848: The Sociology of Literature*. Colchester: Department of Literature, University of Essex.

Williams, R. (1978a) 'Problems of materialism', *New Left Review*, (I) 109.

Williams, R. (1978b) *The Volunteers*. London: Eyre Methuen.

Williams, R. (1979a) *Politics and Letters: Interviews with New Left Review*. London: New Left Books.

Williams, R. (1979b) *Modern Tragedy*. Second edition. London: Verso.

Williams, R. (1979c) *The Fight for Manod*. London: Chatto and Windus.

Williams, R. (1980a) 'Notes on marxism in Britain since 1945', in *Problems in Materialism and Culture: Selected Essays*. London: New Left Books.

Williams, R. (1980b) 'Base and superstructure in Marxist cultural theory', in *Problems in Materialism and Culture*. London: New Left Books.

Williams, R. (1980c) 'Literature and sociology: in memory of Lucien Goldmann', in *Problems in Materialism and Culture*. London: New Left Books.

Williams, R. (1980d) 'Means of communication as means of production', in *Problems in Materialism and Culture*. London: New Left Books.

Williams, R. (1981) *Culture*. Glasgow: Collins.

Williams, R. (1983) *Towards 2000*. London: Chatto and Windus.

Williams, R. (1984a) 'Seeing a man running', in D. Thompson (ed.), *The Leavises: Recollections and Impressions*. Cambridge: Cambridge University Press.

Williams, R. (1984b) 'Crisis in English studies', in *Writing in Society*. London: Verso.

Williams, R. (1985) *Loyalties*. London: Chatto and Windus.

Williams, R. (1989a) *The Politics of Modernism: Against the New Conformists*. (Edited by T. Pinkney.) London: Verso.

Williams, R. (1989b) 'Culture is ordinary', in *Resources of Hope: Culture, Democracy, Socialism*. (Edited by R. Gable.) London: Verso.

Williams, R. (1989c) 'A defence of realism', in *What I Came To Say*. (Edited by N. Belton, F. Mulhern and J. Taylor.) London: Hutchinson Radius.

Williams, R. (1989d) 'Problems of the coming period', in *Resources of Hope: Culture, Democracy, Socialism*. (Edited by R. Gable.) London: Verso.

Williams, R. (1989e) 'Mining the meaning: key words in the miners' strike', in *Resources of Hope: Culture, Democracy, Socialism*. (Edited by R. Gable.) London: Verso.

Williams, R. (1989f) 'The importance of community', in *Resources of Hope: Culture, Democracy, Socialism*. (Edited by R. Gable.) London: Verso.

Williams, R. (1989g) 'Community',iIn *What I Came To Say*. (Edited by N. Belton, F. Mulhern and J. Taylor.) London: Hutchinson Radius.

Williams, R. (1994) 'Afterword', in J. Dollimore and A. Sinfield (eds), *Political Shakespeare: Essays in Cultural Materialism*. Manchester: Manchester University Press.

Williams, R. (2001) 'Film and the dramatic tradition', in J. Higgins (ed.), *The Raymond Williams Reader*. Oxford: Blackwell.

Williams, R. and Eagleton, T. (1989) 'The politics of hope: an interview', in T. Eagleton (ed.), *Raymond Williams: Critical Perspectives*. Cambridge: Polity Press.

Williams, R. and Orrom, M. (1954) *Preface to Film*. London: Film Drama.

Williams, R. and Said, E.W. (1989) 'Appendix: media, margins and modernity', in R. Williams, *The Politics of Modernism: Against the New Conformists*. (Edited by T. Pinkney.) London: Verso.

Wilson, S. (1995) *Cultural Materialism: Theory and Practice*. Oxford: Blackwell.

Wolff, J. (1990) *Feminine Sentences: Essays on Women and Culture*. Cambridge: Polity Press.

Wolff, J. (1993) *The Social Production of Art*. London: Macmillan.

Wolfreys, J. (2000) 'In perspective: Pierre Bourdieu', *International Socialism*, second series, 87.

Women's Studies Group (1978) *Women Take Issue: Aspects of Women's Subordination*. London: Hutchinson/Centre for Contemporary Cultural Studies.

Wood, B. (1998) 'Stuart Hall's cultural studies and the problem of hegemony', *British Journal of Sociology*, 49, 3.

Wordsworth, W. (1952) *The Poetical Works of William Wordsworth*. Oxford: Oxford University Press.

Zhdanov, A.A. (1977) 'Soviet literature - the richest in ideas, the most advanced in literature', in M. Gorky et al., *Soviet Writers' Congress 1934: The Debate on Socialist Realism and Modernism*. London: Lawrence and Wishart.

Index